Antonia Clare
JJ Wilson

speakout

Intermediate
Students' Book

with ActiveBook

CONTENTS

CONTENTS

CONTENTS

>> LEAD-IN

GRAMMAR

1 Read the text and find examples of …

1 the past simple *he saw*
2 the past continuous
3 the present perfect
4 the past perfect
5 a modal verb
6 a superlative
7 a relative clause
8 a passive

There have been some amazing coincidences throughout history, but this might be the best. In 1900 King Umberto of Italy was dining in a restaurant when he saw that the owner looked exactly like him. The man, who was also called Umberto, was born in Turin on the same day as the king and, like the king, married a woman called Margherita. Amazingly, their weddings had been on the same day. The king invited the restaurant owner to an athletics meeting the next day. As the king sat down, he was told that the other Umberto had died in a mysterious shooting accident. Just as the king heard this news, an anarchist shot him dead.

PRONUNCIATION

2A Find pairs of words that have the same vowel sound.

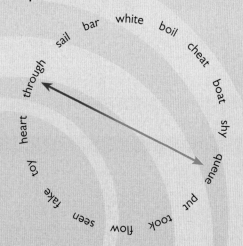

B ▶ L.1 **Listen and check your answers.**

C Work in pairs. Think of other words in English that use the same sounds.

VOCABULARY

3A Complete the common phrases below using the correct verb from the box.

| ~~have~~ | take | check | watch | chat | go | meet |
| play | do (x2) | | | | | |

1 *have* a meeting
2 _____ your email
3 _____ out with friends
4 _____ some sport
5 _____ a colleague
6 _____ some work
7 _____ on the internet
8 _____ a break
9 _____ a DVD
10 _____ some music

B Add phrases 1–10 above to the word webs below.

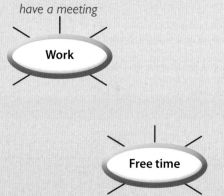

have a meeting

Work

Free time

C Can you add any more phrases to the word webs? Which of these things do you do on a normal day?

COMMON ERRORS

4A Correct the mistakes.

1 She likes listening music.
2 I am architect.
3 Are you feeling allright?
4 When I can visit your house?
5 Let's discuss about this tomorrow.
6 He don't come here often.
7 We come from germany.
8 Where you go yesterday?
9 I live in this town all my life.
10 My wife is a really good cooker.

B Which mistakes are connected with …

a) verb–noun agreement 6   f) articles
b) spelling   g) vocabulary
c) verb tense   h) word order
d) punctuation/capitalisation i) missing auxiliary verb
e) prepositions   j) extra words

UNIT I

UNIT I

identity

speakout DVD

▶ **GRAMMAR** | question forms   ▶ **VOCABULARY** | family   ▶ **HOW TO** | talk about your family

SPEAKING

1A Work in pairs. Take turns to find out as much as you can about your partner. Talk about your family, job/studies, home and likes/dislikes.

B Introduce your partner to the class.

VOCABULARY family

2A Match questions 1–10 with answers a)–j).

1 Do you know a lot about your **family history?**

2 Which do you know best: your mother's or your father's **side of the family?**

3 Where did your **ancestors** come from?

4 Did you ever meet your **great-grandparents?**

5 Do you know most of your **relatives?**

6 Are you **related to** anyone famous?

7 Have you **inherited** any family characteristics?

8 Who in your family do you **take after?**

9 Would you like to know more about your **roots?**

10 Do you live with your **extended family?**

a) Quite a lot. My parents told me a lot of stories about my background.

b) Yes. I'm very shy, like my father and my older brothers.

c) I'd love to, but it's difficult because my parents don't often talk about the past.

d) Yes, I live with my immediate family and my grandparents.

e) No, there are no celebrities in the family!

f) They came from Lagos, in Nigeria.

g) I know about half of them. The others live in New Zealand and I've never met them.

h) My father's. I grew up next door to his sister's family.

i) My mother. We look alike and we have similar characters.

j) No. Unfortunately, they died before I was born.

B Work in groups. Discuss questions 1–10.

▦➡ page 148 **VOCABULARYBANK**

READING

3A *Who Do You Think You Are?* is a BBC programme that gets celebrities to research their family's roots. What kind of things do you think they discover?

B Read the text to find out.

C Read the text again and answer the questions.

1 Who has a royal ancestor?

2 Who has a relative who was a policeman?

3 Who has roots in three continents?

4 Who has a relative who started a second family?

5 Who has an ancestor who built boats?

6 Who has a criminal relative?

---

1 *Who Do You Think You Are?* is a BBC programme that gets celebrities to research their family's roots. They find out about their ancestors, sometimes travelling across the world to interview relatives. They discover that their family histories include every type of person imaginable: heroes, liars, geniuses, soldiers, inventors and even kings.

2 In one episode, model Jodie Kidd learns that she is the great-granddaughter of newspaper owner Lord Beaverbrook, who was a politician during both world wars. Jodie also discovers that her great-grandfather on her mother's side of the family made a fortune from building ships during World War I and received letters from the King of England and Winston Churchill.

3 And on the subject of kings, Olympic athlete Matthew Pinsent finds that he is related to Edward I, one of the most famous kings in British history. Another Olympic gold medallist, Colin Jackson, takes a DNA test and discovers that he is fifty-five percent sub-Saharan African, thirty-eight percent European and seven percent American Indian. The last result comes as quite a surprise!

A Colin Jackson   **B** Matthew Pinsent   **C** Jodie Kidd

D Underline words or phrases in the text that match meanings 1–5 below.

1 a lot of money (paragraph 2)

2 someone who won a gold medal in sport (paragraph 3)

3 making arrangements so someone is safe (paragraph 4)

4 extremely sad (paragraph 5)

5 left someone (or something) in a bad condition (paragraph 5)

6 given a punishment for a crime (paragraph 6)

4 Work in pairs and discuss. Would you like to be on the programme? Why/Why not?

4   Davina McCall, presenter of *Big Brother*, knows her mother's side of the family is from France. She goes to Paris and finds out that her great-grandfather, Celestin Hennion, was famous throughout France as head of the French police. He once received a medal from King George V to say 'thank you' for organising security for the king's trip to France in 1914.

5   Not everyone on the programme finds good news about their family history. Jerry Springer learns of a tragic story: his parents escaped Nazi Germany three days before the start of World War II but other family members died in the war. And Actress Kim Cattrall discovers that her grandfather, from Liverpool, UK, abandoned his family, including three young daughters. He didn't go far. Forty miles down the road in Manchester, he started another family.

6   Finally, Nigella Lawson, a famous chef whose father was a British politician, discovers that one of her relatives was a thief from the Netherlands. After being sentenced to prison, he escaped to England, which is how the Lawsons ended up in London.

| D Davina McCall | E Kim Cattrall | F Nigella Lawson |

LISTENING

5A ▶ 1.1 Listen to an interview with a man describing his family history. Which family members does he talk about?

B Listen again and answer the questions.

1   How many of his great-grandparents and grandparents did he meet?

2   Where did his father's family come from?

3   What three types of job did most of his ancestors do?

4   How many people are in his 'immediate family'?

5   Who does he think tells the best family stories?

GRAMMAR   question forms

6A Read questions 1–6 from the interview. Answer questions a)–e).

1   (Do) you <u>know</u> a lot about your family history?

2   Did you ever meet your great-grandparents?

3   Where did your ancestors come from?

4   What happened to them?

5   Which members of your family do you feel close to?

6   Who tells the best family stories?

a) Underline the main verb in each question. (The first has been done for you.)

b) Circle the auxiliary verbs. Which auxiliaries refer to the past? Which refer to the present?

c) Which two questions are *yes/no* questions?

d) Which two questions end in a preposition: *of, to, by*, etc.?

e) Which two questions use *wh-* words to refer to the subject (the person who does the action) and don't use an auxiliary verb?

▶ page 128   **LANGUAGEBANK**

B ▶ 1.2 Listen to the questions above. Are the question words (*wh-* words) in 3–6 said in a higher or a lower voice?

C Listen and shadow the questions (say them at the same time).

PRACTICE

7A Put the words in the correct order to make questions.

1   do / every / your / family / you / day / see / ?

2   your / anything / did / teach / grandparents / you / ?

3   remembers / who / always / birthday / your / ?

4   read / taught / to / you / who / ?

5   do / do / you / relax / what / to / ?

6   holiday / do / next / to / you / want / go / on / your / where / ?

7   words / you / what / describe / three / ?

8   happy / what / you / makes / ?

9   knows / best / you / who / ?

10 did / speak / first / when / English / you / ?

B Choose three of the questions to ask other students.

SPEAKING

8A Write four dates, four names and four places that are connected with your family.

Dates: *7 May 2008 – My son was born.*

Names:

Places:

B Work in groups. Take turns to explain what you wrote. As you listen, think of questions to ask afterwards.

WRITING emails of introduction

9A When do you need to write a letter or email to introduce yourself? Which of these things have you done or will you do in the future?

- apply for a job/course
- arrange to meet someone for the first time

B Read the emails. Why are the people writing? Which sentences tell us?

To:	CTEBS committee
Subject:	introductions

Dear Colleagues,
As you probably know, next month I will start work as the new director of the Teacher Education Programme. For those of you who don't know me, I would like to take this opportunity to introduce myself. Since 2006, I have worked at the School of Education at Sidis University. My specialisation is in maths and science, and I have been involved in a number of teacher education projects in these fields.

I look forward to working with you.

Yours sincerely,

Nicholas Collett

To:	maxperkin@hotmail.co.uk
Subject:	hi!

Hi Max,
How are you? Zeinab told me it'd be OK to write to you at this email address. My name's Julia. I was at school with Zeinab years ago. I'm coming to Leeds for a week at the end of May. She told me you'd be able to show me some of the sights and help me find my way around. It'd be great if we could meet. Hope to hear from you soon.

All the best,

Julia :)

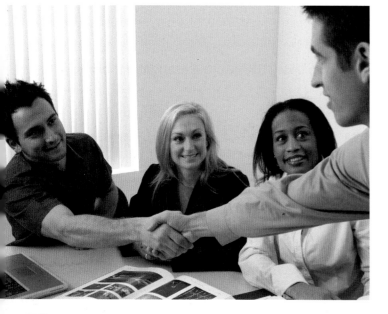

10 Read the five stages of email writing below. Do the emails in Exercise 9B follow all the stages?

1 **A**im for your **a**udience: think about who you are writing to. Is the email formal or informal?

2 **B**e **b**rief: try not to use too many words. Emails shouldn't go on for pages.

3 **C**ommunicate **c**learly: use simple, clear language and simple sentence structure.

4 **D**o two **d**rafts: write a first version and then rewrite.

5 **E**dit **e**verything: check grammar, vocabulary, spelling and punctuation before sending.

LEARN TO write formal and informal emails

11A Look at the emails in Exercise 9B again. Which one is formal and which is informal? How do you know?

B Answer questions 1–4 with formal (F) or informal (I).

1 Which email uses full forms of verbs (*I am*, *I would*) instead of contractions (*I'm* and *I'd*)?

2 Which email leaves out words (e.g. *Hope to* … instead of *I hope to* …)?

3 Which email sounds more like spoken English?

4 Which email uses longer, more complex sentences?

C Complete the notes with phrases from the email.

Greeting (formal): [1]_____.
(informal): Hi/Hello.
Opening line (formal): I am writing to …
(Informal): [2]_____.
Introduction (formal): I would like to take this [3]_____.
(informal): My name's …
Final message (formal): I look forward to …
(informal): [4]_____.
Goodbye (formal): [5]_____.
(informal): All the best.

12 Read the situations below and write the emails. Think about who you are writing to, the reason for writing and if you need to use a formal or informal style.

Situation 1

Next week you start a new job as Project Manager for a publishing company. Your job is to start new book projects and organise teams to work on the projects. Write to your new colleagues. Introduce yourself.

Situation 2

You are going to Sydney, Australia, for the first time. Your brother's friend, Tom, lives there. You've never met Tom. You want him to show you around the city. Write to Tom. Introduce yourself, and say when you are coming and what you want to do.

MEN AND WOMEN

▶ **GRAMMAR** | review of verb tenses ▶ **VOCABULARY** | relationships ▶ **HOW TO** | talk about people in your life

SPEAKING

1A Work in groups and discuss. Do you think male and female brains are different? How? What are the stereotypes of men and women in your country?

B Read the BBC blog and discuss the points you agree/disagree with. Can you think of any opinions to add?

GRAMMAR review of verb tenses

2A Match the underlined verbs below with the tenses a)–d).

1 Scientists recently <u>discovered</u> that there are seventy-eight genetic differences.

2 Men can't remember what they <u>were wearing</u> yesterday.

3 Women <u>hide</u> things in cupboards.

4 A baby <u>is crying</u>.

a) present simple   b) present continuous

c) past simple   d) past continuous

B Complete the rules with the correct tenses a)–d).

> **Rules:**
>
> 1 We use _____ for actions, events or situations that are finished.
>
> 2 We use _____ for things that are going on at a particular moment in the present.
>
> 3 We use _____ for habits, routines and things that are always true.
>
> 4 We use_____ when someone was in the middle of an action at a particular moment in the past.

C Read about state verbs and underline three examples in the blog opposite.

> **Rule:** Some verbs are not usually used in the continuous, e.g. *want*, *like*, *remember*, *understand*, *know*. These are called 'state verbs'.

▶ page 128 **LANGUAGEBANK**

PRACTICE

3A Read the personal profile and put the words in brackets into the correct tense.

My name is Matsuko Tamazuri. I am twenty-three and I [1]_____ (be) a student. I study French and Spanish at university in Osaka, where I [2]_____ (grow up), but at the moment I [3]_____ (learn) English in New York. When I first [4]_____ (get) here, everything [5]_____ (seem) different: the food, the clothes and the weather. Now I [6]_____ (enjoy) it and it feels like home! I have a boyfriend called Josh. I [7]_____ (meet) him three weeks ago when I [8]_____ (look) for an internet café! My hobbies [9]_____ (be) surfing the net and singing. I [10]_____ (sing) every day, usually in the bathroom!

B Work in pairs. Ask questions and write your partner's personal profile. Use the profile above to help.

Scientists recently discovered that there are seventy-eight genetic differences between men and women.

BBC Online News readers suggest what those differences might be.

❝ Women have a multi-tasking gene. Men can never prepare dinner so that everything is ready at the same time. ❞

❝ Men like to have all their stuff (DVDs, CDs) on show to impress their friends. Women hide things in cupboards. ❞

❝ Women have an ability to make men think they are in charge. ❞

❝ Men refuse to pay more than £5 for a haircut because it's not that important. ❞

❝ A baby is crying, a dog is barking, a doorbell is ringing. It doesn't matter: the man of the house is sleeping. Men can sleep through anything. Women can't. ❞

❝ A man can choose and buy a pair of shoes in 90 seconds over the internet. ❞

❝ Women know what to do when someone starts to cry. ❞

❝ Women remember every outfit they've worn for the past twenty years. Men can't remember what they were wearing yesterday without looking on the floor. ❞

❝ Men speak in sentences. Women speak in paragraphs. ❞

LISTENING

4A Read the description of a BBC TV documentary and answer the questions.

1 What is the aim of the documentary?

2 Whose lives does it follow? For how long?

3 What is the purpose of the test?

Child of Our Time

Child of Our Time is a BBC documentary that aims to discover what makes us who we are. The programme follows the lives of twenty-five children and their families for a period of twenty years. During the series, the children and their parents do a number of tests. In this programme, they do a test to discover whether a male brain is different from a female brain and how this affects our character and abilities.

B ▶1.3 Take a piece of paper, listen to Parts 1 and 2 and follow the test instructions.

C ▶1.4 Listen to the explanation in Part 3. Turn to page 158 and check your picture. How many parts did your bike have? Could it work? Does it have a person on it? Compare your picture with other students'.

D ▶1.5 Listen to people discussing their pictures of the bicycle. Who says sentences 1–6? A man (M) or a woman (W)?

1 None of us got the chain, did we?

2 Pedals nor chains, so mine will never work.

3 None of us drew a person.

4 I've got a little bird on my handlebars, though.

5 Yours is the most accurate one.

6 And you've got lights on yours.

5 Discuss the questions.

1 Was the explanation correct for you?

2 Do you agree with the presenter's views about men and women?

> Women think people are important. Men, on the other hand, are more interested in getting the machine right.

VOCABULARY relationships

6A Work in pairs. Look at the words in the box and answer the questions.

~~boss and employee~~ classmates partner team-mates member godfather and godmother mentor and pupil fiancée and fiancé

1 Which pair works together? *boss and employee*

2 Which pair promises to help guide a child through life?

3 Which pair is going to get married?

4 Which pair involves one person learning from the other?

5 Which word describes people who play in the same sports team?

6 Which word describes people who go to the same class?

7 Which word describes a person who is part of a club?

8 Which word is a general word for 'someone who you do something with'?

B Work in groups and discuss.

1 Do you associate the roles with men or women or both?

2 Do you think men and women are different in the roles? How?

I think women bosses are often less aggressive than male bosses and they are better at listening.

C ▶1.6 Listen to six sentences. Number the words in Exercise 6A in the order that you hear them.

D Six of the words have two syllables. Find the words and underline the stressed syllable. Say the words aloud, putting the stress on the correct syllable.

speakout TIP

Remember: most two-syllable words in English have the stress on the first syllable. Hold a hand under your chin. Say the word slowly. The jaw (the bottom part of your chin) drops more on the stressed syllable.

SPEAKING

7A Think about your own relationships. Prepare to talk about one man and one woman in your life. Use the questions below to make notes.

• Who are they?

• What is their role in your life?

• How often do you see them?

• How have they helped you and how have you helped them?

I'm a member of a football club, and we meet every week. Our coach is fantastic and he has helped our team a lot.

B Tell other students about these relationships.

VOCABULARY *PLUS* collocations

8A Work in pairs and do the quiz opposite.

B Turn to page 158 and read the text to check your answers.

9A Look at the quiz again. Find and circle five expressions using *take*, *get*, *do* and *go*.

B Write the expressions in italics in the correct places in the word webs below.

1 *~~on a diet~~, home, off something, for a drink/a walk/a meal, grey*

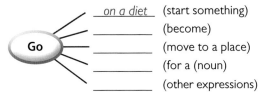

Go
- *on a diet* (start something)
- _____ (become)
- _____ (move to a place)
- _____ (for a (noun))
- _____ (other expressions)

2 *responsibility for, after someone, part in something, a taxi*

Take
- _____ (go in a vehicle)
- _____ (join in)
- _____ (phrasal verbs)
- _____ (other expressions)

3 *married, a job/degree, on with someone, here*

Get
- _____ (become)
- _____ (obtain)
- _____ (go somewhere)
- _____ (phrasal verbs)

4 *exercise, research, housework, someone a favour*

Do
- _____ (activity)
- _____ (responsibilities and tasks)
- _____ (find information)
- _____ (help someone)

➡ page 148 **VOCABULARYBANK**

SPEAKING

10A Think about your classmates. Write down the name of someone who:

- never gets angry.
- does research for his/her job.
- took a test in the last six months.
- went for a meal last weekend.
- took up a new hobby recently.
- always gets here early.
- went for a walk today.
- got a new job recently.

B Work in groups. Ask the other students to check if they agree with your ideas.

What Women Really Think

Stella magazine commissioned YouGov, a research agency, to interview over 1,000 women in the UK about what they really think. How do you think they responded?

1 How many women in the UK would prefer to have a male boss?
(a) less than 30%
(b) about 50%
(c) over 70%

2 How many women have gone on a diet in the past?
(a) 20%
(b) between 35% and 45%
(c) over 50%

3 How many women spend more than seven hours a week doing exercise?
(a) 4%
(b) 15%
(c) 30%

4 What is the biggest challenge for women today?
(a) staying healthy
(b) making enough money
(c) balancing home and work life

5 What do women think is the best age to get married?
(a) between 21 and 24
(b) between 25 and 29
(c) over 30

6 What do 59% of women think fathers should take more responsibility for?
(a) their children
(b) doing the housework
(c) organising holidays

7 According to women, how much housework do they do?
(a) more than 50%
(b) over 75%
(c) nearly all of it

8 How many women aged 45–54 met their husbands through the internet?
(a) 1%
(b) 9%
(c) 16%

5 tips to help you do well at interviews

How do you get into the university or the job of your dreams? Even before the interview, you might need to catch someone's attention. The Dean of Admissions at Harvard University says he often receives flowers and chocolates from potential students. One student sent references every day for three months. Eventually, he even sent a letter from his dentist saying how nice his teeth were. He didn't get an interview.

For those of you who do make the interview stage, here are five top tips:

1 Be prepared. Do some research about the university or company so you know what questions to ask.

2 Dress appropriately. You don't have to dress smartly but you should look clean. And don't wear 'bling' (large pieces of jewellery).

3 Arrive on time. Fifteen minutes early is OK.

4 Shake hands firmly and make eye contact. First impressions are important.

5 Speak clearly and try to offer full answers rather than short responses. This shows your enthusiasm.

SPEAKING

1A What type of interview can you see in the photo? Is it a/an:

- job interview?
- interview for a place at university?
- newspaper/magazine interview?
- interview for a talk show/other television programme?
- police inquiry?
- placement interview for a language course?

B Look at the list of interview types above. Answer questions 1–3.

1 Which types of interview above have you experienced?

2 Which will you experience in the future?

3 Do you think it is possible to show 'the real you' in a short interview? Why/Why not?

VOCABULARY interview advice

2A Work in pairs. Look at topics 1–3 below and match them to the expressions in the box.

> dress smartly 3   speak clearly   answer briefly
> shake hands firmly   send references
> arrive on time   avoid eye contact   do some research
> show enthusiasm   be prepared

1 Should do during an interview

2 Shouldn't do during an interview

3 Might do before an interview

B What else should/shouldn't you do in an interview? Think of as many things as you can in two minutes.

You should try to ask questions.

FUNCTION talking about yourself

3 Read the text and answer the questions.

1 What type of things do people do to get an interview at Harvard University?

2 What should you do before and during an interview?

4A ▶ 1.7 Listen to three extracts from the audio and answer the questions.

1 What types of interview are they?

2 Which interviewee doesn't follow the five tips? What does he/she do wrong?

B Answer questions 1–6. Listen again to check.

Interview 1

1 What does the student want to practise?

2 What types of classes are in the afternoons?

Interview 2

3 What did the girl organise on the summer camp?

4 What 'can be difficult', according to the interviewer?

Interview 3

5 What does the man want to know?

6 Why are online courses more difficult than face-to-face courses, according to the interviewer?

5A Read the extracts from audio 1.7. Underline the expressions that introduce a question.

Extract 1

T: OK. You've got a very good level of English so we'd put you in the advanced class. Is there anything else?

S: <u>Could I ask a question?</u>

Extract 2

I: There are a couple of things I'd like to ask about. Your CV says you have some experience of looking after children?

A: Yes, I was a tutor on a summer camp last year.

I: Can I ask you about that? What type of things did you do?

A: Um, well, I organised games.

Extract 3

I: I think that's about it. Do you have any questions? Any queries?

S: Um, yes, actually I do have a query.

I: Yes, go ahead.

S: It's about online classes at the university.

B Read the extracts below and underline the expressions that are used to introduce an opinion.

Extract 1

S: I've studied English for many years and spent time in Britain, but that was a few years ago. <u>So for me the most important thing is to</u> just refresh … and try to remember my English and practise speaking and listening.

Extract 2

I: OK. And you enjoyed it?
A: Yes.

I: What aspect, what part did you enjoy, would you say?

A: I suppose I'd have to say I liked the games best.

I: And any problems?

A: Um, no.

I: What about the different ages? We often find that different ages together can be difficult.

A: It depends. In my opinion, you can usually get the older children to help the younger ones.

Extract 3

S: If I'm accepted, I saw that there are, that it's possible to take some courses online.

I: That's right.

S: So I wouldn't need to attend classes?

I: Not for the online courses. But … well, one thing I'd like to say is that the online courses are, in many ways, more difficult than face-to-face courses.

⫸ page 128 **LANGUAGE**BANK

6 Put the words in the correct order to make sentences or questions.

1 query / I / a / have / do
2 I / a / could / question / ask / ?
3 like / couple / of / are / about / I'd / things / to / a / ask / there
4 ask / you / I / can / that / about / ?
5 true / this / opinion / my / isn't / in
6 to / I'd / I / agree / have / say
7 thing / that / like / I'd / one / say / is / to / is / course / the / difficult
8 is / thing / important / most / for / the / me / to / study

LEARN TO use two-word responses

7A Match expressions 1–5 with expressions a)–e).

1 Of course.
2 That's right.
3 I see.
4 No problem.
5 Go ahead.

a) Please continue.
b) You're correct.
c) You're welcome.
d) Yes, definitely.
e) I understand.

B Which expressions are more formal: 1–5 or a)–e)? Which do you use regularly? Read audio script 1.7 on page 164 to see how the expressions are used.

SPEAKING

8A Work in pairs and role-play the interview. Student A: read the instructions below. Student B: turn to page 158.

You work for a famous business school. Student B wants to do a course at the school. Interview him/her. Use the following prompts and ask about:

- his/her reason for doing the course
- his/her work experience
- his/her expectations of the course
- his/her plans for the future

Prepare the questions. Remember to ask your partner why he/she is a good candidate for the school and, at the end, if he/she has any queries about the business school.

B Change roles and role-play the interview again.

DVD PREVIEW

1A What can you do in Second Life? Do you think the statements below are true?

1 In Second Life you can **alter** your appearance.

2 You can become more **attractive** than you actually are.

3 You can **pick** a different skin colour.

4 You can wear strange **outfits**.

5 You can **socialise** with people from different countries.

6 You can talk to other **residents** of Second Life.

7 You can make money in Second Life's own **currency**.

B Match the words in bold above with the words/phrases in the box.

clothes	type of money from one country
change	beautiful meet and talk to
choose	people who live in one place

C Read the programme information and check your answers to Exercise 1A.

BBC The Money Programme: Second Life

This BBC programme investigates Second Life, a virtual world with its own communities. In Second Life, you reinvent yourself: you choose a different name, change your appearance in any way you want and get a new personality. What is more, Second Life is a world of endless pleasure. You can go shopping, take English classes, meet and chat to people from all over the world, live in a perfect house on a magical island and even make money. There's only one rule in Second Life: there are no rules!

▶ DVD VIEW

2 Watch the DVD and put pictures A–E in the correct order.

3A Match pictures A–E with sentences 1–5.

1 Once you've created an account, you can create an avatar.

2 You can be female, male or even something called a 'furry': half-animal, half-human.

3 It turns out there are not a lot of unattractive people in Second Life.

4 But it's more fun flying, and with maps I can find almost anything I want.

5 You can go up to anyone and chat.

B Watch the DVD again to check.

4 Work in groups and discuss.

1 Have you been in Second Life? If not, would you like to spend time there?

2 What might you enjoy about Second Life? What would you not like about it?

3 Why do you think people get addicted to Second Life?

speak create a new identity

5A ▶ 1.8 Listen to someone talking about her avatar. Answer the questions.

1 Where did she hear about Second Life?

2 What did she change about her appearance?

3 What job did she decide to do in Second Life?

4 What is the 'one thing that hasn't changed'?

5 What type of building does she talk about?

B Listen again and tick the key phrases you hear.

Keyphrases

(You can) create a different version of yourself.

I reinvented myself as a …

I created a new image of myself.

I didn't change my appearance that much.

One thing I decided to alter was my …

One thing that hasn't changed is …

My avatar is based on …

C Create your own avatar. Complete your profile using the prompts below:

- name
- age
- height
- weight
- hair colour
- eye colour
- clothes
- nationality
- languages spoken
- job and/or hobbies
- favourite places to hang out
- would like to meet (type of people)
- motto or personal philosophy
- one thing no one knows about you

D Talk to other students. Introduce your new (avatar) self. What do you have in common with other avatars in the class?

write answer a questionnaire

6A Read the questionnaire. Choose to be either yourself or your new identity and write answers to the questions. Write 1–2 sentences for each question.

Who are you?

1 What three words best describe you?

2 What is your idea of perfect happiness?

3 What possession is most important to you?

4 What is your greatest achievement?

5 What is your favourite sound, smell and taste?

6 What do you like most about your lifestyle?

7 What do you like least about your lifestyle?

8 What do you always carry with you?

9 Who would be your perfect dinner date? Why?

10 What's your favourite month and why?

11 If you could change one thing about the past, what would it be?

12 If you could learn one new thing, what would it be?

B Share your answers with other students. Decide if the other students' answers are for themselves or their avatar.

FAMILY

1A Complete the sentences with the words in the box.

history	inherited	after
extended	ancestors	relative
great	side	roots	related

1 My parents told me about my family ___history___.

2 My _____ probably came from the place where I was born.

3 I once met my _____ -grandparents.

4 I take _____ my mother, especially my personality.

5 I know someone who _____ a house when their parents died.

6 My family's _____ are in another country.

7 I have a _____ living in Australia.

8 I know someone who is _____ to someone famous!

9 I know my mother's _____ of the family much better than my father's.

10 I have a very large _____ family: lots of cousins, nephews and nieces.

B Tick the sentences that are true for you. Compare with another student.

QUESTION FORMS

2A Find and correct the mistakes in the questions below. Three of the questions are correct.

1 When you started studying English?

2 Who did helped you to learn English?

3 Do you be enjoy learning languages?

4 Did you to learn anything important from your teachers?

5 What annoys you about your job or your studies?

6 In your job or studies, is there anything you are not happy?

7 When you imagine the perfect career, what do you think of?

8 What keeps you awake at night?

B Work in pairs. Choose four of the questions to ask your partner.

REVIEW OF VERB TENSES

3 Find and correct the mistakes. Five of the underlined verbs are incorrect.

12.10.09

I ¹was walking to work this morning when I ²was seeing Mr Gonzalez, my old Spanish teacher. He ³was wearing a leather jacket and carrying a guitar. I ⁴ask him how he was. He said, 'Fine. I ⁵go to my band practice.' I said, 'What band?' He replied, 'I ⁶don't teach any more. It ⁷wasn't really the best job for me. A few years ago I ⁸was starting a band called The Big Easy. We ⁹don't make much money, but I ¹⁰'m liking the lifestyle.' I asked him where he lived and he said, 'I ¹¹'m living in my caravan at the moment. I ¹²travel a lot. I'm a child of the 60s!'

RELATIONSHIPS

4A Put the letters in the correct order to find the names of twelve types of people.

1 tomdogher

2 niface

3 ilupp

4 nraterp

5 ceanife,

6 breemm

7 stamcasel

8 dethagorf

9 sobs

10 emeyloep

11 trenom

12 maatteme

B Work in pairs. Which of these people do you know or have? Which of these are you?

I have a fiancée. We're getting married next summer.

I'm a member of a gym.

TALKING ABOUT YOURSELF

5A Complete the conversations with the pairs of words in the box.

query about	like to	to say
you about	I ask	thing I'd

query about

1 A: I have a|the class. Do I have to bring a pen?

B: No, it's a computer class.

2 A: Could a question? Where does the tennis class meet?

B: At the tennis courts.

3 A: I'd have I'm not sure you're qualified. Why should we employ you for the library position?

B: Because I'm good with children and animals.

4 A: There are a couple of things I'd ask. Firstly, can you work on Saturdays?

B: Is that at the weekend?

5 A: One like to say is that you look good for your age. How old are you?

B: Thirty.

6 A: Can I ask your latest film, *Philadelphia*? Where is it set?

B: In Philadelphia.

B Work in pairs and write a conversation. Use the expressions in Exercises 5 and 7 on page 15 to help.

C Work in groups and take turns to perform your conversations.

UNIT 2

SPEAKING

> Talk about life stories
> Talk about an important news event
> Tell a true story or a lie
> Tell a narrative

LISTENING

> Listen to a radio programme about films
> Listen to news reports
> Listen to people telling anecdotes
> Watch a BBC drama about an art thief

READING

> Read an article about conspiracy theories
> Read a news report
> Read a text about lying

WRITING

> Write a news report
> Write a short narrative

BBC CONTENT

☐ Video podcast: When is it OK to tell a lie?
◉ DVD: Hustle

UNIT 2

tales

▶ **Fact or fiction?** p20

▶ **What really happened?** p23

▶ **I don't believe it!** p26

▶ **Hustle** p28

SPEAKING

1 Work in groups and discuss. Can you think of a film you have seen that has taught you about a person/event in history?

2A Work in pairs and do the quiz. Decide if each question is fact, fiction or partly true. Then check your answers on page 158.

B Discuss. Do you think it is all right for film-makers to change the facts of a story? Why/Why not?

Hollywood versus history

Do you know the difference between what you have learnt from your history books and what you have learnt from watching Hollywood's historically inaccurate movies? Can you tell your facts from fiction?

1 In the film *The Last Samurai*, Tom Cruise plays a US army captain who joins the samurai warriors in Japan in 1876. Was Captain Nathan Algren a real figure from history?

2 In *Shakespeare in Love*, William Shakespeare is inspired to write *Romeo and Juliet* by his real-life relationship with a young actress. Did this happen in real life?

3 In a scene from *Gladiator*, we see the Roman Emperor Commodus die at the hands of a gladiator. Did he really die like this?

4 In the film *Braveheart*, Mel Gibson plays the character William Wallace, leading an army of men with painted faces, and wearing kilts* as he battles to free Scotland from the English. How much truth is there in the story?

5 In the 1995 adventure, *Apollo 13*, we hear the pilot saying the famous words 'Houston, we have a problem.' But were these his exact words?

* **kilt** – a skirt traditionally worn by Scottish men

VOCABULARY types of story

3A Look at the types of film stories in the box below. Match the types of story with the descriptions a)–i).

> biopic   docudrama   disaster   romantic comedy
> period drama   fantasy/science fiction   psychological thriller
> action/adventure   mystery/crime

a) Heroes chase and fight.
b) Characters battle with their minds.
c) Strange things happen in the future or in imaginary worlds.
d) Things that happen in the life of a real person.
e) The good guy (the detective) finds the bad guy (the criminal).
f) People dressed up in old-fashioned costumes.
g) Funny things happen. Two people fall in love.
h) Terrible things happen, but people survive.
i) A documentary made more interesting with some parts acted.

B Work in pairs and answer the questions.
1 Which types of film do you enjoy watching?
2 Can you name films which match each type of story?

LISTENING

4A ▶ 2.1 Listen to the first part of a radio programme about films and answer the questions.
1 What type of film does the programme talk about?
2 Why are these films so popular?

B Work in pairs and discuss. Look at the photos of actors who have played the roles of famous people in films. How do you think they prepared for the role? Do you think it was difficult?

5 ▶ 2.2 Listen to the second part of the radio programme and answer the questions about the actors and the roles they played.
1 Who met a character they would play in person?
2 Who couldn't meet with the character they played?
3 Who became good friends with the character?
4 Who phoned hotels in order to listen to a special accent?

6A Complete the information about the radio programme.
1 Hollywood has always used _____ _____ in its films.
2 Hollywood began making films in the _____s.
3 Some of the best films in recent years have been based on _____ _____.
4 From these films we've learnt about the _____ lives of some of the biggest music legends.
5 Many of these actors have won _____ for their roles.
6 Helen Mirren met the Queen for _____.
7 Josh Brolin phoned up hotels in Texas, to listen to their _____.
8 Tatou wanted to look like Coco Chanel, so that we would recognise her _____.

B ▶ 2.3 Listen and check your answers.

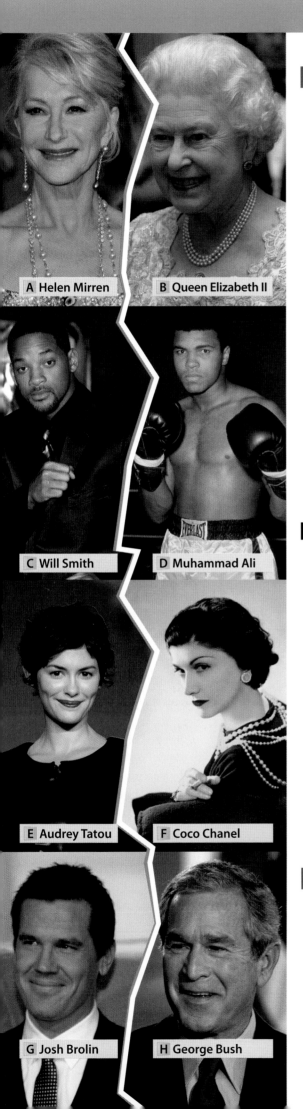

A Helen Mirren

B Queen Elizabeth II

C Will Smith

D Muhammad Ali

E Audrey Tatou

F Coco Chanel

G Josh Brolin

H George Bush

GRAMMAR present perfect/past simple

7A Read the sentences in Exercise 6A and underline examples of the present perfect and past simple.

B Complete the rules with present perfect or past simple.

Rules:
1 Use the _____ to talk about experiences or things that happened before now. The time is not specified or important.
2 Use the _____ to talk about recent events, or an action which started in the past and continues now.
3 Use the _____ to talk about a specific event in the past (we know when the event happened).
4 Use the _____ to talk about an action which starts and finishes in the past.

C Look at the sentences in Exercise 6A again and match them with one of the rules above.

⟶ page 130 **LANGUAGEBANK**

8A ▶ 2.4 Listen to the pairs of phrases. Notice the difference.

1 I lived / I've lived
2 we met / we've met
3 he decided / he's decided
4 they spent / they've spent

B ▶ 2.5 Listen and write the sentences.

C Listen again and check. Then listen and repeat.

PRACTICE

9 Complete the text with the correct form of the verbs in brackets.

Chris Gardner is a successful businessman and a millionaire. But things ¹_____ always _____ (not be) easy. He ²_____ (not meet) his father until he was twenty-eight years old. This experience made him sure about one thing: he ³_____ always _____ (want) to be a good father to his own children. As a young man, Gardner ⁴_____ (experience) hard times. His wife ⁵_____ (leave) him, he ⁶_____ (lose) his job, and at one stage he and his two-year-old son ⁷_____ (sleep) in train stations and airports. He ⁸_____ (come) a long way since then. His life changed when he ⁹_____ (meet) a man driving a red Ferrari and asked him what job he did. The man was a stockbroker, so Gardner ¹⁰_____ (ask) him out to lunch, and the Ferrari driver introduced Gardner to the world of finance. Since he ¹¹_____ (become) successful, he ¹²_____ (spend) a lot of money helping homeless people, and he ¹³_____ also _____ (write) books about his experiences. His story was told in the film *The Pursuit of Happyness*, starring Will Smith.

SPEAKING

10A Work in pairs. Student A: write *Have you ever ...?* questions using the prompts in the box below. Student B: turn to page 160.

be on TV/in a newspaper   do something embarrassing in public
write a poem/story   go to a country on a different continent
collect something as a hobby   see someone commit a crime

B Take turns to ask and answer questions. Try to find five things that you have done and your partner hasn't done.

SPEAKING

11A Imagine you are going to make a film about your life. Choose five events you would like to include. Write some notes in the film strip below.

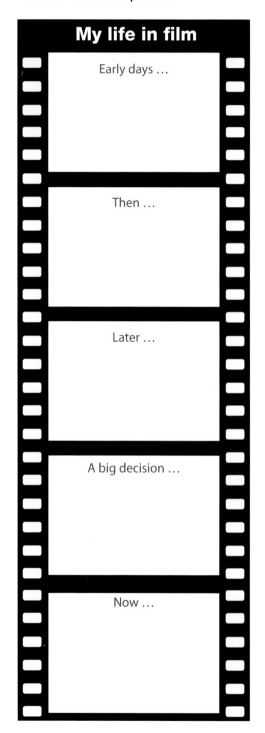

My life in film

Early days …

Then …

Later …

A big decision …

Now …

B Work in pairs. Take turns to talk about the film of your life.

C Think of three questions to ask your partner about the film of their life. Ask and answer the questions.

Why did you choose to … ?

What happened when you … ?

What did you enjoy best about … ?

VOCABULARY *PLUS* prepositions

Preposition + expressions of time

12 Complete the word webs with expressions in the box.

Saturday   the weekend   Monday morning   New Year's Day   July
the winter/the summer   the twenty-first century   lunchtime

12 o'clock

1 _____

at

night

2 _____

the morning

3 _____

2010

in

4 _____

5 _____

6 _____

the 4th of July

on

7 _____

8 _____

> **speak** **out** **TIP**
>
> To help you remember which preposition of time to use, try to memorise this: *on Monday*; *in winter*; *at that time*
> *on* = for specific days, *in* = for time periods, *at* = for specific times

Preposition + noun

13 Complete the sentences with the correct preposition: *on, for* or *by.*

1 It's a book _____ Dan Brown, a film _____ Steven Spielberg, a song _____ Amy Winehouse.

2 I saw it _____ TV. I heard it _____ the radio. I spoke to him _____ the phone.

3 We went _____ a walk, _____ a drive, _____ a run, _____ a swim.

4 They travelled _____ boat, _____ plane, _____ coach, _____ train.

Fixed expressions

14 Match the fixed expressions in bold in sentences 1–10 with meanings a)–j).

1 I dropped it **by mistake.**
2 I did the work **on my own.**
3 He's here **on business.**
4 We met **by chance.**
5 It was made **by hand.**
6 We got there **in the end.**
7 She said it **on purpose.**
8 We arrived **on time.**
9 I'll do that **in a moment.**
10 They're **in a hurry.**

a) finally
b) cannot wait
c) by a person, not a machine
d) it was not a mistake
e) alone, not with other people
f) not early, not late
g) in a very short time
h) accidentally
i) not on holiday, but for work
j) it was not planned

15A Look at Exercise 14 again. Write 6–8 questions with phrases with prepositions.

*Do you usually arrive **on time**, or are you sometimes late?*

*Do you prefer to live with someone, or live **on your own**?*

B Work in pairs. Take turns to ask and answer the questions.

➠ page 149 **VOCABULARYBANK**

▶ **GRAMMAR** | narrative tenses ▶ **VOCABULARY** | the news ▶ **HOW TO** | talk about important events

SPEAKING

1 Discuss the questions.

I How do you keep up-to-date with the news?

2 What have been the most important stories in the last five years?

2A ▶ 2.6 Listen to the excerpts from news reports. Which stories can you see in the photos?

B Work in pairs. What do you know about these news stories?

READING

3A Work in pairs. Read the definition and look at the photos below. Then answer the questions.

> **a conspiracy theory:** a theory or belief that there was a secret plan behind a major event

I What do you think the conspiracy theories were about (the events in the photos)?

2 Which story do you think involved a real conspiracy, according to official reports?

B Read the article to check your answers.

4A Read the article again and answer the questions.

I Who was killed in a crash?

2 Who was shot?

3 Who was arrested?

4 Who was murdered?

5 Who were the suspects?

6 Who was photographed?

B How are these words and phrases related to the stories?

> shadows   stars   a love story
> alcohol   photographs/photographers
> a man with a gun   a flag
> the FBI (Federal Bureau of Investigation)

C Work in pairs. Answer the questions.

I What do you think? Do you believe the official reports or the conspiracy theorists?

2 Do you know any other conspiracy theories? What happened?

The World's best-known conspiracy theories
BBC Focus Magazine takes a look

Man on the Moon

There are claims that Neil Armstrong's 'giant leap for mankind' took place in a studio and not on the Moon at all. Many have doubts about the photographs taken by astronauts on the Moon's surface. The conspiracy theorists say that strange shadows were falling in different directions, and surprisingly there are no stars visible. It also seems that the US flag, planted by Buzz Aldrin, was apparently waving in an impossible wind. However, all of these doubts can be explained logically. The lighting conditions on the Moon were complicated, and 'fluttering' on the flag only appeared when the astronauts moved it.

A Royal Affair

Diana, Princess of Wales, was killed on 31st August 1997, after her car crashed as it was driving through the Pont de l'Alma tunnel in Paris. Conspiracy theorists have claimed that Diana's death was not an accident – that she was in fact killed by MI6 (the British Secret Intelligence Service) because of her relationship with Dodi Al-Fayed. However, an inquiry into the accident eventually concluded that Diana's death was simply the result of driver Henri Paul's drunken condition, and the fact that paparazzi photographers were following them. There was also no evidence that Diana was pregnant at the time of the accident, or that she had planned to marry Dodi Al-Fayed.

The Death of a President

Suspects in the assassination of President John F Kennedy included the FBI, the Cuban leader Fidel Castro, and many others. Kennedy was killed in Dallas, Texas, on 22nd November 1963. He was riding through crowds in his car when a gunman shot him once in the head. Lee Harvey Oswald was arrested almost immediately after Kennedy's death, and was himself murdered two days later. A report in 1964 concluded that Oswald had acted alone. But in 1979, the report and the original FBI investigation were criticised. The new report agreed that Oswald had killed Kennedy, but also concluded that the President was killed 'as a result of conspiracy' by people unknown.

GRAMMAR narrative tenses

5A Read the summary. Find and underline examples of the past simple and the past continuous and answer the questions.

> Princess Diana's car crashed as it was driving through the Pont de l'Alma tunnel in Paris. Conspiracy theorists claimed that M16 planned her death because she was having an affair with Mr Al-Fayed.

1 Which tense do we use to talk about the main events in a story?
2 Which tense do we use to give the background information in a story?

B Read the conclusion and answer the questions.

> An inquiry concluded that Diana had not planned to marry Mr Al-Fayed, and that the crash had happened because the driver was drunk.

1 Which of the verbs is in the past simple?
2 Which of the verbs is in the past perfect?
3 Which tense describes the event that happened first?

C Underline the correct alternative to complete the rule.

Rule: Use the past perfect to talk about actions which happened *before the past time event we are talking about/a very long time ago*.

➔ page 130 **LANGUAGEBANK**

PRACTICE

6 Read an account of an important news event. Complete the text with phrases a)–h).

11 February 2000: Nelson Mandela's release from prison

I was in the crowd on the parade in Cape Town that day. It was a hot day, and ¹_____ to see Mandela walk free from the prison. ²_____ for twenty-seven years. At one point ³_____ but most people stayed calm. People ⁴_____ and singing songs. There was a great feeling of solidarity. There was a large tree in the middle of the parade, and ⁵_____ to get a better view. Suddenly, ⁶_____ and people fell to the ground. But nobody wanted to leave. Nobody wanted to miss the chance of seeing Mandela for the first time. ⁷_____ there was a huge cheer. From where I was standing, it was difficult ⁸_____ but I knew I was there for an important moment in our history.

a) He had been in prison
b) one of the branches broke
c) we heard some shots
d) 50,000 people were waiting
e) to hear what Mandela was saying
f) When he finally arrived
g) were talking to each other
h) many people had climbed onto it

VOCABULARY the news

7A Match the headlines 1–10 with the explanations a)–j).

1 Prime Minister's wife dies in **crash**

2 World Trade Center **attacked**

3 Student demonstration turns **violent**

4 Workers threaten **strikes**

5 Massive **earthquake** hits Los Angeles

6 Most wanted **fugitive** arrested

7 Floods **destroy** crops

8 **Hostages** released after talks with rebels

9 Music legend **shot** outside his New York apartment

10 Businesses hit by **collapse** of banks

a) Someone tried to damage or destroy a building.
b) People who were kept as prisoners are allowed to go free.
c) A musician was killed with a gun.
d) Police catch a man who they suspect committed a serious crime.
e) A natural disaster destroys a city.
f) Economic crisis affects businesses.
g) A woman is killed in a car accident.
h) A lot of farmland is under water.
i) Many people might refuse to go to work.
j) People who are protesting begin to fight on the streets.

B Work in pairs. Describe some stories which have been in the news recently using the vocabulary in bold above.

➔ page 149 **VOCABULARYBANK**

SPEAKING

8A Choose one of the news stories in the lesson or another important news story. Make notes to answer the questions below.

1 What was the news story? Where were you when you heard the news?

2 What were you doing? Who were you with?

3 What did you think at first? How did you feel?

4 Did the news change things for you in any way?

B Work with other students. Tell them about your story.

WRITING a news report

9A Read the news report and answer the questions. Underline the parts of the news report which help you to answer.

1 Who is the story about?

2 What happened?

3 Why did it happen?

4 Where did it happen?

5 When did it happen?

6 What is the situation now?

Fraud fugitive in Facebook trap

A man who was on the run from police in the US revealed where he was hiding through a series of Facebook updates.

Cameroon-born Maxi Sopo falsely obtained credit from banks while he was living in the US. By the time he had finished, he had stolen more than $200,000. He then escaped to Cancun in Mexico, where he was happily spending the money, until he made posts on his Facebook page telling the world that he was 'living in paradise'.

'He was making posts about how beautiful life is and how he was having a good time with his buddies,' said Assistant US Attorney Michael Scoville. 'He was definitely not living the way we wanted him to be living, given the charges he was facing,' he added.

However, during his time in Cancun, Mr Sopo also befriended a former justice department official on the networking site. This man, who had only met Mr Sopo a few times, was able to discover exactly where Mr Sopo was living. As soon as he had this information, he passed it to the Mexican authorities who arrested Sopo last month.

The twenty-six-year-old is currently in custody in Mexico City.

B Read the news report again. Find examples of the following:

1 quotes used to give someone's opinion

2 a concluding statement which gives us information about the current situation

3 an introductory statement which explains in one sentence what happened

4 more information about the background to the story

LEARN TO use time linkers

10A Look at the news report and find examples of the time linkers in the box.

| as soon as   while   during   until |
| by the time |

B Look at the words/phrases in the box above. Which time linker do we use to link an action that:

1 happened previously? _by the time_

2 continues up to that point and then stops? _____

3 happens at the same time as another action? _____

4 happens at some point in a period of time? _____

5 happens immediately after something else has happened? _____

C Complete the sentences with the correct time linker.

1 I came _____ I heard the news.

2 They arrived _____ we were having dinner.

3 Her cat died _____ the night.

4 We waited _____ the lights had gone out.

5 _____ the fire engines arrived, the house was destroyed.

11A Work in pairs. Choose a headline and write six questions asking information you would like to know about the story.

Woman finds suitcase full of money on train

Huge earthquake destroys city

Man shot outside his house

B Give your questions to another student.

C Look at the questions and write a short news report (100–150 words). Look at the ideas in Exercise 9B to help you.

speakout TIP

A good news report will give readers all the key information (why? what? how? when? etc.), in a clear and concise way. Does your news report contain the key information?

D Compare your stories with other students. Who has the best story?

▶ **FUNCTION** | telling a story   ▶ **VOCABULARY** | say/tell   ▶ **LEARN TO** | keep a story going

A   B

VOCABULARY *say/tell*

1A Work in pairs and discuss. How do you know when someone is lying? Do you think their behaviour changes?

B Read the text to check your answers.

How do you know if someone is lying?

From little white lies to lies which can destroy nations, people have lied for as long as they have told the truth. Some people are very good at it. So, how do we know if someone is lying? Here are the things to look out for.

1   The guilty hand: when someone is telling the truth they usually use more body language. They move their hands and their face more. When someone lies, their hands are still.

2   The lying eye: people find it very hard to tell you a lie if they're looking at you straight in the eyes. Normally, they look away just at the moment that they tell the lie.

3   The 'Me': when people tell a story about themselves, they tend to use a lot of 'me' words, like *I*, *me*, and *my*. When they tell a lie, they don't use the 'me' words as much.

2A Match 1–6 with a)–f) to make sentences.

1 I'm terrible at telling	a) 'hello', but she didn't answer.
2 My brother told me	b) a white lie than to upset someone.
3 I think you should say	c) what you mean.
4 Sometimes it's better to tell	d) a funny story yesterday.
5 You should just say	e) sorry.
6 I said	f) jokes. I always forget the punch line!

B Add the phrases with *say* and *tell* from Exercise 2A to the table.

say	tell
'hello'	a story

C Work with other students. Do you agree/disagree with the statements? Why?

1   A lie can travel half way around the world while the truth is putting on its shoes.

2   A good storyteller should mix fiction with truth to make their stories interesting.

3   It's OK to tell lies sometimes.

FUNCTION telling a story

3A Look at the pictures above which tell a story. What do you think is happening in each picture?

B ▶ 2.7 Listen to a woman telling her story. Number the pictures in the correct order.

4A Look at the phrases we can use to help tell the sequence in a story. Add the sequencers from the box to the correct place in the table.

~~This happened when~~   The next thing I knew Anyway,   In the end,   Before long, And then, all of a sudden

beginning
In the beginning, … *This happened when*
describing what happened
Well, … So, …
ending
Finally, …

B Listen to the story again, and tick the phrases you hear.

�⟶ page 130 **LANGUAGEBANK**

5A Work in pairs. Practise telling the story using the sequencers and the pictures to help you. Start like this:

This happened when the woman had an important interview and …

B ▶ 2.8 Do you think the woman was telling a true or false story? Listen to find out.

LEARN TO keep a story going

6A Look at phrases a)–j). Which phrases complete extracts 1–6?

a) ~~What happened then?~~

b) What did you do?

c) Then what?

d) Oh no!

e) Oh dear.

f) How embarrassing!

g) That's really funny.

h) Really?

i) You're joking!

j) You're kidding!

1 **W:** So, anyway, erm … I then got on to the tube, um … to go for my interview.
  M: Right, and ___a)___?

2 **W:** I've woken up shouting the word, 'Mum!'.
  M: No! _____!

3 **W:** At the top of my voice, in a packed, quiet tube.
  M: _____

4 **W:** … they're looking at me in a rather strange way.
  M: Right … _____

5 **W:** My face had swollen up! … It was bright red, … and covered in blotches, spots …
  M: Oh! _____!

6 **W:** Yes, and the pills that my mother had given me were so out-of-date that they had caused an allergic reaction …
  M: Oh! … _____!

B ▶ 2.9 Listen again and check your answers. Notice how intonation is used to sound interested.

C Listen and repeat the phrases. Try to sound interested. Then repeat but try to sound bored. Can you hear the difference?

❝ speakout TIP

How amazing! When someone tells a story, try to use comments and questions to show that you are interested. Remember to check your intonation. Do you sound interested?

SPEAKING

7A Prepare to tell a story. It can be a true story or a lie. Choose one of the situations below. Talk about when you:

- got stuck in a lift
- missed (or nearly missed) a flight
- slept outside
- spoke to someone famous
- got a tattoo
- appeared on television/in the newspaper
- chased/met a criminal
- were mistaken for someone else
- sung karaoke
- tried a very dangerous sport
- found something unusual
- did something embarrassing on holiday

B Think about the details of your story. Think about the questions below and make some notes or practise telling your story.

- Where were you?
- Why were you there?
- What were you doing?
- What happened?
- How did you feel?

C Work with other students. Take turns to tell your stories and listen and respond. Ask questions to decide if it is a true story or a lie.

A: I once got stuck in a lift.

B: Really?

A: Yes. I was …

D Tell the other students if it is a true story or a lie.

DVD PREVIEW

1 Work in pairs. Discuss the questions.

1 What famous fictional thieves/investigators/detectives do you know about?
2 Which are famous in your country?
3 Have you watched any programmes involving them?
4 Do you watch any crime detective dramas? Which ones? What do you like/dislike about them?
5 What are the features of good detective dramas, e.g. interesting characters?

2 Look at the pictures and read about the programme. What problems do you think Finch had when he stole the painting?

BBC Hustle

Hustle is a BBC drama series about a team of criminals who try to obtain and sell things in an illegal or dishonest way. In this programme we meet Finch, a burglar. He's in trouble with Customs, who believe that he has stolen a valuable piece of art. Unfortunately for Finch, when he stole the painting, things didn't go quite according to plan and now he needs the help of a friend.

▶ DVD VIEW

3A Match the words in the two columns to make common crime collocations.

1	guard	a) thief
2	art	b) guard
3	valuable	c) weapon
4	burglar	d) officer
5	customs	e) dog
6	loaded	f) alarm
7	security	g) painting

B Watch the programme. Tick the things above which you see in the clip. Which of the above do you <u>not</u> see?

4A Work in pairs and answer the questions.

1 How does Finch get into the grounds of the mansion?
2 What is the security guard doing?
3 What does Finch do when he breaks into the house?
4 What sets off the alarm?
5 How does Finch escape?
6 What happens at the airport?
7 Why do customs officers search Finch? Do they find anything?
8 What do customs plan to do?

B Watch the DVD again to check.

speakout a narrative

5 Work in groups. Invent details for the story using the questions below to help.

1 What exactly has Finch stolen?
2 Why did he steal it?
3 Is he usually a successful thief?
4 What happens in the airport in Brazil?
5 Where is the painting now?
6 What happens when Finch gets back to the UK?
7 How does Finch plan to get the painting?
8 Does Finch get arrested? Why/Why not?

6A ▶ 2.10 Listen to someone telling the story. How do they answer the questions above?

B Listen again and tick the key phrases you hear. What tense does the speaker use to tell the story? Why is this?

keyphrases

In this story, …
The problem is that …
In fact, …
What he doesn't realise/know is that …
However …
Later, …
Because of this, …
In the end, …

C Work in pairs. Take turns to retell the story (or your own version of the story) using the key phrases and the questions in Exercise 5 to help.

writeback a newspaper article

7A Read about a famous art theft. Who stole the painting? Why did he steal it? What happened in the end?

Famous painting stolen

On August 21st, 1911, Leonardo da Vinci's *Mona Lisa*, one of the most famous paintings in the world, was stolen from the wall of the Louvre Museum, in Paris. At first, the police thought one of the guards might have stolen the painting, but seventeen days after the theft, they arrested poet Guillaume Apollinaire. However, he was released when police could find no evidence that he had committed the crime. Two years later, the real thief, Vincenzo Peruggia, was arrested in Italy. Peruggia had worked at the museum, and had stolen the painting because he was angry about how many Italian paintings were on display in France. He had planned to return the painting to the Italian Uffizi gallery, in Florence. The public was so excited at the news of finding the *Mona Lisa* that the painting was displayed throughout Italy before it was returned to France in 1913.

B Write up the story of Finch's art theft as a newspaper article, using the article above and the key phrases to help.

TYPES OF STORY

1A Add the missing letters to complete the types of story.

1 One of my favourite _ ct _ _ n films of all time is *The Terminator*.
2 Jamie Foxx stars in *Ray*, a great b _ _ p _ c of Ray Charles.
3 *Pretty Woman*, starring Julia Roberts and Richard Gere, is my favourite r _ m _ nt _ c c _ m _ d _.
4 I'm not a great fan of p _ r _ _ d dr _ m _s, but I thought this production of *Jane Eyre* was brilliant.
5 I loved the psych _ l _ g _ c _ l thr _ ll _ r, *Silence of the Lambs*, but I found it very scary.
6 I still enjoy Agatha Christie's *Murder on the Orient Express*. It's one of the best ever d _ t _ ct _ v _ films.
7 I can't watch s _ _ _ nc _ f _ c _ _ _ n films, like *Star Wars* and *Alien*. I can't stand them.
8 I think d _ c _ dr _ m _ s, films like *Nixon*, are a great way to learn about what really happened during important events.

B Work in pairs. Choose five of the genres and make a 'best ever' list of the films in these genres.

PRESENT PERFECT/PAST SIMPLE

2A Look at the phrases below. Have you done any of these things? Write sentences using *I've ...* , *I haven't ...* and *I have never ...* .

• play in a band/write a song
• ride a horse • visit another country
• run a marathon
• walk in the mountains/go skiing
• organise a big family party
• see a famous band
• swim with dolphins/go scuba diving
• meet someone famous
• go to university/change your job
• start a business
• travel on your own
• write a diary/blog

B Choose one thing you have/ haven't done and tell your partner more about it.

I've played in a band. When I was at university I played in a band called 'The Hooligans'.

THE NEWS

3A Underline the correct option to complete the headlines.

1 Postal *collapse/strike* causes huge delays
2 Police attacked during student *demonstration/crash*
3 *Fugitives/Hostages* released after negotiation with rebel leader
4 Hundreds homeless after *earthquake/collapse* hits
5 *Fugitive/Flood* found hiding in forest
6 Train *strike/crash* kills sixty people
7 House *attacked/crashed* with petrol bomb
8 Young criminal *destroyed/shot* by police

B Work in pairs. Take turns to say a word and respond with a headline.
A: crash
B: Sleeping pilot caused plane to crash.

NARRATIVE TENSES

4A Put the verbs in the correct tense to complete the story.

Sasha [1]_____(wake) up late because she [2]_____ (forget) to set her alarm clock. She [3]_____(have) breakfast when the telephone [4]_____(ring). It was her boss. He wanted to know why she [5]_____ (not finish) the report that he [6]_____(ask) her to do. She quickly [7]_____ (leave) the house to go to work. She [8]_____(stand) on the train when she noticed that lots of people [9]_____ (look) her feet. Then, she [10]_____(realise) that she [11]_____(forget) to put her shoes on. She [12]_____(wear) her slippers.

B Can you remember a day when you woke up late? Why? What happened? Tell your partner.

TELLING A STORY

5A Add a word to each speaker's part to correct the conversations.

happened
1 A: This, when I was living in Hong Kong.

   B: Oh really? happened?

2 A: I was having a shower when all a sudden I saw a huge spider.

   B: Oh no. What you do?

3 A: Anyway, before I knew it someone called the police.

   B: Really? What next?

4 A: The next I knew, the man was running towards me and shouting.

   B: don't believe it!

5 A: , anyway I was going up the ski-lift and I fell off.

   B: embarrassing!

6 A: So, in end, I had to pay all the money back.

   B: dear.

B Work in pairs. Choose three of the conversations above and expand the stories.

C Work in groups. Take turns to role-play your conversations.

BBC VIDEO PODCAST

Download the video podcast and view people discussing whether they would ever tell a lie, what lies they've been told and who told them.

Authentic BBC interviews

www.pearsonlongman.com/speakout

UNIT 3

contact

SPEAKING

1 Work in groups and discuss.

1 What problems do teenagers and parents of teenagers have? Why?

2 What is the best thing a parent can do for a teenager?

READING

2A Read the article. Does it mention anything you discussed in Exercise 1? What is the main problem it mentions?

B Complete the summary of the article. Use one or two words for each gap.

> The writer is worried about the way she communicates with her ¹_____. She is always asking them questions about their ²_____, but most of the time they ³_____. She thinks that mobile phones and text messages mean that arrangements are always ⁴_____. In the end, she decides to ⁵_____ her own way of making plans. Next time she arranges to meet someone, she's going to be ⁶_____.

C Are the statements 1–5 true (T) or false (F)?

1 Simon usually arrives late.

2 The mother's teenage children always answer her questions.

3 The mother worries about her children when she doesn't know where they are.

4 The teenagers tend to make their plans early.

5 In the end the mother decides to change her behaviour.

D Find words or phrases in the text that match meanings 1–6.

1 changing an opinion or decision (paragraph 1)

2 manage a situation (paragraph 1)

3 too interested in other people's business (paragraph 5)

4 a fear that terrible things might happen (paragraph 5)

5 plans that you make just before they happen (paragraph 7)

6 if you can't change how people behave, then change your behaviour to be like them (paragraph 9)

3 Discuss the questions.

1 Do you think it is important for parents to know about their teenagers' plans?

2 Do you agree that mobile phones have changed the way that people make plans? How?

Life on planet teen

1 My friend Simon is always changing his mind about things. He's never quite sure where he's going to be or whether he'll be busy, and he never arrives when he says he will. This is sad, but I can cope with it. He doesn't live in my house.

2 But I don't like the same situation when it's happening under my own roof. Every day I ask my teenagers questions like an eager reporter. 'Where are you going? When are you coming back? How are you getting home?' And what do I get? If I'm lucky, a small bit of information.

3 'I think it's football after school,' says my fourteen-year-old. 'Unless that was last week.'

4 'I'm going out on Saturday,' says my sixteen-year-old. But most of my questions, however, go unanswered.

5 I don't want to be nosy. I really don't. But I would so love to have a rough idea of where members of the family are going to be. The problem is that I have an over-active imagination. The logic goes: you haven't got football, you didn't say you'd be late, therefore you must be under the wheels of a bus. But while I'm watching the clock in an attempt to stop my panic, my teenagers are changing their arrangements again …

GRAMMAR the future (plans)

4A Read the conversations about plans and complete the rules with the phrases in the box.

> the present continuous   *going to* + infinitive   *will* + infinitive   *might* + infinitive

1 A: Are you going to Joel's party?

  B: I <u>might</u> stay at home. I'm very tired.

2 A: Have you spoken to your teacher yet?

  B: No, I'<u>m going to speak</u> to her later.

3 A: What time <u>are you meeting</u> Adam?

  B: At six o'clock.

4 A: Do you want to come with us?

  B: No, thanks. I'<u>ll see</u> you at the stadium.

Rules:

1 Use _____ to talk about plans or arrangements which have already been made.

2 Use _____ to talk about a plan or intention. You have decided that you want to do this, but you may not have made the arrangements.

3 Use _____ when you are not sure what the plan is.

4 Use _____ to talk about the future when you have no specific plan, or you make the decision at the time of speaking.

6   Mobile phones and text-messaging means that dates and times are always flexible. 'That's why I don't know what I'm doing on Saturday,' says my eldest. 'I won't know until five minutes before.'

7   I can, of course, keep up with all this instant mind-changing by spending my Saturday nights texting 'R U OK?' But I can't help thinking that they enjoy the last-minute arrangements because it gives parents less time to object ('You're going where?').

8   After a series of questions, I finally give up. It's obvious that while I want to carefully plan the details of our family arrangements, my sons want more freedom.

9   So, if you can't beat them, join them. Simon, I'm going to follow your lead. The next time I arrange to meet someone, I'll be late. Or I might not turn up at all.

B Look at the article above again. Find examples of the structures described below.

1 present continuous for talking about future arrangements
2 *going to* + infinitive for future plans
3 *will* + infinitive for a decision made at the time of speaking
4 *might* + infinitive for a plan which is undecided

▥▶ page 132 **LANGUAGEBANK**

5A ▶ 3.1 Listen and complete the sentences.

1 What _____ at the weekend?
2 We _____ my brother and his family.
3 Where _____ for them?
4 They _____ a party on Friday.
5 _____ with us tomorrow?
6 I'll ask Marion when she _____.

B Listen again. Notice how they pronounce *going to* in fast speech. Does *going to* have the same pronunciation in sentences and questions? Do we always pronounce *going to* like this? When is it different?

C Listen again and practise saying the sentences fast.

What are you going to do at the weekend?

PRACTICE

6 Underline the correct alternatives to complete the conversation.

Pete: Hey Dax. What ¹*are you two doing / will you two do* on Saturday night?

Dax: I don't know. We ²*might / will* go to the Death City Dread concert. What about you?

Pete: ³*I'll have / I'm going to have* a bit of a party. My parents ⁴*are going / will go* away for the weekend, so I've asked a few people to come over to my place. Kris ⁵*will bring / is bringing* his DJ equipment round, so ⁶*we're having / we'll have* music. And everyone ⁷*is going to bring / might bring* some food and drink. Euan ⁸*will come / is coming* with a few friends. Do you think you can make it?

Dax: It sounds great. ⁹*I'm going to text / I'll text* Leyla to ask her what she thinks. Then ¹⁰*I'm calling / I'll call* you back to let you know. Is that OK?

Pete: That's fine. ¹¹*I'll speak / I'm going to speak* to you later. Bye.

7A Write sentences for situations 1–6 below. Think about whether you have made arrangements already, then decide which tenses to use.

1 something you plan to do at the weekend
Some friends are coming to stay. (I've already arranged this)
I might go out for a pizza on Friday night. (I don't know yet.)

2 something you are going to do after the class
3 something you might buy in the near future
4 something that someone in your family is planning to do
5 a plan or ambition you have, related to your work / studies
6 something that you plan to do for your next holiday

B Work in pairs. Compare your ideas. Ask and answer questions to find out more information.

My sister's moving to Poland.
Really? That sounds exciting. Which city?

VOCABULARY communication

8A Match the words in the box with sentences 1–8.

| ~~gossip~~ | compliment | moan | boast |
| argue | warn | chat | apologise |

1 Have you heard about Vicki? She's got a new boyfriend! __gossip__

2 I just wanted to say I'm really sorry I missed the match. _____

3 So, how was your day? Did it go well? _____

4 I was the best rugby player in my school, you know. _____

5 No, that's not true. I didn't say that you could borrow my mp3 player! _____

6 Listen, it's very important that you don't get into cars with people who you don't know. _____

7 You look lovely. That top looks really nice on you. _____

8 And when I got home, the house was in a complete mess. They're so lazy. They never help. _____

B Decide who is talking in sentences 1–8, parents (P) or teenagers (T).

C ▶ 3.2 Listen and notice the intonation. Then listen and repeat.

➡ page 150 **VOCABULARYBANK**

SPEAKING

9A Think about when you were a teenager. Make a note of things you:

• loved/hated/moaned about
• argued about with your parents/friends
• were warned about by parents/teachers

B Think about your life now. Make a note about people you:

• enjoy chatting to/gossiping with
• tend to argue with
• moan about
• have apologised to

C Work in pairs. Compare your experiences. How have your ideas changed since you were a teenager?

A: I really enjoy gossiping with my girl friends about who we like and who we don't.

B: Do you? Me too! It was the same when we were teenagers!

WRITING messages

10 Work in pairs. Look at messages 1–4 and answer the questions.

1 When do you usually write messages to people?
2 What do you think the relationship is between the writer and the person they are writing to in these messages?
3 Are the messages formal or informal?

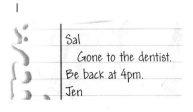

1

> Sal
> Gone to the dentist.
> Be back at 4pm.
> Jen

3

> Hope you had a good day. Dinner's in the oven.
> Fx

2

> Martin
> Please call Tricia on 07679 437 562 asap
> Lucy

4

> Can you pick us up from football tonight?
> See you later
> Ben & Max

❝ speakout TIP

Leave it out! When we write notes and messages we don't always write complete sentences. We often miss out small grammatical words to make the message shorter.

LEARN TO use note form

11A Look at the messages 1–4 above. The words in the box have been left out. Which message do they belong to?

| 1 | We'll | Your | I've | Can you | I'll |

B Rewrite messages 1–4 below using fewer words.

1

> Are you feeling hungry? Do you want to meet me for lunch at Pavarotti's 1pm?
> R x

3

> Pete called to say that he won't be able to come to dinner. Do you think you could call him back on 01954 627 823? Thanks.
> Jayne

2

> **message**
> **We're going to see Elton John in concert. Would you like me to book you a ticket?**
> **Tonya**

4

> I'm really sorry but I can't come to the cinema tonight because I've got too much work to do. I hope you enjoy the film.
> Bess

12 Write short messages for the situations below.

1 You're going away for the weekend and would like your flatmate to water the plants.
2 You want to invite a classmate to the cinema.
3 You need to apologise to a work colleague for missing a meeting.

▶ **GRAMMAR** | the future (predictions) ▶ **VOCABULARY** | future time markers ▶ **HOW TO** | make predictions

LISTENING

1 Look at the photos and answer the questions.

1 What has replaced the objects in the pictures?

2 In your opinion, are the replacements better than the original things?

2A Work in pairs and discuss.

a) In the future how will we communicate with people in other countries?

b) In the future will we still use pen and paper to write?

c) In the future will we watch TV the same way we do now?

B ▶ 3.3 Listen to some people discussing the questions above. Do they mention any of your ideas?

C Find and correct three factual mistakes in the notes. Listen again to check.

> System for translating foreign languages
> Talk to foreigner on the phone & his/her words = translated into your ear
> Online translation services already exist BUT often make mistakes, e.g. English to Chinese

> TV programme says handwriting will disappear in 100 years
> Will use thumbprints/digital signatures, e.g. scans, instead
> Man says people will still carry pens
> Woman says 'kids' (10-12 yrs old) may stop writing

> They think there'll still be a large TV in the living room
> BUT TV programmes will be 'on demand' – watch what you want
> Man thinks it'll change 'in the long term' – a long time in the future
> Woman agrees

3 Look at the words and phrases in the box. What do you think they mean? Use audio script 3.3 on page 166 to help you.

> an intermediary   (that) will stop barriers   thumbprints
> retina scans   the most straightforward way (to do something)
> on demand   a large screen   method of delivery

VOCABULARY future time markers

4A Read sentences 1–9 and underline the time markers.

1 In the near future, there will be a system for translating foreign languages.

2 They don't think that handwriting will exist in the next ten years.

3 This new system for watching TV could happen in a month or two.

4 Certainly in the long term this will be the future.

5 I think these changes will happen in the short term.

6 In ten years' time children won't be able to write with pen and paper.

7 There will still be TV sets a long time from now.

8 I don't think there will be any big changes next year.

9 Phones that can translate languages will be with us shortly.

B Look at the time markers again. Put them under the correct heading below.

1 An exact time in the future

2 Not an exact time in the future – soon

in the near future

in the next ten years

3 Not an exact time in the future – not very soon

C Work in pairs. Ask and answer questions 1–3, using both parts of the question.

1 Will you still live in the same place: a) in the near future? b) in ten years' time?

2 Will you still attend classes: a) six months from now? b) next year?

3 What projects will you work on: a) in the short term? b) in the long term?

GRAMMAR the future (predictions)

5A Read the preview of a programme. What is the programme about?

Visions of the future

In this new BBC three-part series, physicist and futurist Dr Michio Kaku explores the science of today, tomorrow, and beyond. He argues that we are at a turning point in history. In this century, we will move from being passive observers of nature to its active designers. This will give us amazing new possibilities but also great responsibilities.

B Read some of the predictions from the BBC programme. Are they certain (C) or possible (P)?

1 Artificial intelligence <u>will</u> revolutionise homes, workplaces and lifestyles. *C*

2 Robots with human-level intelligence <u>may</u> finally become a reality.

3 The human body <u>could</u> be repaired as easily as a car.

4 We <u>are going to</u> make the … transition from the 'Age of Discovery' to the 'Age of Mastery'.

5 We <u>are likely to</u> live longer because of developments in genetics and biotechnology.

C Look at the underlined words above. Complete the rules with *will, could, to* or *be*.

Rule:

1 We use ____*will*____ + infinitive to make predictions about the future.

2 We use _____ *going to* + infinitive to make predictions when there is present evidence.

3 We use *may* or _____ + infinitive to say something is possible but not certain.

4 We use *likely* + infinitive with _____ to say something will probably happen.

▶ page 132 **LANGUAGEBANK**

PRACTICE

6A Circle the correct alternative, a), b) or c), to complete the programme review.

Dr Michio Kaku says that in the near future we [1]_____ new worlds that look like our own world. To prove it, he flies around in Second Life and tells us that virtual reality is [2]_____ more like real reality.

Kaku then jumps into a remote controlled car, and tells us the car is so intelligent that the words 'traffic jam' and 'traffic accident' [3]_____ from the language.

It isn't just cars that will be intelligent. In a few years' time microchips will be so cheap they [4]_____ into every product we buy – our walls, our furniture, even our clothes. And they [5]_____ to be so small we [6]_____ they exist. The internet, he tells us, will also be everywhere. Kaku says our sunglasses [7]_____ our future home entertainment centre.

Kaku then does a virtual dance using 3-D technology (his dance partner is hundreds of miles away) and explains that one day in the near future, 3-D technology [8]_____ the telephone and [9]_____ air travel.

Then he looks at the popularity of robots. He concludes that, in the long term, some of our closest friends [10]_____ people.

1 (a) will design (b) will be design (c) will to design
2 (a) become (b) going become (c) going to become
3 (a) going to disappear (b) are going to disappearing (c) are going to disappear
4 (a) are could be built (b) could be built (c) could built
5 (a) likely (b) likely are (c) are likely
6 (a) won't to know (b) not will know (c) won't know
7 (a) may become (b) may of become (c) may to become
8 (a) could replace (b) is could replace (c) could be replace
9 (a) reduce might (b) might to reduce (c) might reduce
10 (a) not might be (b) might not be (c) might be not

B Discuss. Which predictions, if they come true, will be good/bad for the world? Why?

SPEAKING

7A Look at the picture of the future above. Is it realistic? Why?

B Think about the topics in the box. How do you think they will change in the future? Make some notes.

> communication   technology   work habits   cities
> the environment   food

C Work in pairs and discuss your ideas.
Communication: I think we will probably have video conference calls on our mobile phones. There probably won't be …

VOCABULARY *PLUS* idioms

Idiom /ˈɪdiəm/ [C]   a group of words that have a different meaning from the usual meaning of the separate words. For example, 'under the weather' is an idiom meaning 'ill'.

8A Read the definition of an idiom and underline the idioms in sentences 1–5.
1 In the future, mobile phones won't only be used for <u>small talk</u> or for taking photos.
2 For people who work against the clock, new ways to communicate will be important.
3 We'll use pen and paper for writing things that are on our mind and for personal notes.
4 Home-made programmes won't be everyone's cup of tea, but that's the future of TV.
5 Music is an issue that's close to my heart because my husband is a musician.

B Look at the underlined idioms and decide if these statements about idioms are true (T) or false (F)?
1 Idioms are usually formal.
2 You cannot usually change the order of words in an idiom.
3 You can sometimes change the verb tense and the subject of an idiom.
4 You can usually guess the meaning from one word in the idiom.

C Work in pairs and compare your answers. Then turn to page 160 to check your answers.

When you learn new idioms write them in a special place in your vocabulary notebook. To remember idioms better, record them in context and add your own examples. Do this for the idioms in Exercise 8A. Then try them out. Make sure it's the right situation and you remember to use the exact words.

9 Work in pairs. Look at the idioms organised by topic. What do the underlined idioms mean?

> PROBLEMS
> 1 We forgot to pay our taxes. Now we're <u>in hot water</u>.
> 2 I said the wrong thing again. I always <u>put my foot in it</u>.
> TIME
> 3 We're <u>working against the clock</u>. We have two hours to finish the project.
> 4 I'm sure we can win this match but we're <u>running out of time</u>.

10 Look at the idioms organised by key words. Match idioms 1–6 with meanings a)–f).

> BODY PARTS
> 1 <u>Keep an eye on</u> him. b
> 2 Can you <u>give me a hand</u>?
> FOOD AND DRINK
> 3 <u>It's not my cup of tea</u>.
> 4 It was <u>a piece of cake</u>.
> ANIMALS
> 5 You're <u>a dark horse</u>!
> 6 I want to get out of <u>the rat race</u>.

a) I don't like it
b) watch
c) help me
d) the competitive world of work
e) you have a lot of secrets
f) easy

11A Find and correct the mistakes. There is a mistake in each sentence.
1 When was the last time you gave someone the hand?
2 Which student do you think is a horse dark?
3 When's the last time you put your feet in it?
4 Which issues are close by your heart?
5 Do you often have to work against the clocks?
6 When were you last in warm water?

B Write an answer to each question. Then compare your answers with other students.
➡ page 150 **VOCABULARYBANK**

37

SPEAKING

1A Work in pairs. Look at the cartoon and read the story. What do you think happened next?

One year a US TV show called *Late Night with David Letterman* was nominated for an award. To celebrate, the eighty people involved in the show went to a restaurant in Malibu, where they sat at twelve different tables and ate outside. That night someone told the show's producer that Johnny Carson, a famous American talk show host, was in the restaurant.

The producer went over to Carson's table and said, 'It would be so nice if you could say hello to David and meet some of the people. It would mean a lot to them.' So at the end of his dinner, Carson came over and said hello. He sat at the table, talked for a while and then left.

At the end of the evening the producer went to pay the bill.

B Read the end of the story on page 160.

C Work in pairs. Retell the story using the words in the box.

> TV show　nominated for an award　celebrate　restaurant
> talk show host　say hello　pay the bill　generous　called
> didn't know　at the table　ten thousand dollars

VOCABULARY misunderstandings

2A Complete sentences 1–8 with phrases a)–h).

1　Make sure you go to the King's Street in the centre of town because …

2　We mistakenly left home at 5.30 because …

3　I was expecting to see Pete, my old school friend, but …

4　I didn't do the homework because …

5　We thought her birthday was 16th July but …

6　I ended up at the wrong house because …

7　When I called Mary Lou, she thought I was a stranger because …

8　I answered the phone but …

a)　it was a **wrong number**.

b)　I'd got the **wrong address**.

c)　we **got the date wrong**.

d)　**we thought** it started at six.

e)　**it was a different** Peter Smith.

f)　there are two streets **with the same name**.

g)　she **didn't recognise** my voice.

h)　I **didn't realise** it was for today.

B Which expressions in bold do you know? Which have you used?

FUNCTION dealing with misunderstandings

3A ▶ 3.4 Listen to four telephone conversations involving misunderstandings. What type of misunderstandings are they?

B Listen again and answer the questions.

Conversation 1

1　Who did the woman want to speak to?

2　Who did she speak to?

Conversation 2

3　How did David make his hotel reservation?

4　What hotel does he want to stay in?

Conversation 3

5　What time does the show finish?

6　What time did the show start?

Conversation 4

7　What does the woman want to rent?

8　What is the date?

C Complete expressions 1–7 with the words in the box.

> tell　that　me (x2)　saying　mean　name　again

1　I didn't catch any of _____.

2　You've lost _____.

3　Could you repeat the last _____?

4　Can you say that _____?

5　What exactly do you _____?

6　I don't get what you're _____.

7　Do you mean to _____ …?

D ▶ 3.5 Listen and check. Then listen again and copy the intonation.

▶ page 132 **LANGUAGEBANK**

THE FELTON

4A There is one word missing in each response. Complete the responses with the missing word.

1 A: Oh no! I can't find the key.

       mean

  B: Do you|to say we're going to be locked out all night?

2 A: And after Jimmy left Minnie, he married Millie, who used to be married to Billy.

  B: You've me. Who are all these people?

3 A: There was a little accident with the spaghetti bolognese and your sofa.

  B: What exactly you mean?

4 A: The boss wants to see you. It's about the money that's missing from the accounts.

  B: I don't what you're saying.

5 A: Um, er, I think my new phone number is, um, 654 0987 6743.

  B: I catch any of that. What's the number?

6 A: My home address is 39 Kings Street, Manchester, Lancashire, M8 2TO.

  B: Can you that again? I didn't hear.

7 A: We're leaving Los Angeles at 11.00p.m., OK? Then we arrive in Sydney at 5.50a.m.

  B: Could you the last part? I didn't hear you.

B Work in pairs. What does speaker A say next? Continue the conversations with your own words.

LEARN TO reformulate

5A Read the extracts from the audio 3.4. Underline five examples of how the speaker reformulates what he/she heard.

1 A: We've got no reservations in the name of Cullinan, and we're fully booked tonight.

  B: <u>So you're saying</u> I can't stay here. This is the Sheldon Hotel, yes?

2 C: Didn't you say it starts at 7.00?

  D: No, it starts at 5.00 and finishes at 7.00!

  C: So what you mean is I've missed the whole show.

3 E: Yes, but today's a holiday and all the cars have been booked already.

  F: Do you mean to tell me that there's nothing at all? No cars available?

  E: There's nothing till tomorrow, I'm afraid.

  F: But I definitely booked a car for today, the third of July.

  E: It's the fourth of July today. In other words, your booking was for yesterday.

B ▶ 3.6 Listen to the phrases. Notice how the words are linked together in fast speech.

So‿you're‿saying …

C Listen again and repeat the phrases.

SPEAKING

6A Work in pairs and role-play the situation.

     Student A   **Student B**

You are a guest at a hotel. Twenty minutes ago you called reception, asking for some soap to be sent to your room. Room service brought you some tomato soup. You want them to take the soup back and bring some soap. Call reception to make your complaint.

You are a receptionist at a hotel. A guest calls to make a complaint. Start the conversation by saying 'Reception. How can I help you?'

Hello. Yes, I'm afraid I have a problem … Explain the problem.

Apologise for the misunderstanding and say you will send someone with soap.

Check details and thank the receptionist for their help.

Confirm details, apologise again and end the call.

B Change roles and turn to page 162.

C Work in pairs and take turns. Student A: ring reception and make a complaint. Student B: apologise and offer a solution. Use the flow charts to help and role-play the situations.

DVD PREVIEW

1 Discuss. How has the internet changed the world?

2A Did you mention any of the following?

1 It **creates wealth**.

2 It allows us to **challenge authority**.

3 It allows authorities to **spy** and **censor**.

4 It has created a generation of **web addicts**.

5 It **opens up new realms of knowledge**.

6 It has allowed the **pioneers** and **key players** in technology to become powerful.

7 It has made **e-shopping** possible.

B Work in pairs. Check you understand the meaning of the words/expressions in bold.

3 Read the introduction to the programme. What is it about? Who does the presenter speak to?

BBC The Virtual Revolution

This BBC documentary looks at the revolutionary impact of the internet. Dr Aleks Krotoski tells the story of the internet from its early days through to its most recent successes and innovations. She looks at the good and bad sides of the internet, revealing statistics that show how much we use it and how it has changed the world. The programme also includes comments from some of the best-known internet pioneers.

▶ DVD VIEW

4 Watch the DVD. Put the statistics in the order they are mentioned.

a) 18 million people read blogs.

b) People in the UK spend a billion pounds a week on the net.

c) A quarter of the planet now uses the web.

d) In the UK 35 million people log on to the internet every day.

e) 5 million people in the UK use a dating website every month.

5A Match the people below to extracts a)–g).

1 Aleks Krotoski, the presenter (x 2)

2 Al Gore

3 Mark Zuckerberg

4 Stephen Fry

5 Bill Gates

6 Steve Wozniak

a) In the ten years that I've been studying the web and writing about it as a journalist I've seen it take our world and shake it apart.

b) Well, the web is how mankind communicates nowadays.

c) It's like the internet has become a brain. It's the smartest brain in the world.

d) It is an empowering tool that has more potential than any other that human civilisation has ever developed.

e) The world is just going to keep on getting more and more open and there's going to be more information available about everything.

f) This is astounding technology and we should just take a moment to celebrate the power and the reach that it gives us.

g) The web is a revolution.

B Watch the DVD again to check.

C Discuss in groups.

1 Do you think there are any negative sides of the internet or is it all positive?

2 What do you like best about the internet: (a) it helps us to communicate, (b) it opens up new realms of knowledge, (c) it creates wealth or (d) other?

3 'Well, the web is how mankind communicates nowadays.' (Bill Gates). Do you agree?

speak**out** communication preferences

6A ▶ 3.7 Listen to a woman talking about how she prefers to communicate (via phone calls, emails, letters, text messages or face-to-face). What does she say about the first four topics below?

- giving good news
- giving bad news
- arranging social activities
- sending a 'thank you' message
- catching up with friends
- making a formal complaint
- asking for information, e.g. to get tickets
- giving opinions on issues

B Listen again and tick the key phrases you hear.

key**phrases**

It depends (on …)
It's much better to …
I prefer to …
On the other hand,
In those circumstances I'd rather …
The best way to do this is to send …
It's more convenient.
People really appreciate …
I like it when …

C How do you prefer to communicate? What does it depend on? Make some notes to prepare for the discussion.

D Work in groups and discuss your opinions. Which ways of communicating are the most popular in your class?

write**back** a memo

7A Your company has decided to have email-free Fridays. Read the notes below. What are the reasons for doing this?

Rules: no internal emails — last Friday of every month
Short memos allowed
Emails OK for external clients
Reasons: Encourage face-to-face communication
Encourage phone conversations
Reduce time spent on emails
Change routine
Additional info: trial email-free Fridays for 6 months. Then review: questionnaire to all staff. Final decision made next year.

B Your boss has asked you to write a memo explaining the idea to the staff. Read the opening lines and complete the memo using the key phrases to help.

Subject: memo

Dear staff,
Starting next month, we have a new initiative.

COMMUNICATION

1 Work in pairs. Take turns to think of three different situations for each verb in the box.

> moan   argue   chat   gossip   warn   apologise   boast   compliment

A: OK. Moan. You moan when it's raining and you have to go on your bike.

B: And you moan when you have too much work to do.

A: Yes, and when the prices of things go up, so everything costs more.

THE FUTURE (PLANS)

2A Complete the paragraphs with phrases from the box.

> 'm going to have   having
> 'm organising   might
> 'm finishing   are going   I'll be
> are coming   will   going to

I ¹_____ work at the end of the month. I've been a teacher here for nearly twenty years, so ²_____ sad when I leave the school for the last time. But in the future, I ³_____ more time to do some of the things I enjoy. My wife and I ⁴_____ travelling. We ⁵_____ visit Australia, which I've always wanted to do.

I'm ⁶_____ be forty next month, so I'm ⁷_____ a big party. Lots of people ⁸_____ that I don't see very often, so I'm really looking forward to it. I ⁹_____ a band, and lots of delicious food and drink, so everyone ¹⁰_____ have a good time.

B Write a short paragraph describing a plan you have for the future. Then compare your ideas with a partner.

FUTURE TIME MARKERS

3A Match 1–6 with a)–f) to make sentences.

1 I might live in *a foreign country* in the long
2 I hope to *be retired* in twenty years'
3 I will finish *this course* in a month
4 I hope to *write my autobiography* a long time
5 I want to buy *a new car* in the near
6 I'm going to *go travelling* next

a) time.
b) year.
c) future.
d) term.
e) from now.
f) or two.

B Choose four of the sentences above. Change the words in italics so they are true for you.

THE FUTURE (PREDICTIONS)

4A Find and correct the mistakes. Seven of the predictions contain grammatical mistakes.

1 Man not will fly for fifty years. (1901)
2 There isn't going be any German reunification this century. (1984)
3 Democracy will to be dead by 1950. (1936)
4 By 1980 all power (electric, atomic, solar) is likely be almost free. (1956)
5 The Japanese car industry isn't likely to be successful in the US market. (1968)
6 Man will be never reach the Moon. (1957)
7 Television won't very matter in your lifetime or mine. (1936)
8 The internet may to become useful for business but never for the general public. (1989)

B Change the verbs so they mean the opposite and become intelligent predictions. You may need to change some other words.

Man will fly within fifty years.

There is going to be German reunification this century.

DEALING WITH MISUNDERSTANDINGS

5A Put the words in the correct order to make responses in dialogues 1–3.

1 **A:** I've heard that a lot of our employees like you.
   B: get / I / saying / you're / what / don't
   A: And I'm looking for someone to take over the business when I retire.
   B: you / do / what / mean / exactly?

2 **A:** The flight should land at 4.00, but it's going to land at 4.15 or 4.20 because of the delay.
   B: didn't / that / I / of / any / catch
   A: Instead of landing at 4.00 we're going to land at 4.15 or 4.20 because of the late take off.
   B: you / that / can / again / say?

3 **A:** David Johnson and Johnny Thomson are going to meet Tommy Davies tonight.
   B: me / lost / you've
   A: Johnson, Thomson and Davies are the company directors. They're meeting to discuss the company's future.
   B: say / do / mean / to / you / they're meeting without me?

B Work in pairs and practise the conversations. Then change roles and repeat.

BBC VIDEO PODCAST

Download the video podcast and view people describing how modern technology has helped or damaged our everyday communication.

Authentic BBC interviews

www.pearsonlongman.com/speakout

SPEAKING
> Discuss the qualities needed for different jobs
> Talk about past habits
> Participate in a meeting
> Describe a day in your life

LISTENING
> Listen to people describing dream jobs gone wrong
> Listen to people making decisions in a meeting
> Watch a BBC comedy about a man's first day in a new job

READING
> Read an article about millionaires
> Read a covering letter
> Read job advertisements

WRITING
> Write a covering letter
> Write about daily routines

BBC CONTENT
> Video podcast: Is your job a 'dream job'?
> DVD: Gavin and Stacey

UNIT

4

jobs

▶ Millionaires   P44

▶ Dream job   P47

▶ That's a good idea   P50

▶ Gavin and Stacey   P52

▶ **GRAMMAR** | *must/have to/should* ▶ **VOCABULARY** | personal qualities ▶ **HOW TO** | talk about work

VOCABULARY personal qualities

1A Read about the qualities people need to do their jobs. Which jobs do you think they are talking about?

Winning is the most important thing for me. I've always been **competitive**, so I love my job. I think I'm **a good leader**. It's important that all the players know what they're doing and it's my job to tell them. The decisions I make are important for the whole team, so I can't be **indecisive**.

I have classes of 80 to 100 children so I have to be **hard-working**. I do my best, because education is so important for the children. You need to be **a good communicator** in my job, so that you can get the children interested in what they have to learn. Often, we don't have very many resources, so we also need to be creative and be able to **think outside the box**.

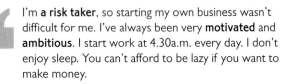

I'm **a risk taker**, so starting my own business wasn't difficult for me. I've always been very **motivated** and **ambitious**. I start work at 4.30a.m. every day. I don't enjoy sleep. You can't afford to be lazy if you want to make money.

B Match the words and phrases in bold above with the definitions 1–9.

1 work with a lot of effort _____
2 have problems making a decision _____
3 think differently or in a new way _____
4 want to be more successful than others _____
5 want to be successful or powerful _____
6 want to achieve something _____
7 person who does things which are dangerous _____
8 person who has the qualities to manage a group of people _____
9 person who can express ideas or feelings clearly to others _____

C Which qualities do you think you have? Work in pairs and compare your answers.

� page 151 **VOCABULARYBANK**

READING

2A Read statements 1–6 about millionaires. Do you think they are true (T) or false (F)?

1 Most millionaires are born rich.
2 Millionaires think that money is more important than love or marriage.
3 They work more than sixty hours a week.
4 They don't like to work when they're on holiday.
5 They do well at school and usually go to university.
6 They like spending money on designer goods.

B Read the article and check your answers.

Have you got what it takes?

1 So you want to be a millionaire, but have you got what it takes? To find out what millionaires are really like and what motivates them, the BBC programme *Mind of a Millionaire* did a survey. Psychologists looked at self-made millionaires to try and understand what qualities are needed to make a million. So, what is really important to a millionaire?

> **You don't have to be born rich to be a millionaire.**

2 The answer, not surprisingly, is money, money and more money. Money is more important than love or marriage. And if you give a millionaire money, they won't spend it, they'll invest it to make more money. But you don't have to be born rich to be a millionaire. Most millionaires come from relatively poor backgrounds. And you don't have to work hard at school either. A lot of successful entrepreneurs were lazy at school and didn't get good results. However, you must have a clear idea of what you want to do (get rich) and you really ought to start early. A lot of millionaires left school early, to start their own businesses.

3   If you want to be a millionaire, not only do you have to work hard, but you should enjoy your work. And you shouldn't take too many holidays. Most millionaires work more than sixty hours a week. Half stay in contact with the office while they're on holiday and 14 percent of them refuse to switch off. Having a good work-life balance is fine for people who only want to be moderately successful, but if you're really ambitious, you have to put in the hours.

4   What are millionaires like as people? The survey found that they are competitive, they like taking risks, and they are aggressive and self-confident. They'll do anything they can to get what they want.

5   Millionaires can break all sorts of rules. The only thing they mustn't do is break the law. Surprisingly, most millionaires are careful spenders. They prefer Gap to Gucci. Many of them choose not to spend money on expensive designer clothes – they would rather find a bargain on the high street. And they don't spend lots of money on expensive meals in restaurants either. They prefer to eat at home. However, they do like to drive Mercedes and go on at least three expensive holidays a year. One last thing: millionaires don't care what other people think of them. So, if you want to be a millionaire, you shouldn't worry about what other people think of you. Just do your own thing.

3 Underline words or phrases in the article that match meanings 1–6.

1   their family didn't have much money (paragraph 2)
2   they never stop thinking about work (paragraph 3)
3   having enough time for work and for the things you enjoy (paragraph 3)
4   work long hours (paragraph 3)
5   find something for a good price (paragraph 5)
6   do what you want without worrying about what other people think (paragraph 5)

4A Work in pairs. Take turns to say things which millionaires do and don't do. Find as many points as possible.
Millionaires think a lot about money. Most millionaires …

B Think of millionaires you have heard of. Do you agree with what the article says?

GRAMMAR   *must/have to/should (obligation)*

5 Match the words in bold in sentences 1–6 with the meanings a)–e). One meaning matches with two sentences.
1   You **don't have to** be born rich to be a millionaire.
2   If you want to be a millionaire, you **have to** work hard.
3   You **must** have a clear idea of what you want to do.
4   You **should** enjoy your work.
5   You **shouldn't** take too many holidays.
6   You **mustn't** worry about what other people think of you.

a) It's a good idea.
b) It's not necessary. You don't need to be/do this.
c) It's necessary. You have no choice.
d) It's important that you don't do this.
e) It's not a good idea.

➡ page 134 **LANGUAGEBANK**

PRACTICE

6A Make sentences with the prompts. Use the positive or negative form of the word in brackets.
1   postmen / get up early in the morning (have)
Postmen have to get up early in the morning.
2   window cleaners / be afraid of heights (must)
3   nurses / be patient and care about other people (should)
4   businessmen often / travel a lot (have)
5   politicians / do their job because they want fame (should)
6   teachers / enjoy working with children (must)
7   doctors / train for several years before they can work (have)
8   teachers / work in the school during the holidays (have)
9   police officers / good communicators (have)

➡ page 151 **VOCABULARYBANK**

B Think about three different jobs. Make sentences to describe what qualities are/aren't important for these jobs. Compare your ideas with a partner.
Teachers have to be motivated. They should be good communicators, but they don't have to be competitive.

Have you got what it takes to be a millionaire?

Can you work your way to success? Try our survey to find out.

1 When your boss goes on holiday, do you:
a) come in later and leave earlier?
b) work as normal?
c) work harder – you want to impress your boss's boss?

2 You see your dream job advertised. Unfortunately, it asks for five specific skills and you've only got two. Do you:
a) resolve to get at least two more of the skills in the near future, so you can apply next time?
b) apply for the job anyway, focusing on the skills you've got and ignoring the ones you haven't?
c) not apply – what's the point of being rejected again?

3 You have gone to a meeting across town, but your client is keeping you waiting. Do you:
a) get angry – why should you wait for anyone?
b) use the time to phone a friend?
c) use the time to make work-related calls?

4 If you don't like a job, do you:
a) leave – nobody should have to work all the time?
b) leave as soon as you've got a better job, or have the finance to start your own business?
c) do nothing – all jobs are miserable?

5 You are helping a friend out in their clothes shop. The store closes at 6p.m. At 5.55p.m. a woman rushes in saying she is looking for a dress to wear for a party. Do you:
a) tell her you are closing and shut up shop?
b) tell her you've got nothing in her size?
c) tell her you've got some in stock and show her?

SPEAKING

7A Work in pairs. Do the survey above. Then check your score on page 159.

B Discuss. Do you agree with what the survey says about your score? Why/Why not? Do you know anyone who would make a good entrepreneur? Why?

VOCABULARY *PLUS* confusing words

8 Read the vocabulary notes and complete sentences 1 and 2.

> **job · work**
> **Work** is what you do to earn money:
> *What kind of **work** does he do?*
>
> A **job** is the particular type of work that you do:
> *Sam's got a **job** as a waiter.*
>
> **Job** can be plural, but **work** cannot.

1 I've finished my degree, so I'm looking for a _____.
2 It's not easy to find _____ when you're my age.

9A Underline the correct alternative in the sentences below. What is the difference between these words?

1 He suddenly *remembered/reminded* that he had to go to the bank.
2 Can you *remember/remind* me to call him later?
3 I've *forgotten/left* my keys in the car.
4 Did you *hear/listen* that noise?
5 Can you say that again? I'm sorry, I wasn't *listening/hearing*.
6 Being ill on holiday isn't much *fun/funny*.

B Turn to pape 159 to check your answers.

speakout TIP

To help you remember confusing words and vocabulary, write them in personalised sentences in your notebook. Write sentences about your life using some of the words from Exercise 9.

10A Complete questions 1–6 with a suitable word from Exercises 8 and 9.

1 What are the best paid _____ in your country?
2 Is there anything you often _____, like phone numbers, or someone's name?
3 If you _____ carefully, what noises can you hear at the moment?
4 Do you write notes to _____ yourself about important things?
5 How much did you _____ for your first job? What did you buy?
6 What do you like doing for _____ ? Do you like playing games?

B Work in pairs. Take turns to ask and answer the questions above.

▶ page 151 **VOCABULARY**BANK

▶ **GRAMMAR** | *used to, would*   ▶ **VOCABULARY** | strong adjectives   ▶ **HOW TO** | talk about past habits

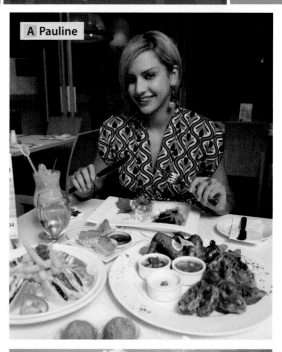

A Pauline

LISTENING

1 Work in pairs. Look at the photos and answer the questions.

1 What are these jobs? Would you like to do them? Why/Why not?

2 What is your idea of a dream job?

2A ▶ 4.1 Listen to people talking about their dream jobs. Match the speaker to the photos opposite.

B What problem does each speaker talk about?

C Listen again and answer questions 1–10. Write Angie (A), Pauline (P) or Monty (M).

1 Who works very long hours? *A*

2 Who got bored of eating restaurant food?

3 Who gave up their dream job?

4 Who travels a lot for their job?

5 Who sometimes works seven days a week?

6 Who thought their job looked exciting?

7 Who is interested in the science of what they do?

8 Who previously worked in a bank?

9 Who has always loved fashion?

10 Who had put on a lot of weight?

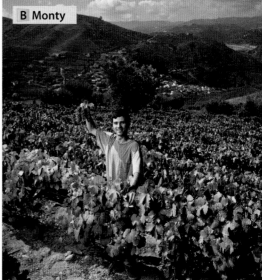

B Monty

VOCABULARY   strong adjectives

3 Read audio script 4.1 on page 168 and find the strong adjectives in bold. Match them to the gradable adjectives below.

1 good: wonderful, _____, brilliant

2 bad: awful, _____

3 big: enormous

4 small: tiny

5 tired: _____

6 hot: boiling

7 cold: _____

8 tasty: _____

9 angry: _____

10 interesting: _____

11 pretty: _____

12 difficult: _____

4A Complete conversations 1–6.

1 A: The food here's very tasty.
   B: Yes, it's _____.

2 A: It's really hot outside today.
   B: I know. It's absolutely _____.

3 A: Was your girlfriend angry?
   B: Yes, she was really _____.

4 A: The view of the lake is really pretty.
   B: Yes, it's _____, isn't it?

5 A: Do you find the job interesting?
   B: I think it's absolutely _____.

6 A: It's difficult to understand what he's saying.
   B: I know. It's _____.

C Angie

B ▶ 4.2 Listen and mark the stress on the strong adjectives. Notice how speaker B emphasises the stressed syllable in their intonation.

C Listen again and shadow speaker B's response.

GRAMMAR used to, would

5A Read the texts. What did the children dream of doing? Have they achieved their dreams?

Childhood dreams

When I was young, I spent afternoons imagining that I had my own rocket ship. I would invite my cousins and my friends to join my crew, and we would lie on our backs inside a very large cardboard box and go through a countdown, blast off into space, spend the whole day exploring other planets, and be back in time for dinner. So that was sort of the beginning – my earliest memories of being fascinated by space.
Chang Diaz, rocket scientist

We used to live in France, and as a child, I always used to collect small insects that I found in the fields near my house. One day I found a butterfly. It couldn't fly, so I put it in a jar and looked after it. The next morning, when I opened the jar, the butterfly opened its wings and flew away. That was when I realised what I wanted to do with my life.
Lowri Davies, veterinary surgeon

B Look at the underlined words in sentences a)–d) and match them with rules 1–3.

a) I would invite my cousins and my friends to join my crew.

b) We used to live in France.

c) I always used to collect small insects.

d) One day I found a butterfly.

Rules:

1 Use the past simple, not *used to* or *would,* to talk about specific events in the past. _____

2 Use *used to* or *would* to talk about a past habit. You can also use the past simple. _____ and _____

3 Use *used to* to talk about a past state. You cannot use *would* to talk about a past state. _____

▶ page 134 **LANGUAGEBANK**

6A Complete the texts. Where possible, use *would*. Where neither *used to* or *would* are possible, use the past simple.

It's every young girl's dream to be an actress when she grows up. I ¹_____ (love) watching beautiful actresses on television. I was so sure that was what I wanted to do that I ²_____ (practise) my Oscar speech in front of the mirror in the bathroom. I ³_____ (use) a shampoo bottle instead of a microphone, and I ⁴_____ (thank) all my family and friends, even my three cats, for helping me!

My family ⁵_____ (live) in Sheffield, just near the football stadium, so as a child, I ⁶_____ (go) to football matches most weekends. I remember the first match I went to, my granddad ⁷_____ (take) me. I was very young, and I had never seen so many people in one place at one time. It was quite frightening, and I don't think I ⁸_____ (watch) the game very much. But I remember that we won, and the crowd went crazy. After that, every week I ⁹_____ (ask) Granddad if he had tickets, and usually he did.

B ▶ 4.3 Listen and repeat. Notice the pronunciation of *used to* /juːstə/. Practise saying the sentences.

1 I used to play football when I was a kid.

2 I used to practise every day.

3 We used to live in London.

4 I didn't use to like classical music.

5 My father used to take me fishing.

6 I used to ski, but now I snowboard.

7 We used to go to the cinema a lot.

C Did you use to do any of the things mentioned above? Tell your partner.

SPEAKING

7 Work in pairs and discuss.

1 What were your childhood dreams? Have you achieved them?

2 Did you have any interests or hobbies in the past which relate to your life (job / studies) now? What were they?

3 How have your ideas, opinions, hobbies, etc., changed? Are there any things that you used to do, which you don't do now? Why did you stop? Would you do these things again?

As a child, I always used to dream about being an artist …

Wanted:
Paradise Island Caretaker

We are looking for someone to work on a tropical island off the Queensland coast. No formal qualifications are needed, but candidates must be willing to swim, snorkel, dive and sail.

- The successful applicant will receive a salary of A$150,000 ($103,000, £70,000) for six months and get to live rent-free in a three-bedroom villa, complete with pool.

- The new recruit will work for just twelve hours a month. Duties include feeding some of the hundreds of species of fish and collecting the island's mail.

- They will also need to prepare a blog, a photo diary and video updates to attract tourists to the area.

WRITING a covering letter

8 Read the advertisement and answer the questions.

1 What kind of person would be good at this job?
2 Would you like to do this job? Why/Why not?

9A Read the covering letter. Do you think this person would be good for the job? Why/Why not?

¹Dear Richard Smith,

²I'm writing to you regarding your advertisement for a caretaker on Paradise Island which I saw on www.findajob.com. I would like to submit an application for the post. Please find my CV attached.

As an experienced photo journalist who has spent the last five years travelling around the world, I believe that I meet all the requirements you outline in your advertisement.

³• Good communicator with broad IT skills: I've published newspaper and magazine articles, given TV and radio interviews and kept a journal and video weblog on my website with up-to-date photos and stories of my travels.

- Interest in nature and conservation: During a six-month stay in Bermuda, I worked for a dolphin conservation programme, where I had hands-on experience of teaching visitors about these amazing animals and why we need to protect them.

- Proven ability in project management: Before travelling the world, I worked for a small company, organising community projects.

⁴If you require any further information, or would like to arrange an interview, please call me on 077895367289 or email me at alisj@yahoo.com. I look forward to hearing from you at your earliest convenience.

⁵Yours sincerely,

Alison Jessop

B Is the wording of the letter formal or informal? Find examples of expressions which tell you this.

C Underline phrases in the letter which match meanings 1–6.

1 about (paragraph 2)
2 I want to apply for the job (paragraph 2)
3 I think I would be good for the job. (paragraph 2)
4 practical experience of doing the job (paragraph 3)
5 I have shown that I am able to do this. (paragraph 3)
6 as soon as you have the opportunity (paragraph 4)

D Underline any other useful phrases.

LEARN TO organise your ideas

10 Match the parts of the letter 1–5 with notes a)–e).

Preparing a covering letter
a) What qualities are they looking for? Write three to four points that show you have these qualities. Use the same words as they use in the advertisement.
b) Address your letter to an individual. Only use 'Dear Sir/Madam' when you can't find out the recipient's name.
c) Finish with a call to action. What is going to happen next? Are you going to call them or should they call you?
d) Explain why you are contacting them. What is the job? Where have you seen it?
e) Use 'Yours sincerely' if you know their name or 'Yours faithfully' if you don't.

11 Look at the job advertisements on page 163 and write a covering letter for one of the jobs. Use the sample letter and useful phrases to help you.

VOCABULARY business

1A Read the review below. What do you think the programme *The Apprentice* is about?

The Apprentice

'This is a job interview from hell. First prize, you get to work for me. Second prize – doesn't exist.' This is how Lord Alan Sugar greets the contestants who have come to join him for the latest series of *The Apprentice* (broadcast on the BBC).

Fifteen young businessmen and women from around the UK have come to London to compete for a job which could earn them a six-figure salary, working for the UK's most difficult boss. Lord Alan Sugar is a successful businessman who owns a vast business empire, and he's looking for an apprentice to work for him and learn business skills. But Lord Sugar is not easy to please. To get their dream job the contestants need to work as a team, but also show that they have individual talent, because in the end there is only one job.

During the competition, the contestants live together in a luxury house. Each week, Lord Sugar sets the teams a task. They have to work as a team to complete the task and earn as much money as possible. The team which wins gets a luxury treat, paid for by Lord Sugar. The team which loses has to go back to Lord Sugar and explain what happened. And each week one of the contestants gets fired.

B Complete the questions with words from the box.

fired   salary   boss   compete   businessmen
interview   team

1 Do you know any successful _____?

2 When was the last time you and your friends worked as a _____?

3 Have you ever worked for a difficult _____?

4 When did you last go for a job _____?

5 Have you ever had to _____ for a job?

6 Which jobs earn a six-figure _____?

7 What kinds of things does someone have to do to get _____ from their job?

C Work in pairs. Would you apply to be on a programme like this? Why/Why not? Take turns to ask and answer the questions above.

FUNCTION reaching agreement

2A ▶ 4.4 Listen to a team having a meeting to decide how to complete the task below. Underline the options they decide on.

Set up a catering company

Your team must start a business that organises and prepares food for customers, either for their businesses, or for events they organise.

Name: Food4events / Italy on the move / Buon Appetito

Company based: in central London / outside central London

Type of catering: company catering / events catering

Speciality Food: British / Mediterranean (Italian) / Indian

B Listen again and tick the option you hear.

1 a) The way I see things, … ✓
   b) The way I see it, …

2 a) That's a good idea.
   b) That's a good point.

3 a) I suggest we think about …
   b) I think we should think about …

4 a) That's fine by me.
   b) That's OK by me.

5 a) I'm not sure that I agree, actually.
   b) I'm not sure that … is a good idea.

6 a) How about if we (call it) … ?
   b) Why don't we (call it) … ?

3 Add the phrases from Exercise 2B to the table below.

Giving opinions
I (really) feel that …

Commenting on other opinions
I (don't) see what you mean.
Exactly!

Suggestions
What about …?
I suggest we focus on …

▮▮▮➤ page 134 **LANGUAGEBANK**

4A Put the words in the correct order to make sentences and questions.

1 decide / I / on / name / we / think / a / should
2 good / a / that's / point
3 you / see / mean / what / I
4 suggest / products / the / on / I / focus / we
5 fine / that's / me / by
6 sure / I'm / that / agree / not / I
7 we / about / don't / it / Why / think / ?
8 business / a / the / about / what / for / name / ?

B ▶ 4.5 Listen to the phrases. Which words are stressed? Listen again and repeat.

LEARN TO manage a discussion

5A Complete the underlined phrases for managing a discussion.

1 <u>First of</u> _____ we need to decide what food we want to sell.
2 <u>Let's</u> _____ on the issue of a theme for our food, you know like Indian, or Mediterranean …
3 OK. So, <u>moving on to the next</u> _____, where do we work from?
4 OK, so _____ <u>recap</u>: the company is called Food4events and we sell at parties, events, weddings, etc. We're based outside London. Erm … What else do we need to think about?
5 <u>I think we need to come</u> _____ to the kind of food we want to sell. I really feel that we need to specialise, so perhaps we could be Italian.
6 So, <u>let's</u> _____ up what we've decided.

B ▶ 4.6 Listen and check your answers.

6 Find and correct the mistakes. One word in each line is incorrect.

1 A: First of it, we need to decide what we want to cook.
   B: That's a good issue. How many people are coming to the party?
2 A: OK. So, let's focus with cooking something really simple.
   B: Yes, that is OK on me.
3 A: So, moving up to the next point. Who's going to bring what?
   B: I think we need to come back for what kind of food we want.
4 A: So, let's review. We're cooking pasta and people are bringing salads.
   B: OK, let's sum for what we've decided so far.

SPEAKING

7A Read the task and write down some ideas.

Set up a company to promote tourism

You are going to set up a tour company to promote tourism in your town/city/country. You need to decide the following:

• the name and location of the company
• what type of tours you will organise (themed tours/language tours/sports tours, etc.) and where they will go
• how you will promote tourism
• how the company will be different from other tour companies

B Work in groups. Read your roles and come up with a plan for the business. You have five minutes.

Student A: It's your job to keep the meeting focused. Try to cover all the points.

Student B: Make sure you make notes about any decisions which are made. You will be the group's spokesperson and will have to sum up at the end of the meeting.

Student C: Try to come up with as many ideas as possible.

C When you are ready, start the discussion like this.
A: Shall we start? First of all, …

D Tell the other groups about your business plan. Which group do you think has the best plan?

DVD PREVIEW

1A Match DVD extracts 1–7 to the correct responses a)–g).

1 Mr Davies, good to see you again. *b)*
2 Did you get your welcome pack?
3 In the event of a fire, my motto is …
4 Ready when you are.
5 Now here's somebody you've not met yet.
6 Parcel for you.

a) It's from my wife.
b) Please, call me Huw. *1*
c) Hi. Nice to meet you.
d) Yeah, I think so.
e) Run for your life?
f) Right, let's show you around.

B What type of situation do you think the DVD clip shows? Read about the programme below to find out.

BBC Gavin and Stacey

*G*avin and Stacey is a BBC programme about a young couple. Gavin comes from Essex, near London, and Stacey comes from Cardiff, Wales. After a long-distance relationship conducted online and by telephone, they eventually get married and Gavin moves to Wales. In this episode, Gavin starts a new job. On his first day, his family want him to do well and be happy at work.

2 Work in pairs and answer the questions.
1 What type of things do you think Gavin needs to learn on his first day at work?
2 Who will he need to meet and what advice will they give?

▶ DVD VIEW

3 Watch the DVD. Tick which of the things below happen.

1 He goes to his office. ✓
2 He meets his new boss.
3 He learns how to use the phone in his office.
4 He speaks to a client on the phone.
5 He finds out what to do if there is a fire.
6 He learns how to use the company's website.
7 He meets the website manager.
8 He meets his personal assistant.
9 He is visited by a family member.
10 He receives a package.

4A Answer the questions.
1 Why is Gavin's wife, Stacey, worried?
2 What does Huw, the boss, give Gavin?
3 Why does Gavin feel embarrassed in front of Huw?
4 What does Owain, the website manager, invite Gavin to do?
5 What does Uncle Bryn bring for Gavin?
6 Who sends Gavin a message in a box? What does it say?

B Watch the DVD again to check.

speakout a day in the life …

5A ▶ 4.7 Listen to someone describing a typical day in her life. Do you think she likes her job?

B Read the key phrases below. Complete each phrase by adding one word.

C Listen again to check. Then tick the key phrases you hear.

D Prepare to tell other students about a normal day in your life. Write notes about:

* hours of work/studying
* tasks you have to do
* people you spend your day with
* problems and challenges
* how you relax
* the best parts of your day

E Tell other students about your typical day. What do you have in common?

writeback your daily routine

6A Read an entry from normallives.com, a website that publishes descriptions of people's daily routines. Is Frank's routine similar to yours? How is it different?

I work as a gym instructor in a sports centre. I **get up at** 5.00a.m. every morning and make a cup of coffee. I can't function until I've had my coffee! I drive to work – it takes about fifteen minutes on a good day – **usually getting there at about** 5.40. **The first thing I do is** switch on the lights and the air conditioning if it's summer (heating if it's winter), and then the radio. We have the radio on all day because our clients like listening to the news and the music. The sports centre opens at 6.00a.m.

I work in a team of four, although only two of us are ever in the gym at the same time. The instructors all wear sports clothes. **It's important to be** comfortable because we sometimes need to show new clients how to use the machines. Apart from this, **our other tasks are** quite simple: we check that everyone has their membership card when they come in, and we check that the machines are clean and safe.

I have a one-hour break for lunch, and I usually do two more hours after lunch. **I go home at about** 2.30.

The best part of the job is meeting people. Our clients range from eighteen-year-old body builders to eighty-year-olds who come to exercise and chat. I've never had any problems at the sports centre. It's a really nice job, though it doesn't pay very well. In the evenings **I relax by** reading a book and cooking for myself, and I'm usually in bed by 9.30p.m.

Frank Carduna

B Write about your daily routine using the sentence starters in bold above and the key phrases to help.

PERSONAL QUALITIES

1 Work in pairs. Take turns to define a word and guess the meaning. Student A: describe a word/phrase from the box in your own words, starting with '*I am/like/enjoy*, etc.'. Don't say the word/phrase. Student B: listen and try to guess the word or phrase.

> hard-working   indecisive
> a risk taker   a good leader
> ambitious   competitive
> think outside the box
> a good communicator

A: *I enjoy working and want to succeed in what I do.*

B: *You're motivated?*

A: *Correct. Your turn to describe a word.*

MUST/HAVE TO/SHOULD (OBLIGATION)

2A Underline the correct alternative to complete the sentences.

1 I *have to/mustn't* call my mother today. It's her birthday.

2 I really *must/mustn't* do more exercise. I'm so unfit.

3 I'm lucky because I *don't have to/shouldn't* get up early in the morning. I'm a student.

4 I think you *should/shouldn't* study harder. Your exam results weren't very good.

5 You *mustn't/should* be afraid of taking risks, or you will never live your dreams.

6 I *shouldn't/don't have to* waste so much time on the computer. I'll never finish my work.

B Complete the sentences so that they are true for you.

1 I have to … this evening.

2 I really must do more …

3 I'm lucky because I don't have to …

4 I think you should … because …

5 You mustn't worry about …

6 I shouldn't waste so much time …

C Compare your ideas in pairs.

STRONG ADJECTIVES

3A Replace the underlined words in the sentences below with strong adjectives in the box.

> brilliant   fascinating   awful
> exhausted   tiny   boiling
> impossible   delicious   furious

1 I'm <u>very tired</u>. I didn't sleep well.

2 Shall we open a window? It's <u>very hot</u> in here.

3 My boss just called. He's <u>very angry</u>.

4 I find phrasal verbs <u>very difficult</u> to remember.

5 The holiday was <u>very good</u>, but the weather was <u>very bad</u>.

6 How can you work in this office? It's <u>very small.</u>

7 I find astronomy <u>very interesting</u>.

8 Did you cook this? It's <u>very tasty</u>.

B Work in pairs and take turns to test each other.

A: *Very big.*

B: *Enormous.*

A: *Correct. Your turn.*

USED TO, WOULD

4A Replace the past simple with *used to* or *would* where possible. Where both are possible, choose *would*.

1 My family lived in Paris, but we moved when I was a teenager.

2 I spent a lot of time with my grandparents when I was younger.

3 For my first job, I washed dishes in a restaurant.

4 I didn't think money was important. Now I have lots of bills to pay.

5 We had a lot more free time before we had children.

6 My best friend at school lived just across the road from me.

B Change four of the sentences so that they are true for you.

C Compare with a partner. Find three things that you both used to do as children, that you don't do now.

REACHING AGREEMENT

5A Complete the conversations.

1 A: The way I s_____ things all cars should be banned from city centres.

   B: E_____.

2 A: I really f_____ that we need to look at immigration.

   B: That's a good p_____.

3 A: The w_____ I see it, the company is making too much money.

   B: I don't see what you m_____.

4 A: I th_____ we should ask for more money.

   B: I'm not s_____ I agree, actually.

5 A: I s_____ we try to meet again next week.

   B: T_____ fine by me.

B Work in pairs and practise the conversations.

6 Work in groups. Look at the questions below and discuss. Try to reach agreement on each answer.

> [1] Should there be a limit to the number of hours people can work in one week?

> [2] Should there be a minimum wage? What should it be?

> [3] How long should men/women be allowed to stay off work after they have children?

> [4] Should everyone be allowed to work from home at least once a week?

> [5] Should employees be allowed to wear to work whatever clothes they want?

BBC VIDEO PODCAST

Download the video podcast and view people describing their dream jobs and describing the good and bad points about the jobs they do.

Authentic BBC interviews

UNIT 5

UNIT 5

SPEAKING
> Talk about different forms of transport and their uses
> Present and answer questions on your area of expertise
> Explain/Solve problems
> Describe a new machine

LISTENING
> Listen to people answering difficult questions
> Listen to conversations about technical problems
> Watch a BBC programme about a race between a car and two people

READING
> Read about how technology changed the world
> Read about a book review

WRITING
> Write an advantages/disadvantages essay
> Write an advertisement

BBC CONTENT
> Video podcast: Are you good at solving problems?
> DVD: Top Gear

solutions

VOCABULARY technology

1A Discuss. How have machines and technology changed the world? Have they made it a better or worse place?

B Work in pairs. Put the words/phrases in the box into the correct word web.

electricity   nuclear power
antibiotics   vaccinations
computer networks   motorbikes
genetic engineering   washing machine
vacuum cleaner   space travel
commercial aeroplanes   solar power
communications satellites

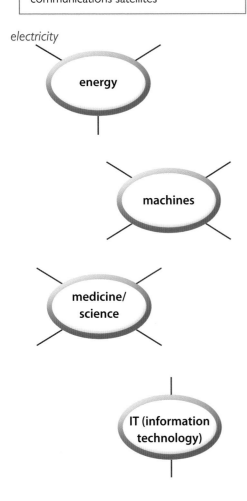

electricity

energy

machines

medicine/ science

IT (information technology)

C Look at the words/phrases above and underline the main stress(es). Sometimes there can be more than one per word/phrase.

electricity   nuclear power

D ▶ 5.1 Listen and check. Then listen again and repeat.

E Work in pairs. Can you add any more words to each word web?

⟶ page 152 **VOCABULARYBANK**

JAMES MAY'S 20th CENTURY

In this BBC series, presenter James May takes a tour of the twentieth century, looking at some of <u>the most surprising</u> and influential technological advances of the past hundred years.

At the beginning of the twentieth century, long-distance travel was only for the military and the very rich. But the invention of commercial aeroplanes and cars changed all that. Travel became <u>easier</u> and more affordable, and the world, as a result, became a little bit smaller. In the programme *Honey, I shrunk the World* James soon discovers that driving a car in those days wasn't as easy as it is today. But shrinking the world wasn't just about travel. For the first time in history, we could bring the world to us via the cinema, then the television, and later the computer.

Each day, 180,000 people move into a city somewhere on the planet. In *Big City, Bright Lights*, James sets out to discover how we've created this high-rise, 24/7 experiment in urban living. He heads for New York – to the top floors of the Woolworth building, once the tallest building in the world. He looks at how, in the last hundred years, our cities have become a lot taller, and how we use electricity to power them.

In the twentieth century the teenager was invented. But how? James May finds out. First, he looks at fashion. The twentieth century introduced fantastic new fabrics in fantastic new colours, made possible by the invention of materials like nylon, which were much cheaper and more colourful than materials we used before. Then, he looks at transport. As a teenager, James always dreamed of having his own motorbike. The motorbike gave teenagers more freedom by allowing them to travel further away from home, and their parents. Finally, he looks at the electric guitar – one of the most important symbols of teenage rock music even today. He talks to Francis Rossi, from the band *Status Quo*, who explains that 'Volume is like speed – you buy a fast car because you want to be faster, you buy a big amplifier because you want to be louder.'

In other programmes, James looks at how advances in medicine have made many people's lives better, and what we have learned from space travel.

READING

2 Read the article on page 56. Tick the inventions in Exercise 1B which are mentioned. Which other inventions does the article talk about?

3A Read the article again and answer the questions.

1 What kind of people travelled long distances in the early twentieth century?

2 What two things happened in the twentieth century to make the world seem smaller?

3 How have cities changed in the last 100 years? Why?

4 What was special about the invention of nylon?

5 Why does James May think that motorbikes are important for teenagers?

6 What invention was an important symbol of teenage rock music?

B Discuss. What do you think has been the most important piece of technology (medicine/education/home/travel) invented in the last 100 years?

GRAMMAR comparatives and superlatives

4A Read the article again. Find examples of comparatives and superlatives.

B Look at your examples and complete the rules. How do we form the comparatives and superlatives of common adjectives?

> Rules:
> 1 Adjectives with one syllable
>   comparatives: add _____,
>   superlatives: add _____.
> 2 Adjectives with two or more syllables
>   comparatives: add _____,
>   superlatives: add _____.

C Look at the sentences below and complete the rules with *small* or *big*.

a) Cities have become *a lot/much/far* taller.

b) The world became *a little/a little bit/ slightly* smaller.

> Rules:
> 1 Use quantifiers *a lot/much/far* to talk about _____ differences.
> 2 Use quantifiers *a little/a little bit/slightly* to talk about _____ differences.

▸ page 136 **LANGUAGEBANK**

PRACTICE

5A Complete the statements with the prompts in brackets.

1 The invention of the bicycle made it _____ (lot/easy) for people to travel from one village to another, to meet new people.

2 The world has become a _____ (much/safe) place to live since the invention of antibiotics. People are _____ (far/healthy) now than 100 years ago.

3 The invention of the washing machine has meant that it is _____ (lot/quick) for people to wash their clothes. I think it's _____ (good) invention of the last century.

4 Although we have computers, paper is still the _____ (cheap) and _____ (flexible) way to record the written word.

5 Electricity is the _____ (important) invention because without it many of the other things we have would not have been possible.

6 The invention of the telephone and the computer have meant that we are _____ (much/busy) now than we were in the past.

B Work in pairs. Choose an invention from the last 100 years. Write sentences to describe how this invention has changed our lives.

C Read your sentences to other students. Which invention do you think has been the best/worst? Why?

SPEAKING

6A Work in pairs. Look at the photos and read about James May's challenge on page 161. Which of these transport ideas exist at the moment?

A **AEROCAR**

speed: +110 mph
consumes: 13 mpg

B **SPACE PLANE**

speed: 15,000 mph
consumes: 0.12 mpg

C **ROCKET PACK**

speed: 60 mph
consumes: 0.06 mpg

D **ROBOT CAR**

speed: 120 mph
consumes: 45 mpg

E **SOLAR CAR**

speed: 60 mph
consumes: n/a

B Turn back to page 161 and complete the task.

C Work in groups and discuss.

1 Which of these forms of transport do you like/like the idea of? Why?

2 Are there any types of ideas here that you would not try? Why not?

3 Think about all the different types of transport you use. Write a list. Which do you enjoy the most/least? Why?

WRITING advantages/disadvantages essay

7A What do you think are the main advantages and disadvantages of technology in everyday life? Write a list.

B Read the model essay. Does it mention any of your ideas?

The advantages and disadvantages of modern technology

1 It's easy to see the advantages of modern technology in our everyday lives. Technology has given us mobile phones, computers, televisions and many other useful things. <u>However,</u> there are also disadvantages with modern technology.

2 <u>One of the main advantages</u> of modern technology can be seen in medical science. The discoveries of antibiotics and vaccinations have saved millions of lives around the world. <u>In addition to</u> this, modern technology has made industry more efficient.

3 <u>On the other hand,</u> modern technology is responsible for the development of weapons, which have caused a lot of destruction. <u>Another disadvantage</u> of modern technology is that it makes people lazy. Nowadays too many people spend their lives sitting in front of computer screens and this is certainly not a good thing.

4 <u>In my opinion,</u> modern technology is a good thing. In general, the advantages outweigh the disadvantages. However, it's important to remember that technology itself is not the problem. <u>The problem is that</u> people use technology for their own benefit and do not think about the harmful consequences.

C Match paragraphs 1–4 with descriptions a)–d).

a) discussion of disadvantages _____

b) conclusion _____

c) introduction ___/___

d) discussion of advantages _____

D Work in pairs. Complete the guidelines for writing an essay with the words in the box.

| personal opinions   examples   notes   beginning   logical order |

1 Sort out the facts – make _____ of all the relevant information you have on the subject.

2 Plan your argument – organise your notes and arrange the ideas in a _____.

3 Give your essay an appropriate _____. Describe what you are planning to say.

4 Decide how many paragraphs you need for your argument. Each paragraph should discuss one point. Use _____ to support your arguments.

5 Write a logical conclusion. Though the style of the essay is generally formal and impersonal, this might be the place to include some _____.

LEARN TO use discourse markers

8A Look at the underlined words and phrases in the essay. Put them in the correct place in the table.

introduce advantages
The most important advantage is …

introduce disadvantages
The main disadvantage is …

contrasting ideas
Although, …

additional reasons
As well as that, …
And another thing, …

personal opinion/conclusion
In general, …
As far as I'm concerned, …

B Underline the correct alternatives.

Satellite TV: good or bad?
More and more people are watching satellite television. [1]*The main advantage / As well as that* is that you can choose exactly what you want to watch, and [2]*in addition to this / however* you can watch programmes in other languages. [3]*However, / Although* this means that whereas people used to talk about programmes with colleagues and friends, now they usually don't watch the same programmes. [4]*On the other hand / And another thing*, there is too much choice. There are so many programmes to choose from that people can't decide what to watch. [5]*This means that / As far as I'm concerned*, they watch too much television. [6]*In my opinion / The problem is that*, satellite television is a good thing, as it gives people more choice. [7]*However, / In general,* people need to be careful that they choose their programmes carefully.

9 Choose one of the titles below and write an advantages and disadvantages essay. Look at Exercises 7 and 8 to help you.

The advantages and disadvantages of:

* modern technology in everyday life
* owning a car/bicycle
* playing computer games
* using a digital camera
* using email/text messages
* cheap flights

▶ **GRAMMAR** | question tags   ▶ **VOCABULARY** | questions   ▶ **HOW TO** | confirm information

SPEAKING

1A Match photos A–F to the questions below.

1 Is it possible to surf a tidal wave?

2 Does cheese really give you nightmares?

3 Why are sumo wrestlers so fat?

4 Do any wasps make honey?

5 Is there an easy way to prove the Earth is round?

6 Why do onions make you cry?

B Work in pairs. How many questions above can you answer in two minutes?

C Turn to page 160 and check your answers.

VOCABULARY   questions

2A Match the pairs of verbs in the box with situations 1–5.

> ~~question/wonder~~   discuss/debate
> respond/reply   research/investigate
> inquire/look into

1 Someone tells you something. You are not sure you agree. *question/wonder*

2 Someone writes you a letter.

3 There is an interesting topic in class.

4 You are writing a thesis for your Master's degree.

5 You need to find some information, e.g. about cinema times or to book a table.

B Five of the verbs above are also nouns. Which five?

'Wonder' is a verb and a noun.

C Look at all the verbs again and write their noun forms. N.B. One verb doesn't have a noun form. Use a dictionary to help you.

'Response' is the noun of 'respond'.

D Underline the correct alternative to complete the sentences.

1 The police officer continued his *investigation/ wonder/inquire* into the robbery.

2 Didn't you get my email? You didn't *response/ look into/reply*.

3 We had a very interesting *discuss/debate/ wonder* about the death penalty.

4 I've nearly finished my *research/investigate/reply* into nuclear particles.

5 When I hear about all these social problems, I have to *inquire/question/respond* the education system.

6 You want a job here? No problem. My cousin is the boss. I'll *inquiry/debate/look into* it for you.

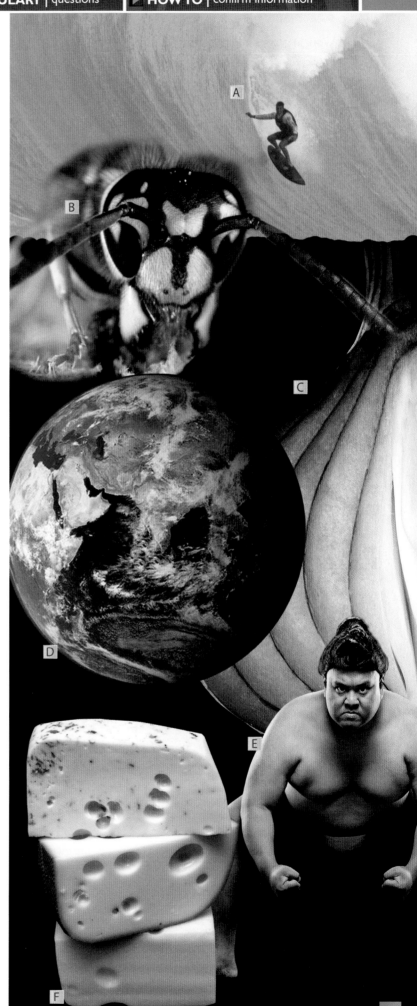

LISTENING

3A Work in groups and discuss.

1 How do you prefer to find information? On the internet, in books or by asking people? What does it depend on?

2 What type of questions do children ask? Think of some examples.

They sometimes ask difficult questions like: 'Why is snow cold?'

B Read a review of a book about questions children ask. How did the author get the idea for the book?

Questions Daddy Can't Answer

It all began with a question asked by Dean, a four-year-old boy: 'Why do ships have round windows?' His father didn't know. And when his sister started behaving badly, Dean asked another question: 'Why can't we just cook her?' On a long drive the boy wondered why the road was so loud. His father replied, 'Because the people who live next to the road have their vacuum cleaners on. The boy's inquiries kept coming: 'Why is the sky blue? Are rainbows hot or cold? What was it like living in the 1940s? What would hurt more – getting run over by a car or getting stung by a jellyfish? Why do police officers like doughnuts?

Eventually, Jamieson decided to write down the questions. He thought it might be fun one day to show them to his son. Then he had a better idea: he'd research the answers. Some people might do their investigations on the internet. Not Mr Jamieson. He contacted experts ranging from astronomers to Buddhist monks to scientists to magicians, and asked lots of questions. He later turned these – and the experts' responses – into a book: *Father Knows Less.*

4A ▶ 5.2 Listen and number the questions below in the order you hear them.

How many hairs are there on the human head?

Why are the windows on ships always round?

Why is there war?

Why did The Beatles break up?

What happens when your plane flies over a volcano?

B Look at the questions again and try to answer them. Compare your ideas with other students.

5A ▶ 5.3 Listen to some people trying to answer the questions in Exercise 4A. Are they the same as your ideas?

B Listen again and complete the notes.

1 Ships' round windows: _____

2 Number of hairs on a human head: _____

3 A plane flies over a volcano: _____

4 The Beatles broke up: _____

5 Reasons for war: different ideologies, a sense of honour, _____

GRAMMAR question tags

6A Complete questions 1–6. Then look at audio script 5.3 on page 168 to check.

1 Round windows are stronger, _____ they?

2 No, it's not that many, _____ it?

3 It depends whose head, _____ it?

4 Nothing happens, _____ it?

5 They got old, _____ they?

6 John Lennon went off with Yoko Ono, _____ he?

B Underline the correct alternative to complete the rules.

Rules:

1 Use question tags to confirm information.

2 To form a question tag, repeat the auxiliary verb. For example, use *do* or *does* for *the present/the past.* Use *will* or *won't* for the future.

3 After the auxiliary verb, use a *pronoun/main verb* (e.g. *he, she, it, they*).

4 If the sentence is positive, the question tag is *positive/negative.*

5 If the sentence is negative, the question tag is *positive/negative.*

➡ page 136 **LANGUAGEBANK**

PRACTICE

7 Look at the statements below and complete the question tags.

1 You're Italian, *aren't* you?

2 You aren't a doctor, *are* you?

3 You don't smoke, _____ you?

4 You play a musical instrument, _____ you?

5 You didn't know any of the other students before, _____ you?

6 Our teacher hasn't taught you before, _____ she?

7 You will be here tomorrow, _____ you?

8 This is your pen, _____ it?

9 You went to bed late last night, _____ you?

10 You've travelled a lot, _____ you?

11 You were good at sport when you were a child, _____ you?

12 It wasn't your birthday recently, _____ it?

8A ▶ 5.4 Listen to two questions. Notice how the intonation goes down when the speaker is sure of the answer. Notice how the intonation goes up when the speaker is not sure.

1 You're Italian, aren't you? (the speaker knows the answer)

2 You aren't a doctor, are you? (the speaker is not sure of the answer)

B ▶ 5.5 Listen to the questions in Exercise 7. Which answers is the speaker sure about? Listen and repeat the questions, using the same intonation.

C Work in pairs. Choose six questions to ask your partner. Make sure your intonation is correct in the question tags.
A: You play a guitar, don't you?
B: Yes, I do. I play bass in a band.

SPEAKING

9 Work in groups and follow instructions 1–4 below.

1 Think of one subject each that you know a lot about. Write your topics on a piece of paper.

tennis, Japanese cars, hip hop

2 Exchange papers with another group.

3 Brainstorm questions to ask the other group about their subjects.

Who is the best tennis player in history?
Which Japanese cars are the most popular?

4 Take turns to ask and answer the questions.

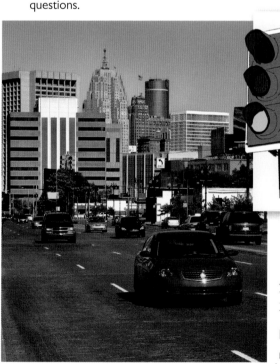

VOCABULARY *PLUS* word-building: adjectives

10A Read the text below. How was the ice cream cone invented?

For over a hundred years ice cream was sold mainly in dishes. Then one day, a creative ice-cream seller turned a hopeless situation into a profitable one. In 1904, at a festival, he ran out of spoons and dishes. He bought some wafers from a vendor next to him and put the ice cream into them. The customers loved them and the idea spread quickly. The world has been thankful ever since!

B Underline four adjectives in the text and add them to the word web below. Can you think of other examples of adjectives that fit these patterns?

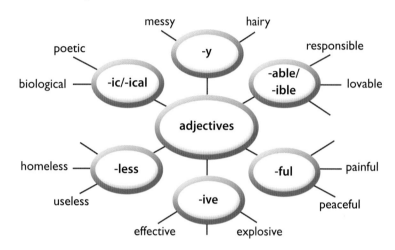

> ❝ **speakout TIP**
>
> Use L1. L1 is your First Language. Some suffixes in your L1 might have similar meanings to suffixes in English. For example, the Italian *-ivo/a* means the same as the English *-ive*. Can you think of any examples from your language?

11 Complete the text. Add suffixes to the words in brackets.

The city of Detroit, USA was famous for its [1]_____ (value) car industry. In the early days, the city was [2]_____ (response) for the majority of cars in the USA, and Detroit's streets were full of cars. A police officer called William Potts saw that the organisation of the traffic was [3]_____ (hope) and the traffic was very slow. So, in 1920, he developed an [4]_____ (effect) system of lights to regulate the flow of cars. He used the same colours as the railway system and put the lights in a tower so that it would be [5]_____ (ease) for drivers to see them even on [6]_____ (rain) days. Potts's system was very [7]_____ (success). When other countries realised how [8]_____ (use) it was, the system spread all over the world.

12A Complete the words by adding suffixes.

Find someone who:

1 has a peace*ful* hobby.

2 is hope____ at maths.

3 is a good, care____ driver.

4 is quite mess____ at home.

5 thinks he/she is quite creat____.

6 is quite knowledge____ about politics.

B Work in groups. Ask and answer questions about the information above.

⫸ page 152 **VOCABULARYBANK**

▶ **FUNCTION** | polite requests ▶ **VOCABULARY** | problems and solutions ▶ **LEARN TO** | respond to requests

2A Do you have problems with your computer when you work/study? What do you usually do when this happens?

B Read the article. What four things do people do when their computer crashes?

Do you get angry with your computer?

As we rely more on computers in the workplace, people are starting to use violence when their PCs break down, say researchers. When faced with technical problems, most people shout at colleagues, hit the PC or even throw parts of the computers. The most frustrating problem was when people lost their work after their computer crashed or froze. The study found that nearly half of all computer users had become angry at some time. A third of people had physically attacked a computer, 67% experienced frustration and anger, and more than 70% swore at their machines. John Blake (UK) says, 'When my computer crashes, I use swear words such as *Windows*, *Microsoft* or, when I'm really mad, *Bill Gates*!'

VOCABULARY problems and solutions

1A Think of two pieces of technology you have used in the last twenty-four hours. Did you have any problems with them? What problems can you have with them?

B Work in pairs. Look at the photos. What is the problem in each case?

C Look at the phrases in bold. Are they problems (P) or solutions (S)? Which phrases can you use to talk about the problems in pictures A–E above?

1 It's **broken down**.
2 It **needs recharging**.
3 It's **out of order**.
4 It **needs fixing**.
5 There is no **reception** (for my phone).
6 **Try switching it off** (and on again).
7 It **keeps making this strange noise**.
8 **It's crashed/frozen**.
9 It **doesn't work** (any more).
10 We have to **sort it out**.
11 **Save it onto a memory stick**.
12 Shall I **print it for you**?

D Work in pairs and answer the questions.

1 Have any of these problems happened to you or anyone you know recently?
2 How did you feel when it happened?
3 How did you try to solve the problem?

FUNCTION polite requests

3A ▶ 5.6 Listen to four conversations. What is the problem in each case?

B Listen again and complete the extracts in the table.

Could you	1 _____ the line, please?
	2 _____ me a refund?
Could you tell me	who I should 3 _____ to?
	what the 4 _____ is?
Do you know	what the problem is?
	if there's another 5 _____ somewhere?
Would you mind	6 _____ at it for me?
	7 _____ him for me?

C ▶ 5.7 Listen and repeat the requests.
⟫ page 136 **LANGUAGEBANK**

LEARN TO respond to requests

4A Read some conversation extracts from Exercise 3. Complete the responses with the phrases in the box.

> Yes, I can   I'm not sure   I'm afraid I can't
> Yes, of course (x2)   Of course not   Sure/OK
> Let me have a look

1 M: Do you know if there's another machine somewhere? I really need to get some money.

   W: Hmm … _____. There might be one in the shopping centre.

2 W: Would you mind looking at it for me?

   M: _____.

3 W: Do you know what the problem is?

   M: _____.

4 W: Could you tell me what the problem is, sir?

   M: _____. It keeps making a funny noise. And it's just not working properly.

5 W: Could you hold the line, please?

   M: _____.

6 M: Could you give me a refund?

   W: _____ do that.

   M: Well, could you tell me who I should speak to?

   W: _____. You need to speak to the manager.

   M: OK. Would you mind calling him for me?

   W: _____. I'll just call him.

B Read audio script 5.6 on page 169 to check.

5A Make polite requests with the prompts in brackets.

1 A: I can't concentrate. (Would / mind / turn / music down)?

   B: Sure. Sorry about that.

2 A: I need to speak to the manager. (Do / know / if / anyone in the office)?

   B: Let me have a look.

3 A: I'm afraid Mr Soul isn't here at the moment.

   B: (Do / know / when / coming back)?

   A: (not/ sure). Do you want me to check?

   B: Thank you.

4 A: (Could / tell / how / machine works)? I don't know how to turn it on.

   B: (Yes / course).

5 A: I need to take this machine to the repair service. (Would / mind / help / me)?

   B: (course / not). Leave it here.

6 A: My computer has frozen (could / tell / who / I / speak / to)?

   B: OK. (Let / have / look).

B ▶ 5.8 Listen to check your answers.

C Does the speaker's voice start high or low? Listen again and repeat the requests copying the polite intonation.

SPEAKING

6A Work in pairs. Read your role and think about the phrases you are going to use. Then role-play the situation below.

Student A   Student B

> Student B: You need to call your sister but you can't get any reception on your phone. Ask Student A if he/she knows where you can get reception.

> Student A: Tell Student B that you have reception on your phone. Suggest that he/she tries standing outside.

> Student B: You still can't get any reception. Ask Student A if you can borrow his/her phone to send a text message.

> Student A: Tell Student B he/she can borrow your phone to make the phone call.

> Student B: Thank Student A for his/her help.

B Change roles and role-play the situation below.

Student A   Student B

> Student A: You can't get onto the internet. Ask Student B if he/she can help.

> Student B: Suggest Student A tries turning the modem off and then on again. Ask if that has worked.

> Student A: It still doesn't work. Ask Student B if you can try using his/her computer.

> Student B: Tell Student A he/she can use your computer.

> Student A: Thank Student B for his/her help.

C Choose one or two situations from Exercises 4 and 5. Write a conversation using the flow charts above to help. Then role-play it with a partner.

DVD PREVIEW

1 Work in pairs and answer the questions.

1 Look at the people at the bottom of pages 64–65. What type of sport are they doing?

2 Would you like to try this sport? Why/Why not?

2 Read about the DVD. Who do you think will win the race? Why?

BBC Top Gear

Top Gear is the BBC's international award-winning television series about motor vehicles, mainly cars. More than 350 million viewers worldwide enjoy watching the presenters Jeremy Clarkson, James May and Richard Hammond with their quirky, humorous style. On the show they compare and test-drive cars, and organise all kinds of crazy races. In this programme, James May, possibly the slowest driver in Great Britain, challenges two freerunners to a race in Liverpool city centre. James has to drive six miles towards the Liver building in the city centre in a Peugeot 207. The two teenagers who try to beat him will run and jump over buildings, taking a much more direct route. Who do you think will get there first?

▶ DVD VIEW

3 Watch the DVD to see if you were right. Number the events in the correct order.

a) The men jump over James's car. ___

b) James arrives at the Liver building. ___

c) James checks his speed. ___

d) The men jump over people eating at a restaurant. ___

e) James stops at a red traffic light. ___

4 Watch the DVD again. What does James May say? Complete the phrases.

1 As we can see, it's a very pretty car, but is it any _____?

2 I'm going to have a race, and it's against the latest French development in urban transport solutions: a couple of young men in silly _____.

3 Parkour: that's a French invention, and it involves that sort of thing. Running around the _____ leaping across buildings and benches.

4 Come on – we're not all _____!

5 I must have averaged ten or twelve miles an hour. I should _____.

6 They are not here. There's no sign of combat trousers man. I've _____!

speakout present a new machine

5A Work in pairs. Answer the questions and complete the tasks.

1 Write a list of jobs you have to do every day.

2 Are there any jobs on this list which you don't enjoy? Could a machine do them for you?

3 Invent a machine which would help you do one of these jobs. Draw a picture of your machine.

B ▶ 5.9 Listen to someone talking about a new machine. What is the invention? What does it do?

C Listen again and tick the key phrases he uses.

keyphrases

I'm going to tell you about …

Basically, …

The way it works is this.

It works like this …

First of all, ….

Then/Also, you can …

All you have to do is …

Make sure you …

The best thing about it is that …

D Prepare and practise a short presentation about your new machine. Use your picture and the useful phrases to explain how it works.

E Present your ideas to the class. Which invention do you think is the best?

writeback an advertisement

6A Read the advertisement and answer the questions. What is the musical shower? How does it work?

The musical shower

If you like listening to music when you have a shower, then you might already have a stereo in your bathroom. But imagine how much better it would be if your shower-head also had an mp3 player attached to it.

It will download your favourite tunes, or radio programmes at night. Then in the morning, your shower will automatically play your favourite tunes for you. Try our musical shower.

There's no better way to start the day.

B Write an advertisement (advert) for your invention (120–180 words). Use the advert above and the key phrases to help.

TECHNOLOGY

1A Complete the words in sentences 1–6.

1 I don't agree with nu_____ po_____. I think it's a dangerous way of making el_____.

2 Sp_____ tr_____ is a waste of money. Why do we need to send people to the Moon?

3 I couldn't live without my wa_____ ma_____. I hate having dirty clothes.

4 I had to have loads of va_____ when I went to Malawi. I didn't want to get ill.

5 I think ge_____ en_____ is a bit worrying. People might start to only want babies which are beautiful and intelligent.

6 Doctors give people too many an_____. So now, some medicines don't work any more.

B Work in pairs. Choose three sentences you disagree with. Tell your partner why.

COMPARATIVES/SUPERLATIVES

2A Look at the information and complete sentences (1–4) using the prompts in brackets.

100 years ago in the US: the average life expectancy was forty-seven years, only 8 percent of homes had a phone, the maximum speed limit in most cities was 10 miles per hour, the average wage was 22 cents per hour, and 90 percent of all doctors had no college education.

1 100 years ago, people didn't live _____ as they do today. (long)

2 It used to be _____ to communicate with people on the other side of the world. (far, difficult)

3 It is _____ for modern businesses to pay their employees. (far, expensive)

4 Nowadays, doctors are _____ than they were in the past. (much, educated)

B Write sentences about how life was different in your country a hundred years ago and compare them with your partner.

QUESTIONS

3A Put the letters in italics in the correct order to find words related to questions.

1 In class last week, we *used discs* ...
In class last week, we discussed ...

2 I can't answer *nose quits* about ...

3 I try to *pen rods* quickly to ...

4 In the next few months I'm going to *took lion* ... (2 words)

5 I recently *quid rein* about ...

6 I *own red* what happened to ...

7 I enjoy a good *tea bed* especially about ...

8 It would be interesting to *sit negative* a crime like ...

B Complete the sentences so that they are true for you.

QUESTION TAGS

4A Complete the sentences with the correct question tag.

1 She wrote the first Harry Potter book in a café, _didn't she_?

2 This man, who is U2's singer, does a lot of humanitarian work, _____?

3 This actor has won an Oscar for *Forrest Gump*, _____?

4 He was probably the greatest basketball player in history, _____?

5 She lived in Calcutta, where she helped street children, but she wasn't from India, _____?

6 He became Cuba's leader in 1959 and he didn't transfer power to his brother until 2006, _____?

7 Her full name is Madonna Louise Ciccone, _____?

8 Her husband was US President, but she probably won't try again to become President, _____?

B Who are these sentences about?
1 J K Rowling

C Work in groups. Play twenty questions. One student thinks of a famous person. The others ask tag questions to find out who it is.
A: You're a man, aren't you?
B: Yes.

POLITE REQUESTS

5A Match requests 1–5 with responses a)–e).

1 Excuse me, could you tell me where I can find the bathroom?

2 Could you call me a taxi?

3 Would you mind helping me with my bags? They're very heavy.

4 Would you mind opening the window?

5 Could you tell me what time the restaurant opens?

a) Sure. It's very hot in here, isn't it?

b) Yes, of course. It's just over there, down the stairs and on the left.

c) Yes, of course. Where do you want to go to?

d) I'm not sure. Let me have a look. Yes, it opens at 11a.m.

e) Of course not. Let me take your suitcase.

B Work in pairs. Take turns to practise the conversations using the prompts below.

Student A:
- where / bathroom?
- call / taxi?
- shop / close?
- get / door?

Student B
- open / window?
- restaurant / open?
- help / shopping?
- tell / platform the train leaves from?

BBC VIDEO PODCAST
Download the video podcast and view people talking about being practical and describing the problems they are good/bad at solving.

Authentic BBC interviews

www.pearsonlongman.com/speakout

SPEAKING
❯ Talk about your emotions
❯ Discuss what you would do in different situations
❯ Introduce/Respond to news
❯ Talk about memorable moments

LISTENING
❯ Listen to a radio show about therapies
❯ Listen to conversations where people hear news
❯ Watch a BBC comedy about a man's terrible day

READING
❯ Read about basic emotions
❯ Read about a BBC programme *The People Watchers*

WRITING
❯ Write a letter of advice
❯ Write a website entry

BBC CONTENT
▢ Video podcast: How are you feeling today?
◉ DVD: My Worst Week

UNIT 6

emotion

▶ **GRAMMAR** | zero and first conditionals   ▶ **VOCABULARY** | *-ing/-ed* adjectives   ▶ **HOW TO** | talk about your emotions

The Six Basic
Emotions

According to BBC Focus Magazine, there are six basic emotions which we all experience, recognise in other people, and show in our own facial expressions. They are:

1 FEAR – probably the most basic emotion, fear activates a part in our brain which allows us to escape from danger.

2 ANGER – our ancestors used this emotion to try and deal with a problem rather than run away from it.

3 DISTRESS – loss or tragedy prompt a feeling of sadness. This often results in tears, a lump in the throat and a feeling of heaviness in the chest. See a sad person and you may feel sad, too.

4 JOY – the simplest things can induce this, like a kind word, or a sunny day. This is the most positive emotion and a great motivator as we will actively try to repeat activities which bring us joy.

5 SURPRISE – life is unpredictable, so surprise is a useful emotion. When something surprising happens to us, we raise our eyebrows to open our eyes wider, to allow us to see what is happening.

6 DISGUST – we will naturally feel disgust at certain objects and smells (like the smell of rotten food). We move away from these things (which may carry disease) so this emotion protects us.

SPEAKING

1A Look at photos A–F. What emotions do you think these people are feeling? Why are they feeling them?

B Read the text and match photos A–F with the emotions.

C When was the last time you felt these emotions? Give some examples.

VOCABULARY   *-ing/-ed* adjectives

2A Work in pairs and complete the questions.

1 What makes you angry or **annoyed**?
2 What sorts of things do you find **relaxing**?
3 Do you enjoy spending time alone, or do you get **bored**?
4 Is there anything you are **frightened** of?
5 What kinds of things make you **worried**?
6 Have you ever been really **embarrassed**?
7 What makes you feel **exhausted**?
8 What sorts of things do you find **confusing**?
9 When was the last time you were **shocked** by something? What was it?
10 Do you find your job/hobbies **satisfying**?

B Look at the quiz again and answer the questions.

1 Which ending is used to talk about feelings: *-ed* or *-ing*?
2 Which ending is used to talk about the cause of feelings: *-ed* or *-ing*?

C Complete the sentences with the correct form of the adjectives above. Remember to use *-ed* or *-ing* endings.

1 It's very ___worrying___ watching the news at the moment. I think there's going to be another war.
2 I'm going to bed. I'm _____ because I've been working late every night this week.
3 My face went bright red when I realised what I'd said. It was really _____.
4 I can't watch sport on television. It's so _____ that I just go to sleep.
5 I don't understand the grammar. I find the rules very _____.
6 I go to yoga every week, because it makes me feel so _____.

D Choose two sentences above and make them true for you. Compare your ideas with a partner.

▶ page 153 **VOCABULARYBANK**

LISTENING

3 ▶ 6.1 **Read the definition and listen to the radio programme. Answer the questions.**

therapy treatment of a physical or mental illness, often without the use of drugs

1 Which two therapies does the programme talk about?

2 The therapies are used in different situations. What situations are mentioned in the programme?

4A Are the statements true (T) or false (F)?

1 Eight out of ten people have trouble controlling their anger.

2 With destruction therapy you use your anger to destroy something in a controlled way.

3 If you think about a situation when you were angry, the therapy will be more enjoyable.

4 In Spain, some companies pay for their workers to build hotels.

5 In Mexico, they use destruction therapy in hospitals.

6 Laughter therapy can help people to feel less pain.

7 On average, children laugh 100 times a day, and adults laugh seventeen times.

B Listen again to check. Correct the false statements.

C Discuss the questions.

1 Do you think destruction therapy and laughter therapy are good ideas? Why/Why not?

2 Would you try any of the ideas in the programme?

GRAMMAR zero and first conditionals

5A Look at four sentences from the programme. Which talk about a general situation (GS) and which talk about a specific/future situation (FS)?

a) When people get angry, they don't know what to do with their anger.

b) When we get there, I'll give you a hammer.

c) If I smash the car to pieces, will I feel better?

d) If people laugh about something, they feel better.

B Underline the correct alternative to complete the rules.

Rules:

1 Use the zero conditional (*If/When* + present simple + present simple) to talk about a *general/specific* situation (fact), or something which is always true.

2 Use the first conditional (*If/When* + present simple + *will/might/could*) to talk about a *general/specific* (possible) situation in the future.

▶ page 138 **LANGUAGEBANK**

6A ▶ 6.2 **Listen and underline the alternative you hear.**

1 If he shouts, *I get/I'll get* angry.

2 If I see him, *I tell/I'll tell* him.

3 When they arrive, *we eat/we'll eat*.

4 When we get there, *I phone/I'll phone* you.

5 If I finish early, *I go/I'll go* home.

B Listen again and repeat. Pay attention to the weak form of '*ll* /əl/ in the contraction *I'll* /aɪəl/ or *we'll* /wɪəl/.

PRACTICE

7A Complete the sentences with the correct form of the verbs in brackets. Mark each sentence zero (0) or first (1st) conditional.

1 a) If I go running every day, it _____ (make) me feel good.

 b) I'm feeling down. If I go for a run, I _____ (feel) better.

2 a) When I finish reading this book, I _____ (give) it to you to read.

 b) When I _____ (finish) reading a book, I usually feel disappointed.

3 a) I'm meeting my boss later. If I tell him about my new job, he _____ (get) angry.

 b) If I _____ (get) angry, I take a deep breath and count to ten.

4 a) If I'm tired, I _____ (like) to eat in front of the television and go to bed early.

 b) I'm planning to drive through the night. If I get tired, I _____ (stop) and sleep.

B Complete the sentences so that they are true for you. Compare your ideas with a partner.

When I get older …

When my English gets better, I …

If I'm happy, I usually …

When I get home this evening …

If I'm stressed, I usually …

SPEAKING

8A Work in pairs. What do you do in situations 1–5? Write three pieces of advice to give to someone in the same situation.

1 You're nervous about a job interview/exam.

2 You're annoyed with someone in your family.

3 It's the weekend and you're bored.

4 You're stressed about your work/studies.

5 You've got too many things to do.

B Work in groups and compare your ideas. Who has the best ideas?

VOCABULARY *PLUS* multi-word verbs

9A Match the following topics: *Clothes, Computers* and *Love and friendship* with paragraphs 1–3.

1_____: I met my ex-boyfriend when he **chatted me up** in a bar. We **got on** really well. We were together for two years and we were planning to **settle down**, but then I **went off** him!

2_____: You have to **scroll up** and then **click on** the arrow icon. And don't forget to **log off** before you **shut down**.

3_____: I love **dressing up** so when I **tried on** that purple suit, I thought it was perfect for my first day at work! So I arrived and the receptionist told me to **take off** my tie because everyone **dresses down** at the company!

speakout TIP

There are different ways to group multi-words verbs (including phrasal verbs) in your notebook. For example, you can group them by topic (e.g. weather, travel, work), or by preposition (e.g. multi-word verbs with *on, over, by*). Decide how you want to group them and then add the phrases to your notebook.

B Match the multi-word verbs in bold in Exercise 9A with the correct definition in the word webs. You will need to use the infinitive form.

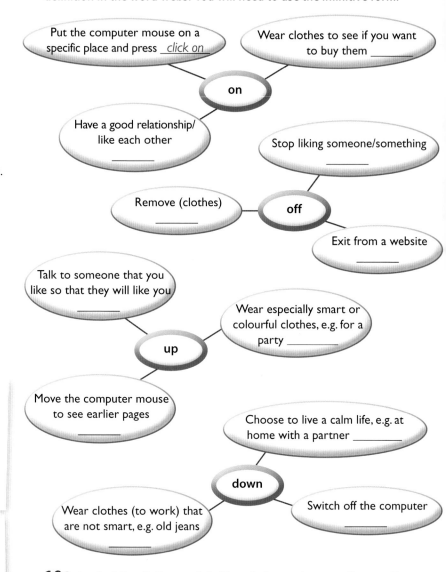

Put the computer mouse on a specific place and press *click on*

Wear clothes to see if you want to buy them _____

on

Have a good relationship/like each other _____

Stop liking someone/something _____

Remove (clothes) _____

off

Exit from a website _____

Talk to someone that you like so that they will like you _____

Wear especially smart or colourful clothes, e.g. for a party _____

up

Move the computer mouse to see earlier pages _____

Choose to live a calm life, e.g. at home with a partner _____

down

Wear clothes (to work) that are not smart, e.g. old jeans _____

Switch off the computer _____

10A Look at the dictionary definitions below and answer the questions.

1 Which verb needs an object?

2 Which verb does not need an object?

3 Which verb can be followed by another preposition?

try sth ↔ **on** *phr v* to put on a piece of clothing to find out if it fits or if you like it: *Can I try these jeans on, please?*

get on *phr v* 1 *Br E* if people get on, they have a friendly relationship: + **with** *She doesn't get on with my mum very well.*

shut down *phr v* if a company, factory, machine etc shuts down, or if you shut it down, it stops operating: *Hundreds of local post offices have shut down.* | **shut** sth ↔ **down** *Did you shut the computer down?*

B Use the dictionary definitions to help you decide which sentences are possible. Mark the sentences with a tick or a cross.

1 I **tried** the suit **on** / I **tried on** the suit.

2 I **get on** really well with Simon / I **get** Simon **on** really well.

3 You need to **shut down** the computer / You need to **shut** the computer **down**.

C Choose 3–4 verbs from above and write your own example sentences. Use a dictionary to help. Then compare them with a partner's.

▶ page 153 **VOCABULARYBANK**

▶ **GRAMMAR** | second conditional ▶ **VOCABULARY** | collocations ▶ **HOW TO** | give advice in hypothetical events

IF you wanted to persuade someone to dress up as a tree in public, what would you do? If you wanted to raise money for charity on the streets, who would you ask to help you? What would you do if you wanted to sell cakes and nobody was buying them? What would you do if you needed to think creatively but didn't have any ideas?

One thing you could do is watch a programme from the BBC series *The People Watchers*. The programme asks the question 'Why do we do what we do?' Through twenty episodes, Professor Richard Wiseman, two psychologists and a neuroscientist do experiments involving members of the public, secretly filming them with a hidden camera. The experiments show why we behave the way we do in everyday situations. If you wanted to know how to get a seat on a crowded train, stop people from jumping queues, get someone to do you a favour, work out if someone is lying, and get a complete stranger to lend you a mobile phone, you could find out by watching.

In one experiment, two of Wiseman's psychologists pretended to be cake-sellers. They stood at a stall on the street and tried to sell cakes for a pound each. No one bought any. So they did what shops do: they held a sale. But it wasn't a real sale. They pretended that one cake cost two pounds, and if you bought a cake, you would get another one free. People started buying! Later they told people that the cakes usually cost two pounds but they were doing a special deal and selling them for just one pound. Again, people bought the cakes. It seems that everyone loves the idea of a bargain even if they aren't really getting one.

Another experiment looked at 'experts' who aren't. Emma, a psychologist, pretended to be a hairdresser. While 'cutting' three people's hair, she talked like a hairdresser, saying all the right things, and dropped a few bits of fake hair. The three volunteers later said they were very happy with their haircuts. In reality, Emma hadn't cut any hair. Richard Wiseman's conclusion? People would do better if they didn't always listen to 'experts'. Instead, they should trust their own eyes.

In another experiment, Jack, a psychologist, had to persuade ordinary people to dress up as a tree. The trick was to 'start small'. First, Jack asked a man to wear a badge; then he asked him to wear a cap; and finally the tree suit. This, Wiseman says, is called 'The foot in the door technique': if you want a big favour from someone, first ask for a small favour!

READING

1A Work in pairs and discuss. What do you think 'people-watching' means? What professions need to be good at people-watching? Why?

B Read the article and check your ideas.

2A Work in pairs and answer the questions.

1 Who is in Professor Wiseman's team?

2 What question does the programme answer?

3 Why did people suddenly start buying the cakes?

4 How much hair did Emma cut?

5 What is 'The foot in the door technique'?

B Read the article again. Make notes under headings 1–3.

1 People involved in the programme

2 Situations

3 Conclusions from the experiments

C Work in pairs and take turns to explain the article using your notes.

VOCABULARY verb–noun collocations

3A Match verbs 1–7 with nouns a)–g).

1	hold	a)	money (for something)
2	raise	b)	experiments
3	do	c)	a programme
4	get	d)	hair
5	jump	e)	a queue
6	cut	f)	a seat
7	watch	g)	a sale

B Which do you do:

1 to sell something cheaply?

2 to avoid standing up in a train/bus/waiting room, etc.?

3 to help a charity?

4 to be informed or entertained?

5 to make someone look more beautiful?

6 to obtain new scientific information?

7 to avoid waiting in a long line (for example, to get tickets)?

GRAMMAR second conditional

4A Read a review of *The People Watchers*. Why does the reviewer like the programme?

Pick of the month

My own favourite series this month? *The People Watchers*. Presented by Professor Richard Wiseman and his rather attractive psychologist friends, the show asks some very interesting questions. <u>If no one saw you, would you take something without paying for it?</u> <u>How close to someone would you stand if you didn't know them?</u> It's all good stuff, but <u>maybe the programme could be even better if we heard from more experts.</u> Unfortunately, for most of the series, we only hear Professor Wiseman's voice. And <u>it would also be nice if we had more statistics.</u> Some of the experiments using hidden cameras show only one or two people in action – not enough to make big conclusions about human nature. But overall, this is good TV: light, easy on the eye, and fun.

B Look at the four underlined sentences above and complete the rules with the words in the box.

would	could	hypothetical	imaginary	past

Rules:
1 We use the second conditional to describe a _____ or _____ situation.
2 In the *if* clause, we use the _____ simple.
3 In the result clause, we use _____ or *'d*.
4 If we are not sure of the result, we can also use _____.

C Find other examples of the second conditional in the article on page 71.

▶ page 138 **LANGUAGE**BANK

5A ▶ 6.3 Listen and complete the conversations.
1 A: What _____ _____ _____ if your laptop exploded?
   B: If my laptop exploded, I'd call for help!
2 A: What would you do if you lost your house keys?
   B: If I lost my house keys _____ climb through the window!
3 A: How would you feel if your car broke down?
   B: If my car broke down, I _____ _____ happy!

B Listen again and answer questions 1–3.
1 How do we pronounce *would* in the question form?
2 How do we pronounce *would* in fast spoken English in positive sentences?
3 How do we pronounce the negative of *would*?

PRACTICE

6 Complete the sentences with the correct form of the verbs in the box.

~~write~~ work do can learn fail have not/rain
see (x2) go like ~~not/have~~ not/be not/work tell

1 I would ___*write*___ my autobiography if I _*didn't have*_ so much work to do.
2 If I _____ enough time, I _____ Japanese.
3 If I _____ go anywhere in the world, I _____ to the Caribbean.
4 If it _____ so much, I _____ to live in Norway.
5 You _____ very happy if you _____ the exam.
6 Who _____ for if you _____ for our company?
7 What _____ if you _____ a UFO?
8 If you _____ a friend stealing something, would you _____ the police?

7A Complete the sentences about your classmates.
1 If _____ could go anywhere, he/she …
2 If _____ wasn't so busy, he/she …
3 If _____ was able to speak to the President of his/her country, he/she …
4 If _____ knew how to, he/she …
5 _____ would feel very happy if …
6 _____'s life would be easier if …
7 _____ wouldn't like it if …
8 _____ wouldn't care if …

B Ask your classmates if your sentences are true.

SPEAKING

8A Work in pairs and discuss. What would you do if …
1 you saw a very young child smoking in the street?
2 you found a bag of money in the street?
3 you inherited a house on the other side of the world?
4 you discovered that one of your colleagues was taking drugs?
5 you heard someone saying bad things about your friend?
6 one of your relatives asked to live with you?
7 someone asked you to take part in a TV programme?
8 you saw someone stealing bread in the supermarket?

It depends. If they looked like they were hungry, I might not say anything.

B Tell other students your ideas. Which dilemmas were the most difficult?

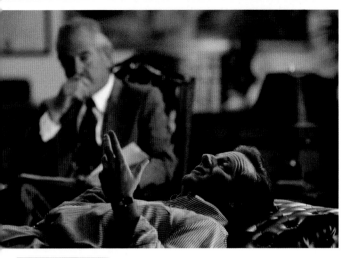

WRITING a letter of advice

9 Look at the photo and discuss. What do you do when you need advice? Would you ever consider getting professional help, going online or asking a relative/friend/experienced older person? What does it depend on?

10A Read the dilemma. What do you think the person should do?

> My cousin has asked me to lend her some money to start an internet business. **She is intelligent and reliable, and I like her, but she is only twenty years old. Also, I know nothing about internet businesses. Should I lend her the money?**

B Read the responses. Which do you agree with? Why?

YES

You have the money. She has the ideas, the energy and the expertise. If I were you, I wouldn't worry about her age. As a young person, in all likelihood she knows more about the internet than you do. And she isn't asking for your advice, only your money. So, come on - you're a member of her family. What do you have to lose apart from a bit of money? And if you're really worried, maybe tell her you want 50% of the money back within two years. If she's reliable, you'll probably get it.

NO

So your cousin wants money. Perhaps you really trust her, but aged twenty, she probably doesn't have much experience in business. If I were you, I'd ask a lot of questions first. I'd find out how much research she has done, how well she knows the market, and who else is involved. It's possible that she will be successful, but over 90% of new companies disappear within the first year. The other thing is time. In all probability, it'll take her a few years to start making a profit. Can you wait that long to get your money back? And think about this: if it wasn't your cousin asking, would you lend the money?

C Tick the things a letter of advice might include. Compare your ideas with other students.

1 a short summary of the situation
2 a few sentences describing your qualifications
3 some ideas about what the person should do
4 some background information explaining your ideas
5 a question for the reader to think about

D Find the things you ticked in the letters of advice in Exercise 10B.

LEARN TO qualify what you say

11A Look at the words/phrases in the box. Find and underline these in the letters of advice in Exercise 10B. Then answer the questions.

> maybe   probably   perhaps   in all likelihood
> It's possible that   in all probability

1 Which words/phrases mean 'there is a strong possibility'?
2 Which two phrases have the same meaning?

B How do you feel about statements 1–4? Qualify them, using the words and phrases above.

1 As life in the twenty-first century gets more complex, people will have more complex problems.
2 In the future, machines will 'read' our emotions and 'know' if we have a problem.
3 In the future, most young people will prefer to talk to strangers online about their problems rather than have face-to-face conversations with family and friends.
4 I'd never write to a problem page if I needed advice.

Most people ask their family and friends for advice. They don't need to write to problem pages.

*Most people **probably** ask their family and friends for advice. **In all likelihood**, they don't need to write to problem pages.*

12A Read the problem below. Work with other students and think of possible solutions.

> I have a problem. **My twenty-six-year-old brother has always loved football, but now it's becoming an obsession. He goes to watch matches every weekend even though the tickets are expensive and he doesn't have much money. At his house, he sometimes watches three or four matches on TV a day! His only friends are football fans, and his last girlfriend broke up with him because of his obsession. I want to help him, but he's older than me and he thinks it's none of my business what he does in his free time. Please can you give me some advice?**

B Write a letter of advice to the letter writer above.

C Work in groups and take turns to read your letters. If you were in the person's situation, which letter would you like to receive?

| ▶ **FUNCTION** \| giving news | ▶ **VOCABULARY** \| life events | ▶ **LEARN TO** \| respond to news |

VOCABULARY life events

1A Look at phrases 1–12. Are they good news (G), or bad news (B)?

1	pass your exams	7	fail a test
2	have an accident	8	split up with a partner
3	be offered a job	9	win a competition/match
4	get a place at university	10	get promoted
5	get engaged/married	11	get a degree
6	lose your job/money	12	buy a house

B Work in pairs and answer the question. Have any of the things above happened recently to you, or anyone you know?

2A Work in groups and discuss. What is the best way to give bad news?

B Complete the article with the phrases in the box. Does it mention any of your ideas?

> give a reason   tone of voice   prepare your listener
> making people too upset   bad news   good news

Good ways to give bad news

It's easy to give someone good news, but what about when you have some ¹_____ to tell? Are there any good ways to give bad news without ²_____? The following steps might help:

- Say something positive: Try to start or end the conversation with some ³_____, so that it's not all bad. For example, 'You did very well in the interview, but unfortunately we've given the job to somebody else.'
- ⁴_____ for the news: Use phrases to introduce what you're going to say, like 'Unfortunately, …', 'I'm really sorry, but …' or 'I'm afraid I've got some bad news.' This gives the listener time to prepare for what you're going to say.
- Try to ⁵_____: People like to know why things go wrong. Try to explain the decision: If someone doesn't get the job, can you explain why? If you have to cancel an arrangement, try to give a reason.
- Use a soft ⁶_____: If you're giving someone bad news, try to use a soft, calm voice to make you sound kind. Say things to show you understand, like, 'I'm really sorry.' or 'I know this must be disappointing.'

C Read the article again. Do you agree with the advice? Why/Why not?

FUNCTION giving news

3A ▶ 6.4 Listen to seven conversations. Match the conversations to pictures A–G.

B Look at the pictures again. What is the good news or bad news in each situation?

4A Look at the phrases the speakers use to introduce their news. Listen again and write the conversation number next to each phrase.

good news	I've got some good news (for you).
	I'm really pleased to tell you …
	You'll never guess what.
bad news	Bad news, I'm afraid.
	I'm sorry to have to tell you, but …
	I'm afraid / Unfortunately, …
	I'm afraid I've got some bad news …
	There's something I've got to tell you.
good or bad news	You know …? Well, …
	I've/We've got something to tell you. 1

B ▶ 6.5 Listen to some of the phrases in the table again. Underline the stressed syllables.

C Listen again. Is the speaker's voice high or low for good news? Is it high or low for bad news? Practise the phrases.

▶ page 138 **LANGUAGEBANK**

5 Put the words in the correct order to make sentences.

1 news / afraid / I'm / bad – / the / we / match / lost
2 to / I'm / the / you / tell / got / pleased / you / really / job / that
3 going / I'm / to / late / we're / be / afraid
4 got / you / there's / tell / I've / to / something
5 never / what / you'll / guess
6 got / news / I've / for / good / you / some
7 was / concert / the / unfortunately, / cancelled
8 lost? / you / the / we / cat / know / we / again / found / him / well,

LEARN TO respond to news

6 How do the speakers respond to the news? Complete the conversations with the words in the box.

> joking   sorry   lucky   annoying   pleased
> Congratulations   done   shame   terrible

1 W: We're getting married.
   M: Wow! That's fantastic. _____!

2 W: We've offered the job to someone else.
   M: Oh. That's a _____. Thanks, anyway.

3 W1: I've just won some money on the Spanish lottery.
   W2: You're _____? … How much did you win?
   W1: 1,000 euros.
   W2: You _____ thing!

4 M1: I've crashed the car.
   M2: Oh no. That's _____.

5 W: They've offered me a place.
   M: That's wonderful news. Well _____! I'm so _____ for you.

6 W1: Steve's lost his job.
   W2: Oh no. That's awful. I'm really _____ to hear that.

7 M: I've got too much work to do.
   W: Oh no. That's really _____.

speakout TIP

Exaggerate! Sometimes when you speak in a foreign language, your intonation can sound flat. This can mean that you don't sound as polite or enthusiastic as you want to. Try to exaggerate the intonation pattern to sound enthusiastic or concerned. Say the responses in Exercise 7A with an exaggerated intonation.

7A ▶ 6.6 Listen to responses 1–4. Notice the intonation patterns.

1 Congratulations!

2 That's fantastic news!

3 That's a shame.

4 That's awful.

B Practise saying the phrases with the correct intonation.

C ▶ 6.7 Mark the main stress on sentences 1–6. Which ones use a higher voice? Listen and check, then listen and repeat.

1 You lucky thing!

2 That's terrible.

3 Well done.

4 I'm so pleased for you.

5 That's really annoying.

6 That's awful. I'm really sorry to hear that.

SPEAKING

8A Work in pairs and role-play the situation. Student A: you interviewed your partner for a job last week. You have asked him/her back to the office to give them the job. Student B: you were interviewed for a job last week, but since then you have been offered a better job with another company, and you have decided to accept their offer.

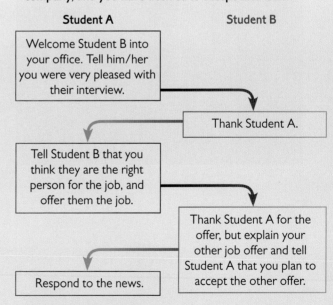

B Work in pairs. First, think of three pieces of good/bad news to tell your partner. Then take turns to give and respond to each other's news using expressions in Exercises 4 and 6.

DVD PREVIEW

1 Read about a BBC comedy. Why is this week supposed to be special for Howard? What's the problem?

BBC My Worst Week

The week before a wedding can be a difficult time, but for publisher Howard Steele, marrying the beautiful Mel, it becomes a complete **nightmare**. Everything that can possibly go wrong does go wrong, even though Howard tries desperately to do the right thing. During the week, Howard accidentally kills his in-laws' dog, puts Mel's granny in hospital, and loses the wedding ring (which has been in the family for many generations) twice. It's not a good start, and what should have been a very special week soon turns into the worst week of his life.

DVD VIEW

2 Watch the DVD then number the events in the correct order.

a) Mel calls Howard in his office. _____

b) Eve tries to take the ring off using soap in the bathroom. _____

c) Howard arrives in his office and shows his secretary, Eve, the ring. _____

d) Mel reminds Howard to collect the ring. _____

e) The ring gets stuck. _____

f) Eve bursts into tears, so Howard lets her try the ring on. _____

3A Who says this: Howard (H), Eve (E) or Mel (M)?

1 'Don't forget the ring.'

2 'It's been in Mel's family for 150 years. They have this rather charming tradition where they (uh) pass it down from generation to generation.'

3 'I always wanted a fairy-tale wedding of my own.'

4 'Try it on. See what it feels like.'

5 'When the vicar asks me to put the ring on my fiancée's finger, it would be very nice if my secretary was not attached.'

6 'No, really – it's stuck.'

7 'I'll get a plumber.'

B Watch the DVD again to check.

4A Complete the sentences about how the characters felt.

1 Mel is worried about …

2 Eve is impressed when she sees …

3 Eve gets upset about …

4 Howard is annoyed when …

5 Eve is anxious about …

6 Howard is shocked when …

B Compare your ideas with another student.

speakout memorable moments

5A ▶ 6.8 Listen to a man talking about a special weekend. Which of the following statements is <u>not</u> true?

1 His brother organised a surprise weekend away.

2 They went on a boat trip to a lighthouse, and slept there.

3 They went shopping with his brother's money.

4 They went to the theatre and then ate an expensive five-course meal.

B Listen again and tick the key phrases you hear.

> **key phrases**
>
> One of the most memorable moments/events in my life was …
>
> The happiest moment of my life was when …
>
> It all started one day when …
>
> I was so embarrased/delighted/shocked/terrified when …
>
> I had absolutely no idea.
>
> The funniest thing that ever happened to me was …
>
> (The) next thing/morning …
>
> That weekend/day is one of my happiest memories.

C Choose one of the following questions. Plan your answer using some of the key phrases.

1 What are your strongest memories of your childhood?

2 Have you ever done anything you regret?

3 What's the most embarrassing/funniest/scariest thing that has ever happened to you?

4 What do you remember about the house you lived in as a child?

5 Can you remember a time when you felt very proud?

6 What is your happiest memory?

D Work in groups and tell your stories.

writeback a website entry

6A Read the website entry. What kind of things do people write about on this website? What was special about Ross's car journey?

> **100 lives: real life, real people, real experiences**
>
> Join people from around the world who want to share their stories and experiences. Read true personal stories, chat and get advice from the group.
>
> **Q: What's your happiest memory?**
>
> One of my happiest memories is of a car journey I took with some friends from Canada down to California nearly fifteen years ago. It was a clear night with a full moon, and as we drove we listened to music, and talked. The roads were empty, and there was a wonderful sense of freedom and adventure. We were driving away from our families and everything we knew so well. We drove with the windows open and I can remember the warmth of the wind on my face, and the sound of the music playing out to the open skies. Even now, when I hear any of the songs on that album, it takes me straight back to that journey, and that feeling. I hope it never goes away.
>
> **Ross, Calgary**

B Choose another question from Exercise 5C and write your story (150–200 words). Use the website entry above and the key phrases to help.

-ING/-ED ADJECTIVES

1A Work in pairs. Use adjectives to describe how you feel in the following situations.

1 you lose your bus/train ticket
2 you get lost at night in a foreign city
3 you wait for a delayed flight
4 you forget someone's name (when you should know it)

B Write situations for the adjectives in the box.

> annoying   worried   boring
> embarrassing   relaxing
> confusing   exhausted
> frightening   satisfied

annoying – When you discover your phone has run out of power, it's …

worried – My exams are tomorrow. I'm really …

C Work in pairs. Take turns to read your situations. Don't say the adjectives they describe. Can your partner guess the adjective?

ZERO AND FIRST CONDITIONALS

2A Match 1–7 with a)–g) to make sentences.

1 If you drink too much coffee,
2 If you go to bed early,
3 If you go to bed late all the time,
4 If you listen to loud music when you study,
5 You won't get fit if you
6 If you don't like your job,
7 You'll have problems at work if you

a) drive everywhere in your car.
b) you won't sleep tonight.
c) it's difficult to concentrate.
d) you'll exhaust yourself.
e) don't finish that report on time.
f) you'll feel better in the morning.
g) look for a new one.

B Look at the sentences in Exercise 2A. Can you think of other ways to complete them? Compare your ideas with a partner.

3 Work in pairs and take turns. Student A: write down three things you would like to achieve this year. Show your list to your partner. Student B: look at Student A's list and make *if/when* sentences to give advice.

A: one: find a new job   two: get fit three: improve my English

B: one: find a new job: If you look on the internet, you might find a new job.

VERB–NOUN COLLOCATIONS

4 Rearrange the letters in blue to complete the sentences with *watch/hold/raise/do/get/cut.*

1 We should go to the concert early so we can est gates. *get seats*
2 They are going to heal loads to sell their old clothes.
3 The schoolchildren decided to ease my iron for cancer research.
4 I'm going home early because I want to grammar two peach on TV.
5 He gave up his job because he didn't want to opened term six on animals.
6 My cousin i shut car for a living.

SECOND CONDITIONAL

5 Work in pairs. Student A: use an *if* clause with the phrases in your box. Student B: respond with the correct *would* clause from your box.

A

> ~~I/be/rich~~   there/be/no war
> there/be/more hours in the day
> I/have/more/energy
> nobody/smoke   I/give up/coffee
> can/paint/well

B

> dance/all night   sleep/better
> people/be/healthier
> do/a portrait of you
> ~~give/money/charity~~
> people/work/more
> the world/be/peaceful

A: If I was rich …
B: I'd give some money to charity.

GIVING NEWS

6A Each conversation has two words missing. Write in the missing words. You may have to change the punctuation.

                    I'm
1 A: Bad news afraid.

   B: What's the matter?

   A: The computers aren't working.

   B: Not again! Annoying.

2 A: You'll never what.

   B: What?

   A: I got the job.

   B: Congratulations! That's news.

3 A: I've got some good news you.

   B: What is it?

   A: I've been promoted.

   B: Well. That's great news.

4 A: I'm to have to tell you, but I'm leaving the company.

   B: What? Why?

   A: The company has got problems, so they're reducing the number of managers.

   B: I'm sorry to that.

5 A: You that exam I did last week?

   B: Yes?

   A: Well, I passed.

   B: Congratulations! I'm so for you.

B Work in pairs and practise the conversations.

BBC VIDEO PODCAST

Download the video podcast and view people talking about emotions and whether they are an optimist or pessimist.

Authentic BBC interviews

www.pearsonlongman.com/speakout

UNIT 7

SPEAKING

> ❯ Talk about success
> ❯ Talk about your abilities
> ❯ Give / Clarify opinions
> ❯ Describe an achievement

LISTENING

> ❯ Understand a radio programme about success
> ❯ Listen to a conversation about memory
> ❯ Listen to a discussion about intelligence
> ❯ Watch a BBC documentary about an achievement

READING

> ❯ Read a biographical text
> ❯ Read about qualifications

WRITING

> ❯ Write a summary
> ❯ Write an internet post

BBC CONTENT

> ❏ Video podcast: What has been your greatest achievement to date?
> ⊙ DVD: The One Show: Water Ski Challenge

UNIT **7**

success

speak**out** DVD

SPEAKING

1A Work in pairs and read the quotes. What do they tell you about success? Do you agree or disagree?

> 'The difference between failure and success is doing a thing nearly right and doing a thing exactly right.'
> **Edward Simmons**

> 'Success doesn't come to you ... you go to it.' **Marva Collins**

> 'The secret of success in life is for a man to be ready for his opportunity when it comes.'
> **Benjamin Disraeli**

B Write the names of three very successful people. Answer the questions.

1 How and why did these people become successful?

2 Do you think they have a special talent, or have they just been lucky?

3 What advice would you give to someone who wants to be as successful as these people?

VOCABULARY success

2A Complete sentences 1–8 with the phrases in the box.

> work hard (at something)   have a natural talent   focus on
> get better at   have the opportunity (to do something)
> believe in yourself   practise (something)   be a high achiever

1 You will never achieve anything, if you don't _work hard_ at it.

2 I don't _____ for languages. I find them difficult to learn.

3 If you _____ and your abilities, then you can achieve anything.

4 It's amazing what children can achieve if they _____ to try different skills.

5 If you want to develop any skill, you have to _____ regularly.

6 I'm sure she will _____. She is determined to do well at everything.

7 When I really want something, I try to _____ my goal.

8 If you keep trying, you'll _____ it. Don't give up!

B Find phrases above to match meanings 1–6.

1 be sure about your ideas/abilities

2 only think about one objective

3 improve

4 do something again and again

5 have the chance to do something

6 be successful in your work or studies

C Choose two of the phrases and make sentences which are true for you. Compare your ideas with a partner.

▶ page 154 **VOCABULARY**BANK

LISTENING

3A Read the introduction to an article about success. What do you think the secret of success is?

What is the secret of success?

BBC Focus Magazine investigates

What makes the most successful people on the planet different from the rest of us? If we were more like Albert Einstein or John Lennon, surely we could enjoy the same level of success they did. In truth, however, we pay too much attention to what high achievers are like, and not enough to where they come from and the opportunities they had along the way. In his new book, Malcolm Gladwell reveals that there is one factor – so obvious that it's right under our noses – that all successful people share ...

B ▶ 7.1 Listen to the radio programme to find out.

C Listen again and complete the summary.

In this new book, *The Outliers*, Gladwell argues that Beethoven, The Beatles and Bill Gates all have one thing in ¹ _____. They ² _____ what they do, and they practised a lot. In fact, Gladwell discovered that in order to be truly ³ _____ in anything, it is necessary to practise the ⁴ _____ for more than ⁵ _____ hours. These people have done that which is why he believes they have been so ⁶ _____.

4A Are the statements true (T) or false (F)?

1 If we want to learn from Bill Gates' achievements, we need to look at where he came from and the opportunities he had.

2 If you're going to be world-class at something, you need to have parents who are high achievers.

3 The Beatles played all-night concerts in Hamburg, and this helped them to master their craft.

4 Bill Gates got into computer programming, and through a fortunate series of events, he was able to do lots and lots of programming.

5 Bill Gates had access to a computer at home during the 60s and 70s when computers were 'the size of rooms'.

6 In order to be very successful, you need a very talented teacher, and enough money to pay for your tuition.

B Listen again to check.

SPEAKING

5 Discuss the questions in groups.

1 Do you have a special skill/interest? How many hours do you think you have spent practising it? (10,000 hours is approximately ten hours per week for twenty years.)

2 Do you agree that if you practise something enough, you can become world-class at it, or do you think you need to have a natural talent?

3 What things have you been successful at? Why?

GRAMMAR present perfect simple versus continuous

6A Read sentences a)–e). Underline examples of the past perfect simple and circle examples of the past perfect continuous.

a) Martina's been playing tennis since she was three years old.

b) She's been going to ballet lessons since she was a child.

c) I've known Max for years.

d) How long have you been studying French?

e) He's always enjoyed playing sport.

B Match sentences a)–e) with rules 1–3. Some sentences will match more than one rule.

> **Rules:**
> 1 Use the present perfect continuous to emphasise that an action has been long and repeated.
> 2 With state verbs (e.g. *like*, *love*, *understand*, *remember*, *know*, etc.), we cannot use the present perfect continuous, so we use the present perfect simple.
> 3 We often use *for, since* and *How long have you …?* with the present perfect simple and the present perfect continuous.

→ page 140 **LANGUAGEBANK**

PRACTICE

7A Complete the sentences with the present perfect simple or continuous form of the verbs in brackets.

1 I _____ (write) books for years, but I haven't written a best-seller yet!

2 They _____ (play) music for hours! I can't get to sleep.

3 I _____ always _____ (love) art, but I'm not very good at it.

4 She _____ (not study) a lot because she's been ill.

5 How long _____ you _____ (know) Sheila?

6 I _____ (learn) Mandarin for two years.

7 I _____ (have) my own car since I was twenty.

8 Will Smith? I've never _____ (hear) of him.

B ▶ 7.2 Listen to check. Notice the pronunciation of *have*. Is it strong or weak? Practise saying the sentences.

8A Make questions with the prompts.

1 how long / you / know / best friend?

2 how long / you / do / your hobby?

3 how long / you / study / English?

4 how long / you / live where you live now?

5 how / you / spend / your days off recently?

B Work in pairs. Take turns to ask and answer the questions above. Think of two or more follow-up questions for each question.

A: How long have you known your best friend?

B: For about fifteen years.

A: Where did you meet?

VOCABULARY *PLUS* verb phrases

9A Choose the correct preposition to complete the verb phrases in sentences 1–7.

1 I don't **have a lot in common** *to/with/for* my sister.

2 We don't **have access** *with/at/to* the internet at work.

3 She**'s world-class** *in/for/at* playing the violin.

4 He works very hard. He **puts** *in/to/with* a lot of hours.

5 I've got a lot to **think** *with/for/about* at the moment.

6 The film **picks up** *on/to/at* the difficulties people experienced during the war.

7 She **has a talent** *about/for/in* finding a bargain.

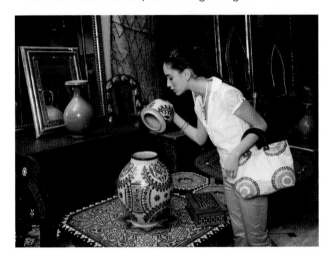

B Add the verb phrases to the correct group below.

1 agree argue _____	with	5 depend rely _____	on
2 worry complain _____	about	6 look laugh _____	at
3 belong pay attention _____	to	7 succeed believe _____	in
4 pay wait _____	for		

speakout TIP

There are many verbs in English which use prepositions. Keep a record of which prepositions go with which verbs in your notebook. Can you add any more phrases you know to the diagram in Exercise 9B?

C Write three questions using the verb phrases above.

*Do you **argue with** anyone in your family?*

*What kind of things do you **worry about**?*

D Work in pairs. Ask and answer your questions.

→ page 154 **VOCABULARYBANK**

VOCABULARY ability

1 Work in pairs. Take turns to ask and answer as many questions as you can about the things you are good/bad at.

When did you start playing the drums? How often do you play? Do you …

2A What do the phrases in bold mean?

1 He**'s an expert in** Italian art. He's written several books about it.

2 He**'s gifted at** painting. He had his first exhibition when he was sixteen.

3 She **has** a lot of **ability** as a dancer. I think she could become a professional.

4 She's the most **skilful** footballer I've ever seen. She can play in any position.

5 He **has an aptitude for** maths. He learns new formulas very quickly.

6 He is a really **talented** musician. He can play six instruments.

7 I'm **hopeless at** geography. I failed my exam three times.

8 I'm **useless at** ball sports. I can't play any.

B ▶ 7.3 Look at the words in bold above. Then listen to the sentences from above and answer the questions.

1 Which parts of the words in bold are stressed? Underline the stressed part.

2 Which five words have two syllables? Where do we normally put the stress on two-syllable words?

C Listen again and repeat the sentences. Focus on the stressed parts.

3A Write the name of:

• an expert in your own area of interest.

• someone in the class who is talented.

• a gifted musician.

• something you are useless at.

• something you have an aptitude for.

B Work in groups. Ask each other to explain what they wrote and why.

READING

4A Work in pairs. Look at the photos opposite and on page 161, then discuss. The men in the photos have been called 'The human camera' and 'The human computer'. What special abilities do you think they have?

B Student A: read the text opposite to see if your ideas are mentioned. Student B: turn to page 161.

The human camera

There is no one quite like Stephen Wiltshire. Born in 1974, Stephen was always different. As a child, he couldn't make friends. In fact, he talked to nobody, showed no interest in school subjects and wasn't able to sit still. Stephen was diagnosed as autistic. He didn't learn fully to talk until he was nine years old and he didn't manage to pass his exams, but he found one thing he liked doing: drawing. Art became his way to communicate.

He started by drawing funny pictures of his teachers, but soon began to draw buildings. His eye for detail was perfect. He could see a building just once and remember everything about it. In 1987, aged twelve, he saw a train station in London called St Pancras. Hours later, in front of TV cameras, he managed to draw this complicated building, with the time on the station clock saying 11.20, the exact time when he was there. The drawing showed every detail perfectly.

Since that television programme made him famous in the UK, many great things have happened to Stephen. He has become a well-known artist, published four books of his drawings, taken helicopter rides above the world's great cities – including London, Rome, Hong Kong and New York – and drawn amazing pictures of them, and opened his own art gallery, where he now works, in London.

His drawings are incredibly accurate – he always manages to draw everything in the right place – but also beautiful to look at. In 2006, he was given an MBE by the Queen of England for services to art.

* **autistic** /ɔːˈtɪstɪk/ *adj* – having a mental condition that makes it hard for someone to understand other people and form relationships

* **MBE** – Member of the British Empire, an award given by the Queen for outstanding achievements

C Student A: read the text above again and answer the questions.

1 How was his behaviour different from other children's?

2 What special talents does he have?

3 How did the public learn about his special talents?

4 What country/countries has he been to and what did he do there?

5 What has he published?

6 What is his 'job' now?

D Tell your partner about your text. Use questions 1–6 to help.

GRAMMAR present and past ability

5 Read sentences 1–9. Which describe present ability and which describe past ability? Which three sentences are negative?

1 If you tell Daniel your birth date, he <u>can</u> tell you what day of the week you were born on. *present ability*

2 He could see a building just once and remember everything about it.

3 As a child, he couldn't make friends.

4 He is able to do extremely difficult mathematical calculations.

5 He was able to calculate 82 x 82 x 82 x 82.

6 He wasn't able to sit still.

7 He always manages to draw everything in the right place.

8 He managed to learn Icelandic in a week.

9 He didn't manage to pass his exams.

▶ page 140 **LANGUAGEBANK**

PRACTICE

6 Complete the text with the words in the box.

| can | isn't | can't | managed | could | to | couldn't | able |

When four-year-old Derek Paravacini heard the sound of the piano, he ran towards it. Although he was blind, he ¹_____ to reach the instrument. He pushed the piano player – a small girl – off her stool, and started to play. Adam Ockleford, a piano teacher, said, 'It was … extraordinary. He was hitting the notes with his hands, his feet, his nose, even his elbows.' Paravacini was ²_____ to play the tune he had just heard and at that moment Ockleford realised the boy was a genius.

Paravacini was born blind and autistic and had great learning difficulties. As a child, he ³_____ do many things that ordinary children do. Even today, as an adult, he ⁴_____ count to ten, and he ⁵_____ able to dress or feed himself. But Paravacini has one incredible gift: music. Like Mozart, he ⁶_____ remember every piece of music he hears.

It started when his parents gave him a plastic organ when he was eighteen months old. He couldn't see the notes, but he managed ⁷_____ play tunes on it. By the time he was four, he ⁸_____ play many pieces on the piano. With Ockleford's help, Paravacini developed his technique and played his first major concert at the Barbican Hall in London, aged nine. He has performed all over Europe and the US and in 2006 recorded his first CD.

SPEAKING

7A Look at the activities opposite and read the instructions below.

1 Put one tick next to the things you can do now.

2 Put two ticks next to the things you could do when you were a child.

3 Put three ticks next to the activities you are very good at.

B Work in groups. Compare your abilities. Say how often you do these things, and which ones you enjoy(ed). Describe any special experiences you have had while doing these things.

change the wheel on a car

paint pictures

run for an hour

Toc! Toc! / Qui est là?

tell a joke in a foreign language

catch and cook a fish

write with your 'wrong' hand

remember important dates from history

1066 1901 1666 1837

climb a mountain

play tennis

ride a motorbike

WRITING a summary

8A Read the summary and answer questions 1–3.

Daniel Tammet and Stephen Wiltshire are two gifted young Englishmen who suffer from forms of autism. These men have one thing in common – they are able to remember large amounts of information – but their talents are very different. Wiltshire has an ability to draw complicated images after seeing them only once, while Tammet has an amazing aptitude for remembering numbers. They have both appeared on television programmes, which helped make them famous, and both published books. While Tammet and Wiltshire experienced difficulties during their childhood, their great achievements are now recognised by the public. And best of all: they both seem happy with their lives.

1 Does the summary explain the main idea of the text(s) (who, what, where and why)?

2 Is the summary shorter or longer than the original text(s)?

3 Does the writer of the summary copy sentences from the original text(s) or does he/she use his/her own words?

B Work in pairs. Look at phrases 1–5 from the summary. What details do these phrases leave out? What information is missing?

1 Wiltshire has an ability to draw complicated images.

He drew a train station in London and pictures of other cities, including Rome, Hong Kong and New York.

2 Tammet has an amazing aptitude for remembering numbers.

3 They have both appeared on television programmes.

4 Both published books.

5 (They) experienced difficulties during their childhood.

LEARN TO make notes for a summary

9A Read the notes and find examples of 1–6 below.

THE MEMORY MEN
Tammet & Wiltshire = very gifted. They are able 2 remember
lots of info. Their abilities → them becoming famous
The artist
Wiltshire remembers things he sees
The mathematician
Tammet remembers numbers & does maths problems

1 an abbreviation

2 symbols for: a) *and* b) *resulted in*

3 a number to represent a word that sounds the same

4 a heading

5 a subheading

6 highlighted information

B Look at suggestions 1–8. Are they good or bad ideas for taking notes? Change the bad ideas.

1 Use abbreviations and symbols.

2 Use diagrams or drawings.

3 Try to write down every word you hear/copy down every word you read.

4 Write fast. Don't worry about handwriting.

5 Don't worry about spelling. You can check later.

6 Highlight important information.

7 Don't use your own words – you might make mistakes.

8 Use a space or a new heading when there's a change of speaker or topic.

10A ▶ 7.4 Listen to three people talking about memory. Tick the things they talk about in the box.

> names   faces   dates   words   birthdays
> directions to places   books you've read   places
> films   jokes   information about products
> things that happened to you when you were very young

B Read the notes about Peggy. Listen again and use the same headings to write notes about John and Tim.

PEGGY
Job
sales rep 4 publishing company

Memory
needs 2 remember lots
not good at directions → used to get lost all the time.
has to remember names & faces of people she talks to +
information about products

C Compare your notes with a partner. What else can you remember about what they say? Use the phrases below to help you.

> ~~Sally or Samantha?~~   makes mistakes
> blocking   all other students
> after an hour of watching a film

She spent an hour calling a woman Sally when her real name was Samantha.

11A Work in pairs. Ask and answer the questions.

1 Do you have a good memory, generally?

2 Which things in the box in Exercise 10A are you good at remembering?

3 Which would you like to be better at remembering?

4 Do you use any special strategies to remember things?

B Write a summary (100–120 words) of what you learned about your partner.

▶ FUNCTION | clarifying opinions ▶ **VOCABULARY** | qualifications ▶ **LEARN TO** | refer to what you said earlier

VOCABULARY qualifications

1A Discuss. Which jobs do you think require the most qualifications?

In my country you have to study for six years to become an architect.

B Read the text. What did Steve Eichel do? Why?

Steve Eichel, a psychologist, was worried about the number of therapists with false diplomas and degrees. He thought it was too easy to get these qualifications. So, one day, he decided to do an experiment. Eichel had a cat called Zoe. Using the name Zoe D Katze (in German, the name means Zoe the Cat), Eichel applied for a number of diplomas and a degree in hypnotherapy for his cat. He completed some forms, paid the money, and invented a CV and a job for Zoe at the Tacayllaermi Friends School (Tacayllaermi backwards spells 'I'm really a cat'). In a few weeks, the cat had two diplomas and a PhD.

2A Work in pairs. What do the words in bold mean? Which words are shown in the photos?

1 What **qualifications** do you have? Apart from school exams, what other exams have you taken or will you take in the future?

2 In your country, when you leave school do you get a **certificate**?

3 Do you have a **driving licence**? What other **licences** can you get?

4 Have you ever done an **online course**?

5 Is **distance learning** popular in your country? Is it more popular than **face-to-face learning**? Which do you prefer?

6 For which professions do you have to **do an apprenticeship**? Does the company usually pay you while you do your training?

7 Do you have a **degree**? From which university?

8 Do you know anyone with an **MA** or a **PhD**? What subject, and in which university, did they do it?

B Discuss the questions in groups.

FUNCTION clarifying opinions

3A Work in pairs and discuss. Do you think people with a lot of qualifications are usually intelligent?

B ▶ 7.5 Listen to two people discussing intelligence. What do they talk about?

a) intelligent animals

b) intelligent people

c) 'intelligent' technology

C Answer the questions, then listen again to check.

1 Why does the man think the boy from Egypt is intelligent?

2 Why does the woman think her two friends are intelligent? What did/do they do?

3 Why are qualifications useful, according to the woman?

4 What does the woman say about 'real life experience, going out and meeting people, talking, travelling'?

4A Complete the phrases in the table.

offering opinions
The [1]_____ I say (he's intelligent) is (that)
For me
In [2]_____ view
I do think
I must say
giving examples
For example,
Let me [3]_____ you (an/another) example.
For [4]_____ thing

B ▶ 7.6 Listen to some three-word phrases from Exercise 4A. Which word is stressed?

C ▶ 7.7 Listen to the full sentences. Copy the stress patterns.

▸▸▶ page 140 **LANGUAGEBANK**

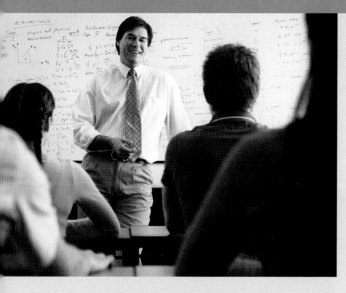

5 Complete the sentences with the words/phrases in the box. Do you agree with the statements?

> ~~must~~   In my   Let me give   The reason I
> For one   For example   I do   For

1 I ____must____ say many creative people are bad students. _____, most artists and musicians don't have many academic qualifications.

2 _____ me, qualifications aren't that important. _____ thing, they don't show a person's character.

3 _____ view, face-to-face learning will disappear. _____ say that is because people want to study from home, so they prefer distance learning.

4 _____ think geniuses usually have personal problems. _____ you an example: Vincent Van Gogh suffered from depression.

LEARN TO   refer to what you said earlier

6 Read the phrases from the audio script and answer questions 1–3.

a) **Like I said,** he doesn't go to school but, for me, he's super-intelligent.

b) **Having said that,** I do think qualifications are useful.

c) Exactly. **That's what I was saying.** Just like the boy from Egypt.

Which phrase shows that you:

1 have already given an opinion that someone else is now giving?

2 have already said something?

3 have said something but now want to give a different opinion?

7 Complete the conversation using the phrases below.

> Like I said,   Having said that,   That's what I was saying.

A: I think online courses are great if you can't travel to class. _____ I prefer to have a real teacher.

B: I agree. You learn more with other people in the room.

A: _____, an online teacher is not the same.

B: I've done some online courses, though. It was really convenient because I could study at home.

A: _____. They're great for people who can't travel.

SPEAKING

8A Read the job advertisement. What qualifications does it mention?

> <u>**Guides needed for Eco-Tours cruise ships**</u>
>
> **Location:**   along the River Nile
> **Salary:**   £20,000
> **Duration:**   6 months (includes four 5-week tours)
> **Date posted:** 18th July 09.22
>
> Duties: introduce tourists to the plant and animal life of the Nile, organise day trips for tourists, write a regular blog. Must speak Arabic and English plus one other language. Must have a tour guide licence, a university degree, and basic qualifications in biology and/or land management.

B Work in groups of three. Student A: read about candidate A. Student B: read about candidate B. Student C: read about candidate C. What benefits can they bring to the job? Are there any skills or qualifications they don't have?

Candidate A
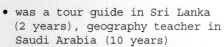
Suresh Perera,
Sri Lanka, 42

- was a tour guide in Sri Lanka (2 years), geography teacher in Saudi Arabia (10 years)
- has a tour guide licence and MA in Geography
- speaks English, Arabic, Tamil
- visited Egypt many times, knows the culture and people
- hobbies: sailing and swimming

Candidate B

Dr. Ahmed Nasari, Egypt, 54

- biologist (20 years), experience in 11 countries.
- PhD in marine biology
- published three books about marine biology, writes regularly for biology journals
- speaks Arabic, English, basic German
- will take the exam for a tour guide licence next month
- wants to research animal life in the Nile

Candidate C
Delilah Olufunwa, Nigeria, 28

- former TV actress and model, then tour guide in Nigeria
- degree in performing arts
- excellent physical fitness (qualified scuba diver, strong swimmer)
- speaks English, Arabic, Spanish, Portuguese, French, is studying Japanese
- loves animals and nature

C Present your candidate to your group. Who should get the job? Why?

DVD PREVIEW

1 Work in groups. Discuss the questions.

1 Do you enjoy sport? Which ones?

2 Have you ever tried to learn a new sport? How successful were you? Why?

3 Have you ever won a sporting competition or attempted a sporting challenge? How did you feel?

2A Read about the programme below. What is Christine's challenge exactly? Why is she doing it? What are the problems?

BBC The One Show: Water Ski Challenge

Sport Relief is a UK charity which asks celebrities to perform sporting <u>challenges</u> in order to raise money for people in Africa. After visiting Uganda with Sport Relief Christine Bleakley, a presenter on *The One Show* (a BBC magazine show), decided to accept a sporting challenge herself. She agreed to water ski across the English Channel from the UK to France. It was an incredibly <u>tough</u> challenge because Christine had never been on water skis before. After a few months training, she <u>attempted</u> the crossing in the middle of winter. Would her physical and mental <u>determination</u> help her to complete the challenge, or would she <u>give up</u> half way? Could she add this <u>outstanding</u> achievement to her already successful career?

B Match the words/phrases in bold in the text with their definitions 1–6.

1 very difficult

2 tried

3 stop doing something (because it is difficult)

4 something that tests your skill or ability

5 excellent/very impressive

6 desire to continue doing something even when it is difficult

▶ DVD VIEW

3 Watch the DVD. Choose the correct summary.

1 Christine completed the challenge without ever falling off her skis.

2 Christine attempted to cross the Channel but failed.

3 Christine crossed the Channel successfully despite falling a lot during the first half.

4 Christine nearly completed the challenge, but fell at the end and broke her leg.

4A Watch the DVD and number the statements in the order you hear them.

a) 'My arms and body hurt so much, but I just don't want to give up.'

b) 'She's fallen in ten times in ten miles, and that simply isn't good enough for this challenge. She has got to (dig in now, and) start to focus.'

c) 'After several falls into the freezing water, I already feel like I can't take much more.'

d) 'I can see France, and nothing is going to stop me.'

e) 'The first woman to water ski across the Channel, in the winter, having only got on water skis four months ago. She is remarkable. It's a truly outstanding achievement.'

f) 'This challenge is incredibly tough. She is going to be operating in sub-zero temperatures for over 90 minutes.'

g) 'I am determined not to fall in, but I soon realise that determination might not be enough.'

B Watch the DVD again and decide who says what. Mark statements with a C (Christine) or a T (trainer).

C Discuss. What do you think of what Christine achieved? Would you do anything like this in order to raise money to help people in Africa? Why/Why not?

speakout an achievement

5A ▶ 7.8 Listen to someone talking about a recent challenge/achievement. Answer the questions.

1 What was her challenge?
2 Was it a good or bad experience?
3 What did she find easy?
4 What problem(s) did she have?
5 Did she succeed?

B Listen again and tick the key phrases you hear.

keyphrases

I found it really easy/quite difficult.
It was the … I had trouble with.
I was/We were very nervous.
At first, I couldn't … but then I started to …
One thing I tried …
I tried to/experimented with … but it didn't work/I couldn't …
I got very frustrated/annoyed/tired.
I didn't know how to …
I'm (so) glad/Eventually I managed it.
It was a (really) difficult challenge/good experience …
For me, it was quite an achievement.

C You are going to talk about a recent challenge/achievement. Before you talk, make some notes on the following:

• What was your challenge? (Were you learning a new sport/how to drive, etc?)
• Where were you?
• How did you feel?
• What was the experience like?/What did the challenge involve?
• Who helped you?
• Did you try any special techniques?
• Did you succeed?

D Work in groups and take turns. Tell each other about your experiences. Who had the funniest/most interesting/most embarrassing experience?

writeback an internet post

6A Read the internet post and answer the questions. What was Jim's challenge? What helped him to learn?

A Beautiful Language, by Jim

I was never very good at languages when I was at school so learning Welsh **was a huge challenge for me. I wanted to learn** Welsh because I was living in Wales and my wife spoke Welsh. **So, I decided** to enrol for a course at the university and go for classes twice a week. I **soon** fell in love with the language – it's so gentle and musical. **I began to realise** how many people living around me loved and treasured their national language. Welsh has beautiful expressions and has often been called the language of poets. **It's not an easy** language **to learn, but it's very satisfying**. I feel like **I've achieved a lot. Now**, when I go into my local shop, I try to speak to people in Welsh. I'm sure **I make a lot of mistakes**, but everyone is very kind to me, and they always smile.

B The *My Story* website publishes stories from the public about their experiences and achievements. Write your own story (120–180 words) to submit to the website. Use the words in bold above and the key phrases to help.

SUCCESS

1A Underline the correct alternative to complete the quotes. Which quotes do you think could be important for you? Why?

1 'When you are not *believing/practising*, remember someone else is *believing/practising*, and when you meet him he will win.'

2 'I was seldom able to see *an opportunity/a talent* until it had ceased to be one.'

3 'Focus *on/in* where you want to go, not on what you fear.'

4 'Some people dream of success, while other people wake up and work hard *on/at* it.'

B Work in pairs and discuss.

1 Do you know anyone who is a high achiever? What have they done?

2 What are you focusing on at the moment in your work/studies?

3 How do you think you can get better at speaking English?

PRESENT PERFECT CONTINUOUS

2A Complete the sentences with the present perfect continuous form of the verbs in brackets.

1 I _____ (practise) learning my lines. Rehearsals start next week.

2 I _____ (visit) patients in their homes.

3 I _____ (mark) homework for hours.

4 I _____ (try) some new ideas for a recipe.

5 I _____ (research) a news story.

B Think of a job to go with each sentence above. Write two or three sentences that this person could say at the end of a busy day. Use the present perfect continuous.

I've been reading all day. I've been saying my lines out loud.

C Work in pairs. Take turns to say your sentences. Can your partner guess the job?

ABILITY

3 Complete the text with the words in the box.

| ~~hopeless~~ | gifted | skilful |
| useless | expert | ability | have |

As a child, I was ¹ *hopeless* at school. I was ² _____ at maths, English, science, everything, because I just didn't ³ _____ an aptitude for that kind of study. One day we were playing football and the ball got stuck in a tree. I climbed the tree to get it, and one of my teachers, John Marston, looking out of the staffroom window, noticed that I was a talented climber. He was an ⁴ _____ in climbing – he'd been in the Alps and up Mount Kilimanjaro – and he invited me to try it one weekend. I really enjoyed it. After a month, he told me I was a very ⁵ _____ climber for my age. I left school three years later with no qualifications, but I kept climbing regularly until I became very ⁶ _____ at it. In my early twenties, I became a professional climber. I'll always remember Mr Marston because he showed me I had an ⁷ _____ which no one else, including me, knew about.

PRESENT AND PAST ABILITY

4A Underline the correct alternative.

1 I *can to/am can/can* type very fast.

2 When I first heard English, I *not able/not could/couldn't* understand anything.

3 Even when I'm stressed, I'm usually *able to/can/able* sleep.

4 I recently had a problem but I *can able to/was able to/managed* solve it.

5 I *'m not able/was able not/wasn't able* to do the job of my dreams (not yet, anyway).

6 Last weekend I *managed to/managed/am managed to* relax completely.

B Tick the sentences that are true for you. Compare your answers with other students.

I can't type very fast, but I don't have to look at the letters when I type.

CLARIFYING OPINIONS

5A Complete the conversations by adding your opinions and giving examples.

1 **A:** I think that, to be happy, people need to have dreams and ambitions.

 B: For me, _____. Let me give you an example: _____.

2 **A:** The most important thing to remember is, if you want to be successful in anything, it's hard work, not talent that gets you there.

 B: I do think _____. The reason I say this is _____.

3 **A:** Being rich or famous is not the same as being successful.

 B: In my view, _____. For example, _____.

4 **A:** There is too much focus on sporting achievement. Games aren't important.

 B: I must say _____. For one thing, _____.

5 **A:** If you want to be successful in your job, you need a good education and you need to understand modern technology.

 B: In my opinion, _____. For one thing, _____. For another, _____.

B Work in groups and take turns. Share your opinions with each other and ask follow-up questions.

BBC VIDEO PODCAST

Download the video podcast and view people talking about their greatest achievements and how they did them.

Authentic BBC interviews

www.pearsonlongman.com/speakout

UNIT 8

UNIT

8

communities

VOCABULARY getting on

1 Work in pairs and discuss.

1 Do you know your neighbours? How well do you know them?

2 Do you have a good relationship with them? Why?

2A Work in pairs. Match sentences 1–6 with the opposite meanings a)–f).

1 I **get on well with** my neighbour – she's always smiling.

2 It's never a problem if I **ask a favour** of my neighbours.

3 I prefer to **mind my own business** so I don't ask the neighbours personal questions.

4 I sometimes **invite** my neighbour **over** for coffee.

5 My neighbour's dog is **a nuisance** – he's always barking early in the morning.

6 We didn't **get to know** our neighbours for years.

a) My neighbour has pets but they never **disturb** me.

b) My neighbour **gets on my nerves** – he's always complaining.

c) We **made friends with** our neighbours immediately.

d) I like to **keep myself to myself** so my neighbour hasn't been in my house.

e) I'm always **doing favours** for my neighbours.

f) I can be quite **nosy** so I often ask my neighbours about their lives!

B Which sentences are true for you? Tell other students.

➠ page 155 **VOCABULARYBANK**

READING

3A Circle the option you think is correct to complete statements 1–4.

1 _____ of people in the UK say they know their neighbours.

   (a) 27%   (b) 50%   (c) 77%

2 If you live in a flat, you probably know your neighbours _____ if you live in a house.

   (a) better than   (b) less than   (c) about the same as

3 _____ year-olds are more likely to know their neighbours than people of other ages.

   (a) 18–24   (b) 30–40   (c) 55–64

4 The people most likely to know their neighbours are: _____.

   (a) women   (b) men   (c) (neither. There is no difference between them.)

B Read the text to check your answers.

4 Answer the questions.

1 What question did the radio programme try to answer?

2 What is ICM and what did it do?

3 Which people who wrote to the website say they have a good relationship with their neighbours?

4 Which person says they had a bad start with a neighbour?

How well do you know your neighbours?

The BBC's iPM radio programme asks its listeners for interesting questions. One question that came up:

'I would like to ask a question about neighbours, by which I mean other people who live in your immediate neighbourhood. Many people we have spoken to have said they don't know any of their immediate neighbours.'

What about you? Do you know any of your immediate neighbours, in the sense of something more than exchanging 'Good morning' or 'Good afternoon', for example?

The BBC liked the question and found the answer. A research group called ICM asked people how well they know their neighbours and this is what they discovered.

Surprisingly, 77% of you say you know your neighbours. It also emerged that if you live in a house, regardless of town or rural area, a massive 80% of you know your neighbours. However, the figure drops to 75% if you're in a flat. The survey also revealed that we appear to get friendlier as we get older. In fact, only 64% of 18–24 year-olds know their neighbours, but for people aged 55–64 this number climbs to 88%. Interestingly enough, it turns out that men are a little less likely to say they know their neighbours than women, and the rich say they are closer to their neighbours than the less well-off.

GRAMMAR articles

5 Look at the words underlined in the sentences below. Match sentences a)–f) with the rules below.

a) The BBC liked <u>the question</u> and found the answer.

b) <u>A research group</u> called ICM asked 1,002 people how well they know their neighbours.

c) <u>Men</u> are less likely to say they know their neighbours than women.

d) Here are a few of <u>the best</u>.

e) We moved into our house in <u>Leeds</u> three years ago.

f) I'm <u>a police officer</u>.

Rules:

1 Use *a/an*:
   - the first time something is mentioned (new information). __b__
   - with jobs. _____

2 Use *the*:
   - when we know which one we are talking about. _____
   - with superlatives. _____

3 Use no article:
   - to talk generally about people or things. _____
   - with most names of places. _____

The topic was very popular with lots of BBC listeners and provoked plenty of comments on the BBC's iPM website. Here are a few of the best:

I only really got to know mine when their house caught fire. We're good friends now.
RxKaren

When we moved into our house in Leeds three years ago, the first remark our neighbour made was, 'So you're moving in? I hope you don't have noisy kids.' We reassured him we had no children and tried to make conversation but with no success.
Loobygraham

I live in a small block of 16 flats. We all know each other and we have 8 nationalities living in these flats so we have our own mini United Nations! If I – or any of my neighbours – needed help or advice or assistance of any kind we could all knock on anyone's door and get it.
Jilcove

I'm a police officer. My neighbours are always extremely friendly. They probably think that if they have any problems, I'll rescue them.
Todd

PRACTICE

6 Complete comments below with *a/an*, *the* or – (no article).

My neighbours have ¹_____ cat that climbs through my window and terrorises my goldfish. It's so annoying! I'm going to buy ²_____ dog next week.

My neighbour is ³_____ doctor. He keeps himself to himself. Once, my son got sick and I asked ⁴_____ doctor to come and have a look and he said, 'My office hours are from 8.00 until 6.00.' Charming!

I have ⁵_____ nicest neighbour in the world. I really get along well with her. She often invites me over for dinner, which is great because she's ⁶_____ professional chef!

⁷_____ People are funny! My neighbours here in ⁸_____ Birmingham have an apple tree that hangs over my garden. Once, some apples fell onto my grass, and they came round to collect them!

My neighbour is ⁹_____ old lady who lives on her own. My wife and I made friends with her and sometimes do favours for her. ¹⁰_____ old lady is always really grateful.

I'm sure that I'm not 11_____ quietest person in the world, but my neighbour is so noisy. She's always playing extremely loud music. I can't escape 12_____ noise! What is wrong with people?

▶ page 142 **LANGUAGEBANK**

GRAMMAR quantifiers

7A Read sentences 1–6 and underline the words that describe quantity.

1 The topic was very popular with <u>lots of</u> BBC listeners.
2 The topic provoked plenty of comments.
3 Here are a few of the best.
4 We reassured him we had no children.
5 We could all knock on anyone's door.
6 Many people … don't know their immediate neighbours.

B Look at the underlined words above and answer the questions.

1 Which mean *a large number/amount*?
2 Which mean *a small number/amount*?
3 Which means *none*?
4 Which two quantifiers can only be used with countable nouns (things we can count)?

▶ page 142 **LANGUAGEBANK**

PRACTICE

8A Underline the correct alternatives in comments below.

1 My neighbour gets on my nerves. She always invites herself over at dinner time so I have to feed her. How *much/many* times have I eaten at her house? *None/No*.

2 My apple tree hangs over my neighbour's garden. There are *a little bit/plenty* of apples for everyone but my neighbours steal them! Once *some/much* of my apples fell on their grass so I went to get them!

3 In fifty years, I've never had *much/many* trouble with my neighbours. But these new ones are a nuisance. They're so nosy – they won't mind their own business. I spend *many of/a lot of* time hiding in the kitchen to avoid them!

4 My neighbour used to leave *a bit of/all of* his windows open. My cat went in there *a few/a little* days a week and played with the goldfish. Then the stupid neighbour bought a dog, and it bit my cat!

5 I'm a doctor. *Several/A bit of* times a year, my neighbours ask, 'Can you give me *a bit of/many* advice?' For free, of course! How do they think I make money? Not by offering free advice!

B Work in groups. Look at the situations above and in Exercise 6 and discuss.

1 Who do you think is the good/bad neighbour in each situation?
2 What makes a good neighbour? What qualities should they have?

VOCABULARY *PLUS* compound nouns

9A Read sentences 1–4. Are they positive (+), negative (-) or both (+/-)?

1 I live next to the <u>main road</u>, so it's a bit noisy.

2 There's a wonderful bookshop near where I live.

3 There's a lovely public swimming pool by my house, and it's free for children.

4 Where I live is good for window shopping but too expensive to buy anything!

B Find and underline a compound noun in each sentence. The first has been done for you.

C Look at the compound nouns and match them with patterns a)–d).

a) noun + noun

b) adjective + noun

c) verb + noun

d) noun + verb

> **speakout TIP**
>
> Compound nouns combine two related words. The first word gives us more information about the second, e.g. *shoe shop, history teacher, paper bag*. What other words make compound nouns with *shop*, *teacher* and *bag*? Compound nouns can be written as one word, two words or with a hyphen. Use a dictionary to check.

10A Which words complete the compound nouns?

1 _____	jam lights	6 sports city	_____
2 _____	park rental	7 high one-way	_____
3 _____	centre mall	8 semi-detached terraced	_____
4 super outdoor	_____	9 housing industrial	_____
5 primary language	_____	10 duty-free gift	_____

B ▶ 8.1 Listen to check your answers. Then think about the stress patterns. Which word is usually stressed: the first or the second? Listen again to check.

C Discuss. Think about the place where you are studying now. Which of the compound nouns does it have nearby?

➡ page 155 **VOCABULARYBANK**

SPEAKING

11A Work in pairs. What features do you like/dislike where you live? Use the photos below to help you. Make notes about the following:

• things you like

a beautiful city centre with lots of trees and parks

• things that are nice but not essential

a good local supermarket

• things you hate

graffiti on the buildings

B Think about your neighbourhood. What would make it:

• more beautiful?

• better for your health?

• more interesting?

• safer?

• more of a community?

I'd really like to see a good shopping mall, where people can meet.

My neighbourhood would be healthier if there was less traffic congestion in the mornings.

C Compare your ideas in groups.

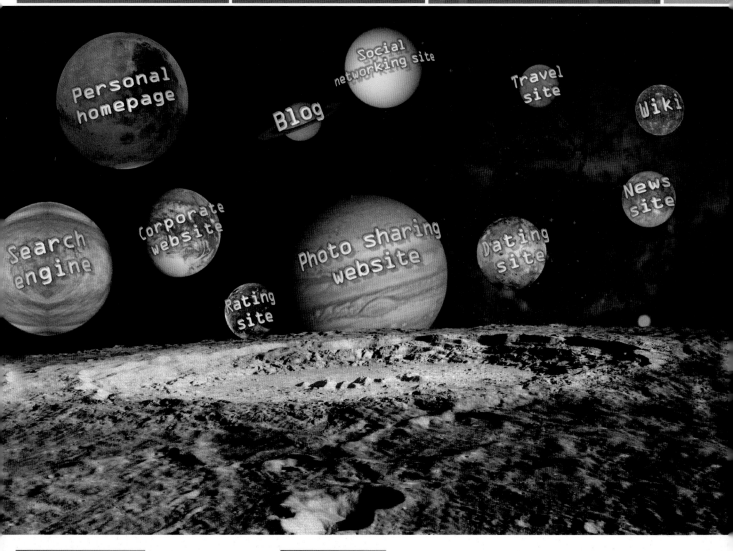

Personal homepage

Social networking site

Travel site

Blog

Wiki

News site

Search engine

Corporate website

Photo sharing website

Dating site

Rating site

VOCABULARY the internet

1A Work in groups. Look at the picture. Which type of website would you use to:

1   find out what is happening in the world?
2   book a holiday?
3   contact friends?
4   show your holiday pictures?
5   meet the partner of your dreams?
6   show your wedding video?
7   find out whether a new film or book is good?
8   find out about a big company?
9   share facts about yourself?
10 read and write opinions about anything and everything?
11 read or write factual information about a topic?
12 find information quickly?

B Discuss. Which of these do you use regularly? Which do you use occasionally? Which do you never use?

LISTENING

2A ▶ 8.2 Listen to four people talking about their online communities and answer the questions.

1   What did Speaker 1, Lynn, do a year ago?
2   What does she say about the community?
3   Why does Speaker 2, Rick, say it's 'a twenty-first-century community'?
4   What does he say about 'the best blogs'?
5   What type of place does Speaker 3, Nathan, live in?
6   What does he like about using the internet?
7   What two things does Speaker 4, Abbie, do on her favourite website?
8   How often does she use it?

B Work in pairs. Listen to each speaker again. When the speaker finishes, take it in turns to use the words in the box to explain what the speakers say.

artists' colony	paintings	business	trust	social networking	cheap
loyal readers	engaged	shop online	bloggers	pictures	grows

3 Discuss the questions.

1   Do you think websites are real communities?
2   What are the benefits of online communities?
3   Are there any dangers or problems in spending a lot of time in online communities?

GRAMMAR relative clauses

4 Read about the origins of a website. Why did the website become successful?

The rise and rise of YouTube

Early in 2005, three friends, Chad Hurley, Steve Chen and Jawed Karim, who were also colleagues, were having problems trying to email a video clip. Within two hours they came up with an idea which would solve the problem and change internet history. They decided to create a video sharing platform and YouTube was born. It's a familiar story for anyone who follows the development of the internet: technology-minded entrepreneurs under thirty, a garage or bedroom, where dreams become reality, little money and a big communicative need. The site was an instant success. The key was a number of features: links to the videos, which made them easy to email; tell-a-friend functions; a feature that allowed YouTube videos to be played on other social networking sites; and another feature that let users comment on the videos. This helped to develop the site's sense of community: YouTube was a place where you posted videos but also chatted about them, complained, smiled (☺) or laughed out loud (LOL). Two years after the launch, Google Inc., bought YouTube for $1.65 billion.

5A Look at the underlined clauses in the sentences below. Which is a defining relative clause and which is a non-defining relative clause?

a) Chad Hurley, Steve Chen and Jawed Karim, <u>who were colleagues</u>, were having problems trying to email a video clip.

b) YouTube was <u>a place where you posted videos</u>.

B Read rules 1 and 2 to check your answers. Then complete rule 3 with *which, who, where* and *that*.

Rules:
1 Defining relative clauses tell us exactly which thing, person or place we are talking about.
2 Non-defining relative clauses add extra information to a sentence. They tell us what a thing, person or place is or does. The sentence is still grammatically possible without the extra information.
3 _____ is used to talk about places

  _____ is used to talk about people

  _____ is used to talk about things

  _____ can be used to talk about places, people or things (in defining relative clauses only)

C Read the text in Exercise 4A again. Find and underline eight relative clauses. What type of relative clauses are they: defining (D) or non-defining (ND)?

▮▮▶ page 142 **LANGUAGEBANK**

PRACTICE

6A Circle the correct alternatives to complete the text.

For people who liked to send and receive very short messages, Twitter.com was a dream come true. This social networking site, ¹*that/which was/who was* the fastest growing site in 2009, became amazingly popular in a short space of time. So how does it work? You write your message, ²*of which must be/what must be/which must be* no longer than 140 characters, onto your profile via a web, SMS or phone application. Then the message, ³*what is called/this is called/which is called* a 'Tweet', is sent automatically to your subscribers or 'followers'. The people ⁴*use/that use/are who use* Twitter say it's fantastic. Jerry Jones, ⁵*who works for/who works where/which works for* an internet company, describes it as 'a mini-revolution'. He says that when Twitter arrived, it was the moment ⁶*which online/for online/when online* communication changed. No more boring blogs, ⁷*what go/where people go/who people go* on and on about nothing. 'Me and my friends, ⁸*who all use/all use/we use* Twitter, have a saying: Keep your Tweet short and sweet!'

B Discuss the questions.
1 Do you or does anyone you know use Twitter?
2 What social networking websites do you know?
3 Which are the most popular now?

7A ▶ 8.3 Listen for the pauses where there are commas. Tick the sentence you hear.

1 a) The travel site which we developed is really popular.
  b) The travel site, which we developed, is really popular.

2 a) Those children who spend too much time on the net don't communicate well.
  b) Those children, who spend too much time on the net, don't communicate well.

3 a) Video sharing sites which are free are a great resource for students.
  b) Video sharing sites, which are free, are a great resource for students.

4 a) On that dating site where I met my wife there are hundreds of single people.
  b) On that dating site, where I met my wife, there are hundreds of single people.

5 a) Bloggers who write regularly often get their stories from news websites.
  b) Bloggers, who write regularly, often get their stories from news websites.

B Work in pairs. Take turns to choose a sentence from Exercise 7A and read it aloud. Your partner says which sentence you read, a) or b).

SPEAKING

8A Look at the activities in the box below. Do you prefer doing them online or in the real world? What are their advantages/disadvantages?

> shopping   meet new people   find out the news   learn a language
> book flights/hotels   watch films/programmes   speak to friends
> look up information   explore new places

B Work with other students. Discuss your opinions.

I prefer shopping online because I don't have to leave my house, park the car and deal with crowds of people. It's really convenient and easy.

WRITING a website review

9A Read the website review and answer the questions.

1 What type of website is it?
2 Why does the writer recommend it?
3 Who uses the website? Why?

Website of the Month for January is **magportal.com**. It's a website which you can use to find magazine articles on lots of different topics. One reason I'd recommend it is the range of subjects, which include health, finance, entertainment, science and technology, sports and even pets and animals.

The best thing about magportal.com is that the design is very simple, which makes it really easy to use. There's a menu of categories and a search engine if you want something specific. Another excellent feature is that you can get articles by typing the date – the most recent ones are shown first – or the name of a specific magazine.

I know several journalists who use magportal.com for research. I suggest that readers try it out; there's something for everyone.

B Number the features of a review in a logical order.
a) Say the purpose of the website. ____
b) Say who you'd recommend the website to. ____
c) Introduce the name of the website. ____
d) Say what special features the website has. ____

C Find and underline three phrases we use to recommend something.

LEARN TO use complex sentences

10A Compare the pairs of sentences. Which sounds more fluent: a) or b)?

1 a) It's a website. You can use it to find magazine articles. The articles are on lots of different topics.

   b) It's a website which you can use to find magazine articles on lots of different topics.

2 a) I know several journalists. They use magportal.com. They use it for research.

   b) I know several journalists who use magportal.com for research.

> **speakout TIP**
>
> Think about using complex sentences. Simple sentences can be effective, but when we use many simple sentences together, it sounds childish: *I swim every day. I love the water. It's good exercise.* We can make sentences more complex by using conjunctions (*and*, *because*, *but*, etc.) and relative clauses: *I swim every day **because** I love the feel of the water **and** it's **also** good exercise.* How have the b) sentences in Exercise 10A been made more complex?

B Rewrite sentences 1–4 to make them sound more fluent.

1 The website is well-designed. The good design makes it user-friendly.

2 The site has too much animation. This makes it very slow. It takes a long time to upload.

3 The website's content comes from its users. Users send in their photos.

4 The site feels friendly. It has user profile areas. Here, users can say who they are.

C Work in pairs and compare your answers.

11A What is your 'Website of the Month'? Choose a website and think about the questions below.

1 What type of website is it (photo sharing, social networking, etc.)?
2 Why do you like it?
3 How often do you visit it?
4 Is there a community of users?
5 Who would you recommend it to?

B Write your review (120–150 words). Show it to other students. Which websites sound interesting to you?

▶ **FUNCTION** | being a good guest ▶ **VOCABULARY** | welcoming ▶ **LEARN TO** | accept apologies

VOCABULARY welcoming

1A Match phrases 1–6 to situations a)–f).

1 Make yourself at home.

2 Excuse the mess.

3 Be my guest.

4 Help yourself.

5 Have a seat.

6 Put your feet up.

a) You are apologising for how your home (or office) looks.

b) You know someone is tired and you want them to relax.

c) You are inviting someone to sit down, maybe at work.

d) You want someone to feel relaxed in your house.

e) You give permission for someone to use something that is yours.

f) You are offering someone food.

B ▶ **8.4 Listen to the phrases and notice how words ending in a consonant sound (e.g. /f/) link together with words beginning with a vowel sound (e.g. /æ/ or /ə/) so there is no pause between them. Then listen and repeat.**

*Make yourself‿at home.   yoursel **fat** home*

C ▶ **8.5 Listen to the conversations. Listen again and repeat the final line.**

FUNCTION being a good guest

2A Work in pairs. Discuss the questions.

1 When was the last time you were a guest? What was the situation?

2 When was the last time you had a guest? Was he or she a good guest? Why/Why not?

3 What type of things do good and bad guests do?

B Read the text. Did you mention any of these ideas in your discussion?

How to be the world's best guest

Do you want to be a sensitive, popular guest who gets invited back? Read our six top tips for being a good guest.

1 Clothes – if you are in a formal situation, dress smartly: a suit and tie for men, a long skirt and jacket for women.

2 Gifts – if you are going to stay in someone's house, don't arrive empty-handed. Bring a small gift if you are staying for a short period of time, a bigger gift for longer periods. Expensive chocolate works in most situations.

3 Greetings – to shake hands or to kiss? Wait to see what your host does.

4 Food – always accept it when offered, whether it looks horrible or delicious. Try to eat all of it and say it tastes good. Most people are proud of their cooking even if they shouldn't be. Don't hurt their feelings.

5 Names – in formal situations, don't use first names. Always use titles (Doctor, Professor, Chairperson) until the person tells you not to.

6 Leaving – the most important tip for being a good guest is to know when to say goodbye. The secret is to leave while the host is still enjoying your company and wants you to stay longer.

3 Discuss the questions.

1 Which pieces of advice are useful? Are there any that you think are incorrect?

2 Can you add any other advice? Think about personal space, smoking, paying the bill, speaking a foreign host's language or one of your own topics.

4 ▶ **8.6 Listen to six situations. Which speakers did something wrong? Which speakers are asking for advice?**

5 Listen again and complete the notes below.

1 She says her family doesn't …

2 He wants to know if he should bring …

3 He should come back in …

4 She forgot to take …

5 In the restaurant you have to …

6 It's Thanksgiving but her family doesn't eat …

6 Look at the phrases in the table and tick the ones you heard in the conversations in Exercise 4. Read the audio script 8.6 on page 173 to check.

asking for advice	
question	answer
Is it OK if I (do this)?	Yes, of course./No, you'd better not. It's considered a bit rude.
What should we do (in this situation)?	If I were you, I'd …
Do I need to (bring a dish)?	Yes, you should./No, it's not necessary.
Did I do something wrong?	No, of course not./It's OK. We can sort it out./Don't worry about it.
Is this a bad time? I can come back later.	Can you come back in ten minutes?/Not at all. It's fine.
apologising	
Sorry about that. I didn't know.	
My apologies. I didn't realise.	

➠ page 142 **LANGUAGE**BANK

7A Complete conversations 1–5 by adding two words from the box to each one.

> that   were   it   OK   rude   should   about
> at   wrong   realise

1 A: Is OK if I take a call during a meeting?
   B: Not really. It's considered a bit.
2 A: I just called the boss by his first name, John. Did I do something?
   B: Not all. That's normal here.
3 A: Sorry about. I didn't know you were waiting.
   B: Don't worry it.
4 A: My apologies. I didn't this was your seat.
   B: No, it's. You can sit there.
5 A: You know I can't eat butter and cheese, right? What I do if they offer me these?
   B: If I you, before your visit I'd tell them you don't eat dairy products.

B Practise the conversations with a partner.

LEARN TO accept apologies

8A ▶ 8.7 Listen to the extracts from the audio script. Number the phrases a)– f) in the order you hear them.

a) It's no problem.
b) Not at all.
c) That's all right.   *1*
d) You really don't have to …
e) It's fine.
f) It's nothing.

B Work in pairs, Read situations 1–4 below and take turns to apologise and accept the apology.

1 You agreed to meet your partner for dinner. You are thirty minutes late.
2 You accidentally wake up your partner by singing loudly. You didn't know he/she was asleep.
3 You borrowed your partner's book. You accidentally ripped one of the pages.
4 You are buying something in a shop. You accidentally walk in front of your partner because you didn't realise there was a queue.

SPEAKING

9A Read the situations. Have you experienced either of these? Work in pairs and discuss what you would do/say.

Situation 1

You are staying with a host family abroad. The family seemed nice at first but now there are some problems and they don't talk to you much. You want to study, but the family is very noisy. They smoke inside even though you asked for a non-smoking house. In the morning, there is never any hot water left for your shower. You decide to talk to the mother of the family.

Situation 2

A foreign student is staying with you. He keeps saying that the food, the coffee, and the weather in your country are terrible. He seems lonely, never socialises and eats his meals in his room. You want to help him, but he doesn't want to talk. You decide to talk to the director of the school where the student is studying. You want to know what to do.

B Choose one of the situations. Use the flow chart below to plan and role-play your own situation.

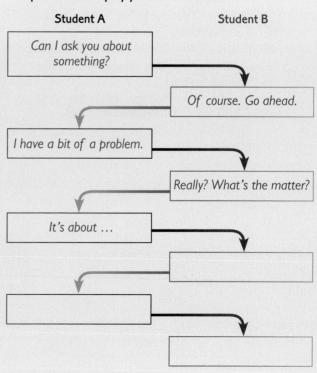

Student A — Student B

Can I ask you about something?

Of course. Go ahead.

I have a bit of a problem.

Really? What's the matter?

It's about …

▶ DVD PREVIEW

1A Work in groups. Look at the photos. Where do you think this is? What do you think life is like for people on an island like this? Do you think their lives are changing in today's modern world?

B Read the programme information. What does Bruce Perry hope to learn from visiting the tribe?

BBC Tribe: Anuta

Tribe is a BBC programme in which presenter Bruce Parry goes to some of the world's most isolated places. In this episode, he goes to the Pacific island of Anuta, one of the most remote communities on Earth. There, he learns about their traditions, and discovers how the community survives. There are just twenty-four families on Anuta. Bruce meets them all, and experiences how their customs help to bind the people together.

2 What do you think the words in the box mean? Match them with definitions 1–6.

tribe isolated remote customs survive bind (people together)

1 form a strong connection between people
2 continue to live normally even when there are great problems
3 something that people in a particular society do because it is traditional
4 a group of people with the same race, language and customs, who live together in the same area
5 far away from other places (can also describe a person who is lonely and can't meet other people)
6 far away from other places (usually used to describe places)

▶ DVD VIEW

3 Watch the DVD and number the scenes in the correct order.

a) Bruce meets the children.
b) Bruce meets the community leaders.
c) Bruce catches a fish.
d) Bruce helps to repair a wall in the water.
e) Bruce arrives on the island.   *1*
f) Bruce says 'I'm in Paradise'.

4A Circle the correct answer, a) or b).

1 When visitors arrive in Anuta, what must they do?
   (a) Shake everyone's hand.
   (b) Bring gifts to the community leaders.
2 What do the community leaders tell Bruce?
   (a) Their island is like Paradise and he is welcome.
   (b) He can stay in Anuta.
3 What happens during a 'community fish drive'?
   (a) The men catch fish and the women cook.
   (b) Everyone in the community helps to catch fish.
4 What do they do with the fish?
   (a) It is divided amongst all the families.
   (b) The islanders all sit and eat together.

B Watch the DVD again to check.

5 Discuss the questions.

1 Do you think it is good that Bruce visited Anuta? Why/Why not?
2 Would you like to visit this place? Why/Why not?
3 Can the modern world learn anything from places like Anuta?

speakout design a community

6A Read the paragraph from a news report. What is going to happen? Why?

Mohamed Nasheed, the new President of the Maldives, has a very difficult task: to find a place for the population to live. Most of the two hundred inhabited islands of the Maldives are about three feet above sea level. Scientists have explained that in the future, the Maldives will be under water because of global warming. No one will be able to live there and nothing will remain.

B What would you do if you had to start a new community? Think about the questions below.

1 Where would it be?
2 Who would live there? Would it be a large or small community?
3 What laws would there be?
4 What type of government would the community have?
5 What special customs would there be? How would these bind the community together?

7A ▶ 8.8 Listen to two people discussing the first three questions above. What do they decide for each question?

B Listen again. Tick the key phrases that you hear.

keyphrases

I'd probably choose …
I'd go for a place that …
It'd need to be somewhere …
They'd need to be able to …
The most important thing would be …
Ideally, there would be …

8 Work in pairs and plan your community. Present your ideas to another pair.

writeback a web advert

9A Read about a project that was the subject of a BBC documentary. What type of community is it?

Tribewanted is a community tourism project on Vorovoro Island, Fiji. The members of *Tribewanted* work with the local people to build a village community. This community combines Fijian traditions with international ideas for environmentally-friendly living. Visitors can stay between one and twelve weeks. While there, visitors work on projects, look after the gardens on the island, feed the pigs and chickens, help with the construction of buildings and write for the *Tribewanted* blog. They can also learn Fijian songs, relax in a hammock, and enjoy the incredible sunsets and sea. It is the adventure of a lifetime.

B You are recruiting people for the *Tribewanted* project. Write a web ad for people to apply. Use the key phrases and the prompts below.

- Amazing opportunity for adventurers!
- We are looking for …
- We need people who …
- We also want people who are able to …
- Your responsibilities on the island will include …
- The community is special because …
- The community will …
- By the end of your stay you will …
- Please send …
- Interviews will be …
- Other information …

GETTING ON

1A Use words to make phrases connected with 'getting on'. You can use the words more than once in any order.

get	to	well
ask	over	favour
do	on	own
disturb	with	business
make	a	nuisance
mind	your	nerves
invite	yourself	nosy
keep	friends	
know	people	
be		

B Use the phrases to write four questions to ask other students.

Do you get on well with your dad?

ARTICLES AND QUANTIFIERS

2A Choose the correct option, a), b) or c), to complete the text.

For sixteen weeks, the only thing we saw was ^{1}_____ sea. One night, fifty miles from ^{2}_____ Solomon Islands, ^{3}_____ storm hit us and ^{4}_____ ship swayed like a drunk soldier. ^{5}_____ of the sailors were washed into the sea, and ^{6}_____ of us were exhausted. The next day we found a hundred fish on the deck, a ^{7}_____ of them still alive, mouths open. We ate them with a ^{8}_____ bread and salt. A week later, we were attacked by pirates. They didn't kill anyone but they stole ^{9}_____ our food. The captain said there was ^{10}_____ for one week, and we were two weeks away from land.

1   (a) a (b) the (c) –
2   (a) a (b) the (c) –
3   (a) a (b) the (c) –
4   (a) a (b) the (c) –
5   (a) Little (b) Few (c) Some
6   (a) little (b) much (c) all
7   (a) plenty (b) few (c) all
8   (a) little (b) lot (c) few
9   (a) a lot of (b) many (c) lots
10 (a) plenty of (b) too (c) enough

B Work in groups. Write 3–4 sentences to end the story.

THE INTERNET

3A Complete the sentences with the words in the box.

> sites   blog   search   travel
> video   networking

1   Have you ever booked a holiday using a _____ site? Was it a success?

2   Do you ever use _____ sharing sites, like YouTube.com? Do you have a favourite clip?

3   What _____ engine do you usually use? Do you know others, apart from Google?

4   Do you like social _____ sites? Do you ever get bored of them?

5   Have you ever contributed to a _____? What was the topic and what did you write?

6   What do you think of dating _____? Do you know anyone who uses them?

B Work in pairs. Ask and answer the questions.

RELATIVE CLAUSES

4A Underline the correct alternative.

1   _____ is *which/when/that* four wolves and a lamb vote on what to have for lunch.

2   _____ is a place *that/ how/where* animals study humans.

3   _____ is a ship *who/ what/that* is big enough for two people in good weather but only one person in bad weather.

4   _____ is the hour *where/ which/when* the traffic stops.

5   _____ is a man *whose/ where/who* has stopped thinking.

6   _____ is a person *who/ whose/which* job is to lend you an umbrella when the sun is shining and take it back when it rains.

B What or who do sentences 1–6 describe? Complete the sentences with the words in the box.

> rush hour   a zoo   a banker
> friendship   an expert   democracy

5 Work in pairs. Look at the list below and take turns to define things. Your partner guesses what/ who you defined.

• a person in the room
• an object in your bag
• a room in the building
• a famous book or film
• a famous singer
• an object on the table
• a town or city
• a person in the news

He's the singer who ...

BEING A GOOD GUEST

6A Match comments/questions 1–5 with responses a)–e).

1   Did I do something wrong?

2   Sorry about that. I didn't know that was the boss's chair.

3   My apologies. I didn't realise I had to shake everybody's hand.

4   Is this a bad time? I can come back another time.

5   Do I need to bring gifts?

a) No, it's not necessary. We don't expect them in our country.

b) Don't worry about it. She didn't mind at all.

c) No problem. You said hello to everybody, so that's OK.

d) Can you come back tomorrow? I'm busy for the rest of the day.

e) Yes, you did. No one talks during the national anthem, but don't worry – we can sort it out.

B Work in pairs. Cover responses a)–e). Take turns to read the comments/questions in 1–5 and to reply with the correct response/one of your own.

BBC VIDEO PODCAST

Download the video podcast and view people talking about their neighbourhood relationships.

Authentic BBC interviews

www.pearsonlongman.com/speakout

SPEAKING
> ❯ Talk about important events in history
> ❯ Talk about your own history
> ❯ Compile and do a quiz
> ❯ Describe a role model

LISTENING
> ❯ Listen to descriptions of past decades
> ❯ Listen to people doing a quiz about history
> ❯ Watch a BBC documentary about a great artist

READING
> ❯ Read about important moments in history
> ❯ Read about time travel
> ❯ Read a quiz about history

WRITING
> ❯ Write a short essay
> ❯ Write a wiki entry

BBC CONTENT
> ▭ Video podcast: Do you think life is better now than in the past?
> ⦿ DVD: The Divine Michelangelo

UNIT

9

history

▶ GRAMMAR | third conditional   ▶ VOCABULARY | history   ▶ HOW TO | talk about imaginary past situations

VOCABULARY history

1A Work in pairs and look at the photos. What important developments in history do they show? What do you think are the three most important events in history?

B Read the comments below. Are any of your ideas mentioned?

> A lot of **revolutions** have been important. For example, the Industrial Revolution was a great **turning point** in history.

> The **development** of the internet. The **spread** of the net has been so fast.

> For me, the greatest **advances** in history have been about social justice. There have been some really important **movements**, such as the Civil Rights Movement. These have made the world a better place.

> I'd choose the **invention** of the wheel. It's the **foundation** of most transport and machines.

> Maybe the **discovery** of fire? I think it was the most important thing in human beings' **progress**.

C Put the words in bold above in the definitions below.

1 A moment of great change: _revolution,_ _____

2 When someone makes or finds something new: _development,_ _____ _____

3 Something getting better: _advance,_ _____

4 When a group of people work to achieve an aim, e.g. human rights: _____

5 The basic idea behind something: _____

6 When something increases and affects more people: _____

D Complete sentences 1–5 in any way you choose. Compare with other students.

1 The biggest turning point in my country's history was …

2 A discovery that changed my life is …

3 My favourite invention is …

4 One thing I hope <u>won't</u> spread is …

5 My country has made progress in …

 ➜ page 156 **VOCABULARYBANK**

READING

2A Read the introduction to an article from *BBC History Magazine*. What 'alternative moments' do you think the historians will choose?

> *Giant Leaps for Mankind* looks at why we should be celebrating the Moon landing of July 1969 and asks twelve historians to nominate alternative moments in the past that they consider to be giant leaps for mankind.

B Student A: read the texts on the opposite page and make notes with the prompts below. Student B: turn to page 159.
- What?
- Where?
- When?
- Why was it important?

3A Work in pairs. Cover your texts. Look at the notes you made in Exercise 2B. Take turns to tell each other what you read. As you listen, make more notes.

B Work in pairs and answer the questions.

1 Which two books helped the spread of new developments?

2 Which advances help us to study things?

3 Which developments happened mainly because of one person? Which happened because of many people?

C Discuss. Which of the four big moments did you know about? Which do you think are the two most important?

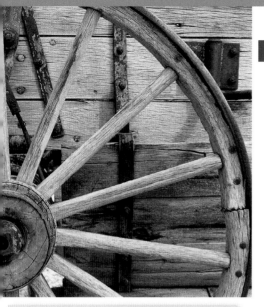

Learning to eat meat

Humans are badly designed animals. We are slow, we have weak teeth, and we don't have tails. That's why we need something extra to match other animals. And that's why eating meat – a development that probably started in Africa around 2.5 million years ago – became so important. Meat gives you fats and proteins that you can't get with other food. But more importantly, meat-eating led to hunting, and hunting helped to develop our imaginations. When you hunt, you need to see what isn't there, to see what's behind the next tree or over the next hill. We wouldn't have become the most imaginative – and the most intelligent – of the animals if we had continued eating only plants.

Teaching people to read

Until the end of the twelfth century, Latin was very difficult to learn. Students read and memorised texts for years. Then a Frenchman called Alexander de Villedieu developed a fast method to teach Latin: he used simple rules and wrote them in verse so the students could remember them more easily. Seeing the success of his method, Alexander wrote a grammar book, *Doctrinale*, published in France in 1199. It became a bestseller and spread quickly through Europe, and started a great literacy movement. This new type of learning became the foundation of modern education. If he hadn't written *Doctrinale*, education would probably have remained the same for hundreds of years.

GRAMMAR third conditional

4A Read the sentences below. Do they describe an imaginary situation in the past or an imaginary situation in the present?

1 If he hadn't written *Doctrinale*, education would probably have remained the same.

2 If Galileo hadn't defended his theories, he would have been a free man.

B Look at the sentence patterns and find one other example in your texts.

If + subject	had(n't) + past participle			would(n't) + have + past participle	
If we	had invented	the wheel earlier, life	would have been		easier.
	hadn't discovered	fire, man's progress			slower.

C Read two more sentences from the article. How is the grammatical structure different from the sentences in Exercise 4A?

1 We wouldn't have become the most imaginative of the animals if we had continued eating only plants.

2 Life would have been different if we hadn't invented the steam engine.

➡ page 144 **LANGUAGEBANK**

PRACTICE

5A Complete the sentences with the correct form of the verbs in brackets.

1 Machu Picchu _____(remain) unknown if Hiram Bingham _____(not explore) the Andes in Peru.

2 If the 'I love you' virus _____(be) found earlier, forty-five million computers _____(not crash).

3 The first experiments in cloning _____(be) impossible if Gregor Mendel _____(not discover) genes.

4 If John Lennon _____(not meet) Paul McCartney, they _____(not form) The Beatles.

5 The invention of the mobile phone _____(not be) possible if Alexander Graham Bell _____(not invent) the telephone.

6 If the Nestor Film Company _____(not open) a film studio there in 1911, Hollywood _____(remain) a quiet community.

B ▶ 9.1 Listen and check your answers.

C Listen again and repeat. Pay attention to the pronunciation of *had, hadn't, would* and *wouldn't have*. How are they pronounced in fast speech?

6 Make a note of three things that have happened to you in the last year. Write third conditional sentences about how your life would have been different if they hadn't happened to you.

I got a new job. If I hadn't got a new job, I would have been bored in my old job!

SPEAKING

7A Work in pairs. You are going to describe a big moment in history. Choose an important historical event. If you need help, Student A: turn to page 163; Student B: turn to page 160. Think about the questions below.

1 Why was this event important?

2 What happened before and after the event?

3 Would the world have been different if this event had not happened?

B Describe your big moment to other students.

WRITING a short essay

8 Work in pairs. Put the six stages of essay-writing in order.

a) Write a second, final draft. _____

b) Proofread before you submit your work. Look for errors in grammar, spelling and punctuation. _____

c) Look carefully at the task/title you are given. What do you need to do: analyse, compare, argue? _____

d) Check that the sections of the first draft are well-organised. Think about how you can reorganise any unclear parts. _____

e) Brainstorm ideas. Write down lots of thoughts quickly and don't worry if they are not all good ideas. _____

f) Write a first draft quickly – it doesn't have to be perfect. _____

9 Read the short essay below and answer the question. What does the writer think would have happened if China had reached the Americas before the Europeans?

WHAT IF ... Chinese explorers had landed in the Americas first?

Once, China led the world in technology. Centuries before Europe, they had printing and gunpowder. They also had the compass, which meant they could navigate without relying on the position of the Moon. Furthermore, they were brilliant shipbuilders. This ability to build large, strong ships went hand in hand with their other talent: exploration.

In 1405, a Chinaman called Zheng He went on a journey. The idea was to create new trade routes for China. On his first trip, he took 28,000 men in sixty-two ships. Zheng He landed in India and brought home many things that were new to the Chinese: plants, animals, even people.

Zheng He made seven westward journeys. If he had continued to explore, he would probably have reached the Americas before Columbus and the Europeans. However, for political reasons, China stopped exploring. Its leaders believed that China didn't need to trade with these simple, uncivilised people so the country became isolated.

Now, let's imagine Zheng He had reached the Americas first. What would have happened? He would have seen the incredible size of the land and the riches in the ground. He probably would have returned with more men and farmed the land. They would have got rich. The new Chinese colony would have grown and grown, and perhaps they would have later spread to other lands.

Would China have created the next great empire if Chinese explorers had landed in the Americas first? We will never know.

LEARN TO structure paragraphs

10A Read the paragraph below. Then complete statements 1–3 using the labels from the key.

> Chinese ships were extremely advanced compared to ships in other parts of the world. Firstly, they were larger; the biggest was 400 feet long and weighed 1,500 tons. They were also better designed; unlike European ships at the time, they had rooms which were 'watertight' – water could not get inside them. What's more, Chinese ships had better equipment: they all had compasses, which meant the sailors would never get lost.

Key:
◯ = linking words
▢ = topic sentence
▰ = supporting sentence 1
▰ = supporting sentence 2
▰ = supporting sentence 3

1 Each paragraph should have a _____ _____ that explains the main idea. Often this is the first sentence.

2 Each paragraph needs several _____ _____ to provide examples that illustrate the main idea.

3 The examples should connect well, using _____ _____.

B Label the parts of the first paragraph in the essay in Exercise 9 using the labels above.

11A Read instructions 1–4 for a *What if ...?* essay.

1 Choose an important development in history: an invention, a discovery or an event.

2 Think about the world without this development. How would life be different? How would people's ideas or actions be different? Brainstorm ideas.

3 Plan and write your essay.

4 When you finish, follow the instructions in the Speakout Tip.

speakout TIP

1 Check the 'big' things first: did you answer the question in the title? Are the paragraphs in the right order? Is there anything missing?

2 Check the 'little' things second: grammar, spelling, punctuation, missing words.

B Exchange your essay with another student and check each other's work.

▶ **GRAMMAR** | active vs passive ▶ **VOCABULARY** | periods of time ▶ **HOW TO** | talk about your personal history

GRAMMAR active versus passive

1 Write three words or ideas that you associate with teenagers. Compare them with other students.

2A Read the paragraph and choose the best title.

1 Music through the ages
2 How the young found their voice
3 The Death of James Dean

The word 'teenager' was invented in the 1950s. This was the first decade in which teenagers had their own style, their own heroes, their own music and their own way of looking at the world. The 'safe' world of adults was rejected by teenagers, and their heroes were more likely to be actors Marlon Brando on a motorbike (in *The Wild One*, 1954) or James Dean, who was killed in a car crash in 1955, aged twenty-four. The business world immediately saw its opportunity. Magazines, cosmetics and cars were designed to appeal to teenagers, who could usually be found in coffee bars listening to Elvis Presley songs. The truth is that young people want to be different. Many styles in music and fashion have been created since the 1950s: punk music, techno, hip hop. It's safe to say the teenager is here to stay.

B Read the sentences below and answer questions 1–3.

a) The word 'teenager' was invented in the 1950s.
b) Teenagers had their own style.
c) The 'safe' world of adults was rejected by teenagers.
d) The business world immediately saw its opportunity.
e) Many styles in music and fashion have been created since the 1950s.

1 What are the main verbs in each sentence? Find and underline them.
2 Two of the sentences don't say who 'did' the action (because we don't know or it's not important). Which two?
3 Which sentences use active verbs? Which use the passive?

C Look at the sentences again. Complete the rule.

Rule: We form the passive with: subject + the verb _____ (in the present, past or other tense) + past participle.

D Find three more examples of the passive in the text.

▸ page 144 **LANGUAGEBANK**

PRACTICE

3A Rewrite the sentences below using the passive.

1 People all over the world wear jeans.
   Jeans are worn by _____ people all over the world _____.
2 Companies are designing mobile phones especially for teenagers.
   Mobile phones _____.
3 The media has always influenced teenagers.
   Teenagers _____ by_____.
4 In Sweden they made a great film about a teenage vampire.
   A great film about a teenage vampire _____.
5 In the past, we saw children as mini-adults.
   In the past, children _____.
6 In the future, the government will prevent people from smoking until they are twenty-one.
   In the future, people will _____.
7 In Mexico they hold a party called *quinceañera* when a girl reaches the age of fifteen.
   In Mexico, a party called quinceañera *_____.*
8 Teenagers will design many of the computer games of the future.
   *Many of the computer games of the future _____
   by _____.*

B ▶ 9.2 Listen and check your answers.

C Listen again and notice the pronunciation of *are* /ə/, *has been* /hæzbɪn/, *was* /wəz/ and *were* /wə/? Then listen and repeat.

VOCABULARY periods of time

4A Put the words and phrases in order from the shortest to the longest periods. Use a dictionary to help you.

> a decade   a millennium   an era   a century   a quarter-century
> a fortnight   an age   the nineteen-seventies/eighties (1970s, 1980s)
> the seventies/eighties (70s/80s)   a generation

B Finish sentences 1–8 with your own words.

1 The best thing about this decade so far has been …

2 The worst thing about this decade so far has been …

3 The thing I remember most about the nineteen-nineties is …

4 One thing I don't know or understand about the nineteen-nineties is …

5 My parents' generation criticises my generation for our …

6 My generation will criticise the next generation for their …

7 One thing that represents my parents' era is …

8 One thing that represents this era is …

C Compare your sentences with other students. Are there any that you agree on?

LISTENING

5A Look at photos A–C. Which decades do you think they are from?

B ▶ 9.3 Listen to three people speaking about different decades. Which decades did they grow up in? Generally, do they feel positive or negative about that decade?

speakout TIP

Before listening, read the task. Which are the most important words? Listen for those words and for their synonyms or words with a similar meaning. For example: *North Americans = people from the United States*; *films = movies*; *environmental problems = pollution and the hole in the ozone layer*; *fashion = clothes/hairstyles*. Read the task in Exercise 5C and listen for the key words and synonyms.

C Listen again and answer the questions.

1 What 'two important aspects' of his life does Speaker 1 mention?

2 What 'celebrations' do you think Speaker 1 is talking about?

3 Where is Speaker 2 from?

4 Which musician was 'an icon' for Speaker 2?

5 What two things did Speaker 3 think he didn't like during the 80s (he later changed his mind)?

6 What trend did Madonna start in the mid-eighties?

6A Read the underlined sentences in audio script 9.3 on pages 173–174 and answer the questions.

1 Which decade do you think was good for film and music?

2 What was 'one of the most memorable moments' of the decade in which you grew up?

3 Were things 'developing and getting better' for your generation?

4 What part of your past do you like 'in retrospect'?

B Discuss your answers with other students.

SPEAKING

7A Choose a period when you were a child, a teenager or in your twenties. What did you listen to/do/watch/wear? How did it change as you got older? Make some notes about the following:

- music
- sport
- fashion
- TV and/or films
- technology
- issues in the news

B Work with other students and talk about your personal history. What do you have in common with other students? Tell the class.

VOCABULARY *PLUS* collocations

8A Read the text and answer the questions.

1 According to the writer, why is time tavel difficult for people to believe in?

2 Why is time travel probably boring?

3 Why is it probably not the solution to man's problems?

B Read the text again. Find and underline eight phrases with *come*, *give*, *have* and *make*. The first two have been done for you.

Time travel

All theoretical physicists have the same dream. They want to travel in time. Normal people like you and me have trouble believing that time travel is possible. The idea is outside our imagination and such thoughts just <u>don't come naturally</u> to us. We can't imagine seeing our parents as little children taking their first steps, or our grandparents' youthful faces as smooth and unlined as glass. We can't imagine watching Stone Age men dragging dead animals to their caves, or watching Alexander the Great conquering half the world, or seeing Mozart at his piano. And the truth is, even if we could travel in time, unless we could also choose an exact moment in an exact place, it would probably be very boring. When we read history books, the past always sounds exciting. But humanity makes progress slowly. And Stone Age man didn't own TVs for entertainment.

If time travel is ever possible in the future, time travellers are probably with us now, today. And if they exist, they have <u>come back</u> from a time in the future and are watching while we make a mess of the world. Why don't they give us directions on how to save the planet? Why don't they give instructions about the environment or how to stop war? Here's a sad thought: maybe they don't know the answers either.

C Look at the underlined phrases and add them to the word webs below.

come
- back (return)
- _____ (ways to travel)
- naturally (easily)
- _____ (win)

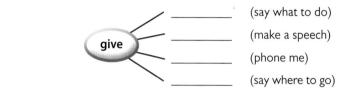

give
- _____ (say what to do)
- _____ (make a speech)
- _____ (phone me)
- _____ (say where to go)

have
- _____ (enjoy yourself)
- _____ (future ambition)
- _____ (have problems)
- _____ (relax for a short time)

make
- _____ (choose)
- _____ (make untidy/dirty)
- _____ (improve)
- _____ (get more money than you invested)

D Look at the words in the box and add them to the word webs above. Then add any other phrases with *come*, *give*, *have* and *make* you can think of.

| by car   first   a talk   a break   a profit   a good time |
| a decision   (someone) a call |

➡ page 156 **VOCABULARYBANK**

9A Complete the topic headings 1–10.

1 How to have a good t_____ in your home town

2 How to give i_____ to children

3 How not to get fired when you're having t_____ with your boss

4 How to make p_____ when you've been learning English for years

5 How to give d_____ to the best restaurants in town

6 How to relax and have a complete b_____ from work

7 How to give a t_____ to an audience of a hundred

8 How to make a p_____ on your investments

9 How to come f_____ in a competition or game

10 How not to make a m_____ when you're cooking

B Which of the topics above do you know more about? Choose one or more and prepare to talk about it/them.

C Work with other students. Tell them which you chose and explain how to do it.

▶ **FUNCTION** | expressing uncertainty   ▶ **VOCABULARY** | describing people   ▶ **LEARN TO** | react to information

SPEAKING

1 Work in pairs and discuss.

1 What are the most famous quiz shows in your country? Do you like them?

2 What type of questions do they ask (history, general knowledge, culture, etc.)?

3 If you had to answer quiz questions on one subject, which subject would you choose?

4 If you had to answer questions on one famous person in history, who would you choose?

I'd choose Walt Disney because I loved his films when I was young and I read his biography.

VOCABULARY describing people

2 Work in pairs. Do the quiz about famous people in history. If you don't know the answers, guess or look at the photos opposite to help.

1 Which highly **original** writer was once kidnapped in France?
(a) Geoffrey Chaucer (b) Isabelle Allende
(c) Jane Austen

2 Which **influential** political thinker was famously messy?
(a) Karl Marx (b) Confucius (c) Machiavelli

3 Which **innovative** and **inspirational** actor and film-maker was stopped by the US government from entering the US?
(a) Jodie Foster (b) Charlie Chaplin
(c) Yoko Ono

4 Which **charismatic** scientist spent his free time playing the violin when he wasn't changing the world?
(a) Galileo (b) Albert Einstein
(c) Isaac Newton

5 Which **brave** and **exemplary** freedom fighter went on a road trip across a continent before becoming famous?
(a) Che Guevara (b) Nelson Mandela
(c) Joan of Arc

6 Which amazingly **creative** artist rarely finished the work he started?
(a) Pablo Picasso (b) Edgar Degas
(c) Leonardo da Vinci

3A Work in pairs and look at the quiz again. What do the words in bold mean? Use a dictionary to help you.

B Think of one famous person for each of the adjectives in Exercise 2A. Compare your ideas with other students.

Diego Maradona – He is probably the most influential sportsperson in the history of Argentina.

FUNCTION expressing uncertainty

4A ▶ 9.4 Listen to someone giving the answers to the quiz to her friend. Which answers did the friend know?

B Look at the phrases in the box. Match them to the groups of phrases below.

> I don't know   I used to know   I know it isn't …
> I'm not sure but I think …

1 _____, I have no idea, I haven't a clue

2 _____, I'm not a hundred percent certain but it might be …, I'm fairly sure it's …

3 _____, It's definitely not, I'm sure it isn't

4 _____, I can't remember, I've forgotten

C Listen again and tick the phrases you hear.

➡ page 144 **LANGUAGEBANK**

5A Complete speaker B's responses in the conversations by adding the pairs of words in the box.

~~have no~~	fairly sure	percent certain · sure it
haven't a	I've forgotten	I can't it's definitely

I A: Which sculptor is famous for the statue of David?

Was it Leonardo da Vinci or Michelangelo?

have no

B: I idea. I don't know anything about art.

2 A: What's the name of that American politician who

made a film about the environment?

B: Oh, um, remember. Was it Rumsfeld? No, um, Bush?

3 A: Who was the white South African leader who freed

Mandela?

B: I'm it was Botha, wasn't it?

4 A: Who's that Mexican actor who was in *Amores Perros*?

B: Oh, his name but I know who you mean. He's quite

small and good-looking.

5 A: Which company invented the CD-ROM?

B: I'm not a hundred but it might be Sony.

6 A: Do you know who wrote *The Lord of the Rings*?

Wasn't it William Golding?

B: I don't know, but not Golding.

7 A: Who won the last football World Cup?

B: I'm wasn't England.

8 A: What was the name of that Steven Spielberg film

about dinosaurs?

B: I clue. I don't watch Hollywood movies.

B Work in pairs and answer the questions. Then turn to page 160 to check your ideas.

C Work in pairs and practise the conversations.

LEARN TO react to information

6A ▶ 9.5 Read the extracts from audio 9.4 below. Then listen and notice the intonation patterns speaker B uses.

I A: It was Chaucer. I think he worked for the British

government.

B: Did he? I didn't know that.

2 A: It was Karl Marx.

B: Oh really?

3 A: It was Einstein. He was a very good violinist,

apparently.

B: Was he? That's interesting.

4 A: Yeah, Guevara was a medical student …

B: Oh yes, I knew that. I just couldn't remember.

5 A: Who went on a road trip with his friend?

B: Ah, that's right.

6 A: It was da Vinci. He invented the parachute.

B: Oh yeah, I was just about to say that!

B Answer the questions.

I Which information did speaker B know already?

2 Which information was new?

SPEAKING

7 Work in pairs. Student A: you are going to ask your partner the questions below. First, add two more questions of your own. The answers can be found on page 158. Student B: turn to page 162.

Geography

1 What's the capital of Australia? Is it Sydney,
   Melbourne or Canberra?

2 Which country has the *second* biggest population?
   Is it China, India or Russia?

3 Which one of these countries is *not* next to the
   sea: Venezuela, Ecuador or Paraguay?

4 _____

5 _____

DVD PREVIEW

1 Discuss. What do you know about the painting at the bottom of page 113, and the artist who created it?

2 Read the sentences about Michelangelo. What do you think the words in bold mean? Which two pairs of words have opposite meanings?

1 His work is **unique** – no one has ever done anything similar.

2 Some said his work was **divine** because only God could create such beauty.

3 His fame is **eternal**. He will never be forgotten.

4 The sculptures are **extraordinary**. They are incredibly beautiful and realistic.

5 Although he was **mortal**, his work will never die.

6 His art is **awe-inspiring**. We feel small when we look at it.

7 His painting on the ceiling of the Sistine Chapel is an incredible **feat**.

8 In those days, many normal men worked with stone, but he was far from **ordinary**.

9 Even as a child, he had **aspirations** to be a great artist.

10 As a young man in Florence he began his **quest** for fame.

3 Read about the BBC programme, *The Divine Michelangelo*. What is the contrast between Michelangelo's life and his art?

BBC The Divine Michelangelo

This BBC documentary examines the life and work of Michelangelo Buonarroti, one of the greatest artists in history. It looks at his background as a child in Florence, and how he went on to produce works such as the statue of David, the awe-inspiring ceiling of the Sistine Chapel, and the dome of St Peter's Cathedral, described here as 'the jewel in the crown on the Roman skyline'. The programme also reveals Michelangelo's tempestuous life, his fights with rivals and with his own demons, showing that an imperfect life can produce perfect art.

▶ DVD VIEW

4A Which of these sentences do you think are true?

1 Michelangelo was a sculptor, painter and architect.

2 He said he was divinely inspired (inspired by God).

3 He lived and worked three hundred years ago.

4 His mother died when he was a child.

5 He was from a rich family.

6 His father always wanted him to be an artist.

B Watch the DVD to check.

5A Read the notes. Which words do you think are missing?

Who was Michelangelo?

... a tempestuous genius ... he wanted eternal fame and [1] _riches_

... an outsider who created works so big and so [2] _____ nobody believed they were produced by a mortal

... NOT an ordinary labourer or honest, [3] _____ stonecutter

Background
... had an [4] _____ childhood
father, Ludovico, was a lowly-paid local official

What did he do?
... persevered and produced works which showed an extraordinary [5] _____
... created a unique vision of heaven on [6] _____

B Watch the DVD again and complete the notes.

C Work in groups and discuss. What do you think of Michelangelo's work? Have you ever seen any of his work? How do you think his work has influenced other artists?

speakout influential work

6A ▶ 9.6 Listen to someone talking about someone whose work influenced her. Who does she talk about? How did this person's work change her life?

B Listen again and tick the key phrases you hear.

keyphrases

I fell in love with his novels.

That book really made its mark on me.

It had a big impact on me.

He's one of the best-known writers.

I'm a big fan of that type of writing.

The style is brilliant.

It was very influential.

He/She/Their work (really) inspired/influenced me … / to (do) …

C Plan to describe someone whose work influenced you. Write brief notes about the following:

- what they did
- their place in history
- what you learned from them
- how it has influenced the way you do things

D Work in groups and take turns to describe your person.

writeback a wiki entry

7A Read the proposal.

Subject: proposal

Dear student,
We are compiling a student wiki about world-famous, influential people in the arts and sciences. Please write a short piece (no more than 200 words) including information about where they live(d), when they did their work, their place in history, why they are influential, and who they have influenced. Do not write about political leaders, sports stars or businesspeople. Send your entry to the web address …

B Read an example entry. Does it fit the requirements in the proposal? Is anything missing?

Ravi Shankar is probably India's most famous musician. A sitar-player, composer, performer, musical director and teacher, he is best known in the west for his collaborations with George Harrison of *The Beatles*, who studied sitar under him and later produced some of Shankar's records.

Born into a wealthy family in 1920, at the age of ten Shankar went to Paris with his brother's dance group. By thirteen, he was part of the group, working as a dancer and playing different instruments. A few years later he decided to focus full time on the sitar and soon became a master of the instrument. In the 1950s and 60s he toured the world, giving Indian classical music a wider audience. It was during this time that he met and influenced Harrison and other well-known musicians from the UK and the United States.

Shankar wrote film scores and recorded numerous popular albums. He was deeply committed to playing live music, and even performed at Woodstock during the hippie era. In his seventies and eighties he was still performing regularly. He has been very influential because he helped to bring Indian music to the rest of the world.

C Now write your wiki entry about the person whose work influenced you. Use the wiki above and the key phrases to help.

HISTORY

1A Work in teams. Write ten sentences. Each sentence must use a different word from the box. The first team to finish wins!

revolution   turning point
development   movement
spread   advance   invention
foundation   discovery   progress

B Read your sentences to the class.

THIRD CONDITIONAL

2A Complete the sentences with your own words.

1 Dayo left his job because …
2 Lily didn't pay for the meal at the restaurant because …
3 Cristian asked for a replacement phone because …
4 I didn't go on my free holiday to Jamaica because …
5 Kim didn't go to see U2 because …
6 I stopped talking to my mother because …

B Exchange sentences with a partner. Write third conditional sentences for each of the situations your partner completed.

Dan left his job because he didn't like his boss. If he had liked his boss, he wouldn't have left his job.

PERIODS OF TIME

3A Complete the sentences with words for periods of time.

1 In which d _ _ _ _ _ were you born?
2 What can you remember about the n _ _ _ _ _ _ _-n _ _ _ _ _ _ _?
3 How did you celebrate the new m _ _ _ _ _ _ _ _?
4 What's your favourite e _ _ in history?
5 If you could go back in time for a f _ _ _ _ _ _ _ _, where and what c _ _ _ _ _ _ would you choose?
6 What do you think your g _ _ _ _ _ _ _ _ _ are/will be famous for?

B Work in pairs. Take turns to ask and answer the questions.

THE PASSIVE

4A Complete the sentences with the correct passive or active form of the verbs in the box.

~~discover~~   assassinate   become
build   climb   declare   destroy
elect   release   identify

1 The tomb of Tutankhamun _was discovered_ in the Valley of the Kings, Egypt.
2 US and French scientists _____ the AIDS virus.
3 A wall _____ between East and West Germany.
4 Edmund Hillary and Tenzing Norgay _____ Mount Everest.
5 The Titanic _____ after hitting an iceberg in the North Atlantic.
6 Nelson Mandela _____ from prison.
7 Mahatma Gandhi _____ by a terrorist.
8 Margaret Thatcher, the UK's first female prime minister, _____.
9 The UK and France _____ war on Germany.
10 Two-year-old Pu Yi _____ Emperor of China.

B Match the events above with the dates in the box.

~~1922~~	1908	1912	1939
1948	1953	1961	1979
1984	1990		

1922: The tomb of Tutankhamun was discovered.

C Work in groups. Compare your answers and correct each other's work if necessary.

EXPRESSING UNCERTAINTY

5A Put part B's words in the correct order to complete the conversations.

1 A: Where's the nearest bank?
   B: no / I / idea / have / sorry,
2 A: Is there anywhere you can smoke in this building?
   B: allowed / it's / definitely / no, / here / not
3 A: What time does this school open in the morning?
   B: at / fairly / opens / sure / I'm / it / 7.00a.m.
4 A: What was your last teacher's name?
   B: remember / can't / I
5 A: Do you know where the nearest restaurant is?
   B: clue / sorry, / haven't / I / a
6 A: What's the school director's name?
   B: it / not / a / might / I'm / percent / but / certain, / be / hundred / Timothy
7 A: How far away is the nearest supermarket?
   B: isn't / it / sure / far / I'm
8 A: What was yesterday's homework?
   B: forgotten / sorry, / I've

B Work in pairs. How many of your partner's questions can you answer?

BBC VIDEO PODCAST

Download the video podcast and view people comparing life now to the past and saying when they would've like to have lived and why.

Authentic BBC interviews

www.pearsonlongman.com/speakout

UNIT
10

world

VOCABULARY the environment

1A Work in pairs and discuss. How important is 'green living' to you?

B Look at the sentences below and try to explain the meaning of the words/phrases in bold. Then use a dictionary to check.

1 How much of the food you buy is **pre-prepared** or **processed**? How much is **organic**?

2 How much of the food you eat is produced in the country you live in?

3 How is your home heated? Do you use **energy-saving light bulbs**?

4 Is your house **insulated** and/or **double-glazed**?

5 Do you turn lights/machines off or leave them **on standby**?

6 When you're buying a product, do you consider how to recycle the **packaging**?

7 How often do you buy, sell or give away **secondhand items**?

8 How much of your rubbish is **recycled**?

9 How many hours, on average, do you spend flying a year?

10 How often do you use a car?

C Answer questions 1–10 above.

D Work in pairs and compare your answers.
⟩ page 157 **VOCABULARYBANK**

READING

2A Justin Rowlatt, a BBC journalist, decided to try living a greener lifestyle for a year. What changes do you think he made?

B Read the article to find out.

C Work in pairs and answer the questions below.

1 Why did Justin decide to try living ethically for a year?

2 Did he and his family enjoy the experience?

3 What kinds of things did they try to change?

4 What kinds of challenges does Justin say that other journalists have to face?

5 Did Justin and his family manage to reduce their impact on the environment?

6 Did the 'experiment' change the way that they have decided to live?

D Discuss. Do you think the 'Ethical Man' experiment is a good idea? Why/Why not?

1 Hi – I'm Justin Rowlatt and I'm the BBC's 'Ethical Man'. So, what does living ethically mean? Giving up the car, recycling wine bottles, not using plastic bags? I spent a year trying to find out.

2 I want to be clear about one thing right from the start – it wasn't my idea to become the BBC's ethical man. I had just started working for the BBC and on my first day the editor asked me to come into his office.

3 What did I think about the idea of a journalist trying to live as ethical a lifestyle as possible for a year, he wanted to know. He asked me if I liked the idea. What did I think? It was my first day; I said I thought it was a great idea!

4 That's why my family (Bee, my wife, thirty-five, and daughters Eva, five and Zola, four) and I agreed to spend a year doing everything we could to try to reduce our impact on the environment. We changed the light bulbs in our house to energy-saving bulbs. We changed the way we heat and power our home. We stopped flying and we got rid of the car. Instead we walked, used bicycles, or took public transport. We did our supermarket shopping online, ate organic vegetables and I even stopped eating meat (for a month). My heavily pregnant wife, Bee, walked two miles to hospital in the middle of the night, to give birth to our third daughter, Elsa. When we went on holiday to France, instead of choosing a two-hour flight, we went on a nightmarish twelve-hour journey on the train, in a heatwave.

5 You expect to face challenges as a journalist. Many of my colleagues regularly report from war zones. Others have just minutes to prepare before they are expected to give a clear explanation of complex economic data. Some have to work with criminal gangs. But few journalists have faced the sorts of challenges I have during my 'year of living ethically'.

6 It has been a tough year. I put my family through hell and there were many rows and arguments. But the overall result? We managed to reduce our carbon footprint by 37 percent – nearly double the total we had hoped to achieve a year ago.

7 Being forced to go green has shown me that anyone can achieve more than we think. However, I believe most people are too busy to go through all this without being compelled – as I was – to give it a go.

8 Having said that, we don't regret doing it, we aren't planning to get the car back and many of the other changes will remain, too.

3 Read the article again. Underline words/phrases in the text that match meanings 1–6.

1 the amount of damage we do (by our actions) to the air, water and land on Earth (paragraph 4)

2 threw away or destroyed (paragraph 4)

3 terrible – like a bad dream (paragraph 4)

4 period of very hot weather (paragraph 4)

5 made my family go through a bad experience (paragraph 6)

6 be forced to do something (paragraph 7)

GRAMMAR reported speech

4A Complete the table to show how tenses change in reported speech.

direct speech	reported speech
'We ¹_____ planning to get the car back …'	He said they **weren't planning** to get the car back …
'Many of the other changes ²_____ remain.'	He said many of the other changes **would** remain.
'My heavily pregnant wife, Bee, ³_____ two miles to hospital.'	He said he that his wife **had walked** to hospital.
'I **think** it's a great idea!'	He said he ⁴_____ it **was** a great idea!
'It ⁵_____ been a tough year.'	He said it **had been** a tough year.
'I ⁶_____ just started working for the BBC.'	He said he **had** just **started** working for the BBC.
'Do you **like** the idea?'	He asked me if I ⁷_____ the idea.

B Check your answers using the article in Exercise 2B.

C Look at the table again and underline the correct alternatives to complete rules.

Rules:

1 When we report speech, we often move the tenses *back (backshift)/ forwards*, e.g. present simple → past simple, present continuous → past continuous, present perfect → past perfect, *will → would*.

2 If what the person says is still true, we can *keep the tenses the same/change the tense to a future form*, e.g. 'It's the 16th.' → She said it's the 16th.

3 In reported speech, we may also need to change *names and places/ pronouns and time references*, e.g. 'I'll see you <u>tomorrow</u>.' → He said he would see her <u>the next day</u>.

4 In reported questions, the word order is *the same as/different to that* for statements.

▸ page 146 **LANGUAGE**BANK

5A Complete the sentences by adding one word.

1 I'll see you in my office. [Editor to Justin]

He said he would see Justin in ___*his*___ office.

2 I've got a new job. [Justin to his wife]

He said he _____ a new job.

3 We're going to try and live a more ethical lifestyle. [Justin to Bee]

They said that _____ were going to try and live a more ethical lifestyle.

4 I'm going to take a taxi to hospital. [Bee to Justin]

She said she _____ going to take a taxi to hospital.

5 We're hot. [children to parents]

The children said _____ were hot.

6 We've achieved a lot. [Justin and Bee]

They said they _____ achieved a lot.

7 I didn't eat meat for a month. [Justin]

Justin said he _____ eaten meat for a month.

8 I had expected to face challenges as a journalist. [Justin]

He said he _____ expected to face challenges as a journalist.

B ▶ 10.1 Listen to check your answers. Listen again and shadow the sentences.

SPEAKING

6A Work in two groups. Group A: look at the photo, read the fact file below and discuss the questions. Group B: look at the photo and read the fact file on page 162.

The plastic bag problem

Did you know ...?

- The world uses 1 million plastic bags per minute.
- The 'Pacific Ocean Garbage Patch' is an area in the Pacific Ocean filled with waste plastic. The area may be as big as 5 million square km (more than twice the size of the USA). Millions of marine animals die when they eat the plastic, become caught in it, or feed it to their young.
- Plastic bags can now be found in all parts of the world, from the top of Mount Everest, to the bottom of the oceans, and the deserts of Mongolia. Each plastic bag takes more than 1,000 years to disintegrate and never completely disappears.

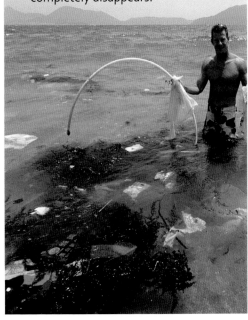

1 Why does the problem exist?
2 What should be done about it?
3 What laws/schemes would you introduce to deal with the problem?

B Work in pairs with a student from the other group. Tell them about the discussions you had in your group, and any ideas you had.
We talked about the problem of plastic bags. We thought it would be a good idea to make people pay for plastic bags in shops.

VOCABULARY *PLUS* word-building (prefixes)

7A Look at the example sentences 1–10 and underline the prefixes.

un-
1 It's very unusual to have snow in April.
2 The whole situation was completely unreal.

re-
3 Most glass bottles and aluminium cans can be recycled.
4 Don't throw away the bottles. They are reusable.

dis-
5 Roth doesn't like anybody who disagrees with him.
6 She would never disobey her parents.

mis-
7 Don't misunderstand me. I want to help.
8 I always mispronounce his name.

over-/under-
9 She hardly eats anything, and she's very underweight.
10 I think I've overcooked the pasta.

B Match the prefixes above with meanings 1–5.
1 not: ___*un-*___ and _____
2 again: _____
3 too much: _____
4 too little: _____
5 wrong: _____

8 Add prefixes to the words in brackets to complete the sentences.
1 He's lying. His story about how he cycled across Africa was completely _____ (believable).
2 It's easy to _____ (judge) somebody's character by looking at the clothes they wear.
3 Much of the snow in the Arctic has completely _____ (appeared).
4 These organic potatoes are delicious. Be careful not to _____ (cook) them.
5 Jessica decided not to accept the job because the company's policies were _____ (ethical).
6 I think I've done this all wrong. I probably _____ (understood) the instructions.
7 My house is always _____ (tidy). I don't have enough time to organise my things.
8 She walks to work every day, despite her _____ (ability).

speakout TIP

Use prefixes to guess the meaning of words you don't know. Look at the words in bold below. Can you use the prefix to guess their meaning?

9 Work in pairs and take turns. Ask and answer the questions.
1 Which professions in your country do people often **mistrust**?
2 Who in your country is very famous now, but was **unknown** last year?
3 What kinds of documents do you sometimes need to **renew**?
4 Do you believe scientists have **overestimated** or **underestimated** the problem of climate change?
5 Do you **disapprove** of people who drive their cars everywhere? Why/Why not?

⟶ page 157 **VOCABULARYBANK**

READING

1 Work in pairs and discuss.

1 What countries do you think the food in the pictures comes from?

2 Would you eat these dishes? Why/Why not?

2A Read the text. Why is Osaka the world's greatest food city?

> **What's the greatest, most exciting food city in the world today?**
>
> There used to be one great food city in the world, and that was Paris. At least, that's what most people believed. People now agree that there is incredible food all around the world. Michael Booth, a writer, traveller and food-lover, thinks that the Japanese city of Osaka is the best.
>
> With its busy food halls and small, exclusive restaurants, Osaka is 'bursting' with amazing places to eat. All around the city, you can find delicious fast food dishes which were invented here. Osaka is the city that invented both sushi and instant noodles in the same year (1958), but there are many more local dishes, too.
>
> In Osaka, people love life and they love their food. They even have a saying, '*kuidaore*', which means 'eat until you are bankrupt' because they love to spend money on food. So, what about you? Which city is your culinary favourite?

B Read the text again and answer the questions.

1 What type of food is Osaka famous for?

2 Where can you eat it?

3 How do the people of Osaka describe their food?

LISTENING

3A ▶ 10.2 Listen to two people talking about their favourite food city. According to the speakers, which city, Hiroshima (H) or Madrid (M), has the following:

1 a small, cheap restaurant which serves wonderful seafood?

2 informal restaurants where you order lots of dishes which everyone shares and eats from the middle of the table?

3 something to eat which is like a cross between a pancake and a pizza?

4 people getting together at Sunday lunchtime to have a few bites to eat?

5 a restaurant which specialises in grilled chicken?

B Listen again and complete the extracts below. Then check your answers in the audio script on pages 174–175.

1 They've got the very famous sushi that everyone thinks about when they think of Japanese food, but they've got so much else to _____.

2 Hiroshima is really _____ for its *okonomiyaki*.

3 *Tempura* is prawns and _____ deep fried in a really light, fluffy batter.

4 I lived in Madrid, in Spain for around _____ years on and off.

5 The quality of the food is _____.

6 *Tarta de Santiago* is a great pastry _____.

7 I once tried pig's ear, which I have to say was possibly the _____ thing I've ever tasted.

C Do you know any cities which are good for food? What types of food are they best known for? Which areas have good restaurants? Plan to talk about your favourite food city. Use these phrases from the listening to make some notes.

> My favourite food city is …   They've got all sorts of …
> XXX is really famous for its …   It's a kind of …
> It's really good (for) …   I think my favourite restaurant in … is …
> One of my favourite restaurants is a place called …, which specialises in …   It's a cheap/basic/smart/expensive …   You can get …
> I'd love to take you to XXX; you'd love it!
> I know a really good … that I should take you to.

D Work in groups and take turns to talk about your favourite food city.

VOCABULARY reporting verbs

4A Match the verbs with the statements.

1 offer   a) I can't eat anything else, thank you.

2 warn   b) Would you like a coffee?

3 refuse   c) Be careful. It's hot.

B Look at the statements/questions below. Rewrite each statement in reported speech using a verb from the box.

warned explained refused promised invited suggested offered

1 'You have to be careful not to eat too much.'

She _____ us not to eat too much.

2 'Why don't you come to Palermo and I'll take you to my favourite restaurant?'

He _____ us to Palermo, and he _____ to take us to his favourite restaurant.

3 'It will definitely be good value for money. I'm 100 percent certain of that.'

She _____ that it would be good value for money.

4 'I think Lima could be one of the greatest food cities in the world.'

She _____ that Lima could be one of the greatest food cities in the world.

5 'The restaurant specialises in grilled chicken.'

He _____ that the restaurant specialises in grilled chicken.

6 'I don't believe that there is any better food than in Singapore.'

He _____ to believe that there was any better food than in Singapore.

GRAMMAR verb patterns

5A Look at the verb patterns in bold in sentences a)–e). Then complete the table below with the sentences.

a) We **explained that** it was our first trip to the area.

b) He **agreed to show** us around Palermo.

c) She **suggested trying** some of the local dishes.

d) They **promised to cook** for us.

e) He **warned us not to eat** the chillies.

verb + infinitive with *to*	verb + *-ing*
She offered to show us around.	They recommended taking the bus
1 _____	3 _____
2 _____	
Verb + object + infinitive with *to*	Verb + *that*
They invited us to stay.	She decided that she would stay.
4 _____	5 _____

B ▶10.3 Listen to the sentences above and underline the stressed words.

C Listen again and check your answers. Pay attention to the weak forms of *to* /tə/, *for* /fə/ and *that* /ðət/. Then listen and repeat.

D Some verbs use more than one pattern. Find two examples in Exercise 4B of verbs which can use different patterns.

*Agree: She **agreed to** show us around. They **agreed that** it was a good idea.*

▶ page 146 **LANGUAGEBANK**

PRACTICE

6 Complete the second sentence so that it means the same as the first. Use the correct form of the verbs in bold.

1 'During the festival, street vendors sell nothing but chocolate.' **explain**

She _____ during the festival street vendors only sell chocolate.

2 People should come to the Tomatina festival in Spain. **suggest/visit**

Beatrix _____ Spain during the Tomatina festival.

3 You shouldn't eat anything before the cheese-tasting festivals. There are more than 1,000 cheeses to try. **warn/eat**

He _____ us not _____ anything before going to the cheese-tasting festivals.

4 'We'll definitely go to the Mango festival in India in July.' **promise/take**

He _____ me to the Mango festival.

5 'Would you like me to show you around the Eurochocolate festival?' **offer/show**

The tour guide _____ us around the Eurochocolate festival.

SPEAKING

7A Read the comments about food below. Do any of the people have similar ideas to you?

'I love good food, but I never cook it myself. I would rather go to a restaurant.'

'Food isn't at all important to me. I just eat when I'm hungry.'

'Food is like a passion for me. I love cooking for lots of people.'

'People who eat in restaurants are lazy. It's such a waste of money.'

B Work in pairs. Tell your partner how you feel about food and cooking. Try to give examples.

C Work with another student. Tell them about your last partner.

WRITING a restaurant review

8A Match headings a)–e) with questions 1–5 to complete the guide to writing a restaurant review.

a) Information about the price
b) Information about the menu
c) Details of the restaurant
d) Information about the service
e) Information about the atmosphere

1 _____: Where is it? How can you contact them? How do you get there? What are the opening hours?

2 _____: What's the décor like? Is it child-friendly? Is it noisy? Is it romantic?

3 _____: What kind of food does it serve? Are there any specialities? Do they serve vegetarian food? Are there any particular dishes you recommend?

4 _____: Are the staff friendly? Do you have to wait a long time?

5 _____: Is it good value for money? How much does it cost per person? Are there any special offers?

B Read the reviews below. Try to answer the questions above for each restaurant. Which one would you like to visit and why?

Are you hungry? You will be at some point. Here's a guide to some of the best restaurants in town.

4,550 Miles from Mumbai (Indian): Boxhill Way, 0265 958 834

An unusual name for an unusual Indian restaurant, 4,550 Miles from Mumbai offers diners a totally different kind of curry experience. This restaurant has such incredibly stylish and modern décor that it goes against everything you expect from an Indian restaurant, and they even have jazz music playing in the background. Whilst the food is not cheap, it's delicious, so considering the surroundings, it is reasonably priced. They also offer different kinds of Indian treats such as deep fried stuffed green chillies and salmon tikka.

Feast (Vegetarian), Long Row, off Market Square, 0265 955 101

Feast specialises in vegetarian and vegan food and offers mainly light meals and snacks. Although the room is quite small, the atmosphere is cosy, due to the size of the room. And the coffee and homemade cakes which they serve during the day are so good that you'll want to come back. Feast becomes more of a bar in the evening, so look out for different DJs during the week.

Marcelo's (Italian), Lower East Street, 0265 979 994

Marcelo's is a large restaurant that is good at catering for big parties. They serve a wide variety of Italian food, and all pizzas and pasta dishes are reasonably priced. The restaurant itself is decorated in an elegant Mediterranean style and has such an authentic Italian atmosphere, complete with soft Italian music in the background, that you could easily forget which country you're in. They do a two-for-one deal on selected meals throughout the week so be sure to check which nights these are available.

LEARN TO link ideas

9A Look at the examples and answer questions 1–3.

*The food was **so** delicious **that** I didn't mind spending more than usual.*

*It was **such** an enjoyable meal **that** I would recommend this restaurant to anybody.*

*It was so expensive that I wouldn't go back there **unless** I wanted to impress a client.*

***Although** it's a five-star restaurant, the service was appalling.*

***While** the staff are friendly, and the atmosphere is fun, the food isn't anything special.*

1 Which linking words do we use to connect ideas which contrast with each other?

2 Which do we use to talk about the consequences of a situation?

3 Which do we use to suggest a condition?

B Read the reviews in Exercise 8B again. Find and underline the linking words.

C Write sentences to connect the five pairs of ideas below. Use the words in brackets to help.

1 Starbucks has been very successful. Now they want to open new stores in China. (so)

2 The restaurant has had very bad reviews. Nobody wants to go there. (such)

3 The food was very bad. I will only go back there again if they get a new chef. (unless)

4 The food was delicious. The service was poor. (although)

5 The restaurant had a good atmosphere. The food was disappointing. (while)

10 Choose a restaurant in your town/city. Write a short review (80–100 words). Use the guide in Exercise 8A to help you. Use the linking words in Exercise 9B to connect your ideas.

► **FUNCTION** | giving advice/warnings ► **VOCABULARY** | airports ► **LEARN TO** | make generalisations

VOCABULARY airports

1A Discuss the questions.

1 Do you ever travel by plane?

2 Do you enjoy it?

3 What do you like/dislike about air travel?

B Complete the questions/statements you might hear in an airport with the words in the box.

proceed	aisle	card	passport
priority	X-ray	hand	gate
check	boards		

1 Can I see your _____?

2 Your _____ number is 42.

3 In a few moments we will be calling all passengers with _____ boarding.

4 Would you like an _____ seat or a window seat?

5 Your flight _____ at 09.30.

6 Please have your boarding _____ ready for inspection.

7 How many bags do you have to _____ in?

8 Do you have any _____ luggage?

9 Please _____ to gate number 30.

10 Put your hand luggage through the _____ machine.

C Put the phrases in the order you might hear them in an airport.

FUNCTION giving advice/warnings

2A Work in pairs. Write a list of three things you must and mustn't do in an airport.

B Read the article. Does it mention your ideas?

C Work in pairs and discuss. Do you agree with the advice? Have you ever experienced any of these problems?

Ten things NOT to do in an airport

1 **Pick the wrong terminal** – Most airports have more than one terminal, so check which terminal you need before your taxi drops you off and drives away.

2 **Annoy the check-in desk** – They may be taking a long time, but getting annoyed with them will get you nowhere.

3 **Make jokes about bombs or drugs** – You might end up in jail instead of enjoying your holiday.

4 **Take more than one bag** – If it says one bag only for hand luggage, then you can't bring your handbag and shopping bags, too.

5 **Go crazy on liquids** – 100 ml is the limit. No extra bottles of suncream, shampoo and hair conditioner.

6 **Waste people's time** – Take off your jewellery, watch and belt before you go through the X-ray machine, so people don't have to wait while you go through the machine again and again.

7 **Leave things in the trays** – Don't wait until you get to the departure gate before you remember that you left your phone, iPod, keys and passport in the tray.

8 **Use the airport internet terminals** – They are slow and expensive, and you'll soon wish you hadn't bothered.

9 **Shop because you're bored** – You got cheap flights and a budget hotel, so why waste money on things you don't need, like giant-sized chocolate bars?

10 **Leave the toilet stop until it's time to board** – You'll keep the other passengers waiting, and then have to make that embarrassing walk down the aisle when you finally board.

3A ▶10.4 Listen and match conversations 1–4 with situations a)–d).

a) crime in a city
b) the journey to Heathrow airport
c) travelling in the north of the country
d) arriving at the airport

B Listen again. What problems do they talk about in each conversation?

4A Match 1–10 with a)–j) to complete the warnings/advice.

1 Watch out for
2 Make sure
3 Don't … (or else)
4 You'd better
5 If I were you,
6 Be careful
7 Don't forget to
8 Whatever you do,
9 You need to
10 The most important thing is

a) when you take trips into the jungle.
b) you find out how much the journey is supposed to cost.
c) watch out for groups of young children on the streets.
d) the taxi drivers who tend to hang around outside.
e) I'd allow about an hour and a half.
f) don't drink the water.
g) leave plenty of time.
h) get in until you've agreed the price with the driver, or else you could …
i) to remember to hold on to your handbag.
j) take your malaria tablets.

B ▶10.5 Listen and check your answers. Then listen and repeat the phrases. Which words are stressed?

▸ page 146 **LANGUAGEBANK**

5 Find and correct the mistakes. There is one mistake in each sentence.

1 The most important thing to remember is not going out alone.
2 If I were you I'll bring waterproof clothes.
3 Make sure if you wear a helmet and protective clothing when you ride a bike.
4 Be carefully when you're on the main roads. They're always very busy.
5 Don't forgetting to keep your luggage with you at all times.
6 Whatever you are do, don't buy food from the street sellers. It's terrible.
7 Watch out for people try to sell you fake watches.
8 You'll better leave your valuables in the hotel.

6A Look at how the speakers make generalisations. Cross out the alternative which is <u>not</u> possible.

1 Watch out for the taxi drivers who *tend to/are tend to/ have a tendency to* hang around outside the airport.
2 You'd better leave plenty of time, because *often/never/ usually* there are delays on the tube.
3 Be careful when you take trips into the jungle. *Sometimes/ Generally/Always* there are a lot of mosquitoes there, so remember to take mosquito nets and insect cream.
4 *On the whole/It doesn't often happen/It's not very common*, but don't walk around the city obviously carrying money in a big money belt or anything.
5 There isn't really much crime. *On the whole/For the whole/ Generally*, it's a pretty safe city.

B ▶10.6 Listen and underline the words/phrases the speakers use.

❝ speakout TIP

English speakers often make generalisations because they want to 'soften' a statement. Generalisations sound less direct and less aggressive. Can you use any of the phrases in italics in Exercise 6 to talk about travelling in your country?

7 Look at the sentences below. Then make generalisations using the prompts in brackets.

1 Men use the internet more than women. (tend)
Men tend to use the internet more than women.
2 I go to bed early in the winter. (whole)
3 The beaches are clean and safe. (generally)
4 The trains to the airport are not delayed. (not common)
5 Criminals target tourists. (tendency)
6 English people complain about the weather. (often)

SPEAKING

8A Work in pairs and role-play the situation. Student A: read the instructions below. Student B: turn to page 160.

Student A: you are a tourist. You want to go on a tour in the Australian Outback. Ask the Tourist Information for advice, e.g. Are there any animals to be careful of? What special clothes/equipment do you need?

I'd like some information about going into the Outback. First of all, what animals do I need to be careful of? …

B Change roles and role-play the following situation. Student A: you work in a diving centre. A customer would like to go snorkelling on the reef. Give him/her some advice using the prompts below:

1 most important thing / wear T-shirt / don't get sunburn Suncream / washes off in the sea
2 whatever do / not / touch the coral / break pieces off
3 watch out / stingrays – they can give you nasty sting
4 careful – strong currents – make sure / you can swim to shore/the boat
5 make sure / take underwater camera – take photos

DVD PREVIEW

1 Read about the BBC documentary. Why do you think life gets difficult for the polar bears?

B B C Nature's Great Events: The Great Melt

This BBC nature documentary, narrated by Sir David Attenborough, shows how life changes when the Arctic ice melts in the summer. This is the greatest seasonal change on the planet. During the long winter, the sun never rises, and temperatures plummet to minus 40 degrees. When the ice melts in the summer, the landscape changes completely and life gets difficult for the polar bears.

▶ DVD VIEW

2 Watch the programme and answer the questions.

1 Why is the melting ice a problem for the polar bears?

2 Is the problem worse than it was in the past?

3A Complete the sentences using the words in the box below.

ice	flicker	rises	drown	summer	sea	islands

1 The Northern Lights _____ across the sky.

2 Polar bears are in their element, hunting for seals on the frozen _____.

3 In February, the sun _____ for the first time in four months.

4 At the height of _____, even the permanent ice-caps are touched by the power of the sun.

5 Over 2.5 million square miles of ice have melted away, uncovering thousands of _____, surrounded by open ocean.

6 A mother bear and her adolescent cub rest on a fragment of _____.

7 If future melts are as extreme as this one, bears like these may either starve or _____, lost at sea.

B Watch the programme again to check your answers.

4 Work in groups and discuss.

1 Do you think man can do anything to improve the situation? What?

2 Do you think television programmes like this help to change the situation? How?

speakout an endangered place

5A ▶ 10.7 You are going to give short presentations about 'Places to see before they disappear'. First, listen to someone else's presentation. Which question below does he not answer?

1 What is the place?

2 Why is it in danger?

3 Why should you go there/see it?

4 How much does it cost to go there?

5 What can be done to change the situation?

B Listen again and tick the key phrases you hear.

keyphrases

One of the most beautiful places … (is under threat)

One of the most endangered places is/has …

One of the biggest problems …

Something that everyone should have the chance to see is …

The problem is that …

Fortunately/Unfortunately, …

Interestingly/Hopefully, …

Many/Much of the … have/has been

We have an opportunity to …

In the past, … but now …

… before it's too late.

6A Work on your own and plan a three-minute presentation. Do some research if necessary, or turn to page 163 for ideas. Use the prompts below and the key phrases to help.

*   What is the place?

*   Why is it in danger?

*   Why should you go there/see it?

*   What can be done to change the situation?

B Work in pairs and take turns.

Student A: practise your presentation. Use your notes, but try not to read all the information. Try to look up when you're talking.

Student B: help your partner improve their presentation. Time the presentation. Was it long enough? Give him/her feedback about his/her style and language.

Then change roles, and practise your presentations again.

C Give your presentation to the whole class. Watch the other students' presentations. Which places would you like to visit?

writeback email for action

7A Read the email and answer the questions. Where is Little Green Street? What is the problem?

Little Green Street is an old cobbled street just outside the centre of London. It is only 2.5m wide, and the houses here were built more than 225 years ago. The street, with its pretty, painted houses, and cobblestones, survived World War II. But now it is under threat from a developer who plans to build a car park and houses on the land near to it. The houses on Little Green St are protected by law (nobody can get permission to demolish them), but the street itself is not. In order to build his car park the developer plans to send heavy work lorries and machinery up and down this little old street. We are in no doubt that the lorries would destroy the street, and possibly the houses along with it. If you would like to join us in our protest against these plans, please sign your name at the bottom of the email. Thank you.

B Write an email calling for action to protect one of the places talked about in Exercise 6. Use the email above and the key phrases to help.

THE ENVIRONMENT

1A Complete the words/phrases in bold with the missing letters.

1 I only eat **o_____c** food because it's grown without using chemicals.

2 I buy **p__-r_____d** food because I don't have time for cooking.

3 I don't use **e___g-s____g** light bulbs because they're expensive.

4 My house isn't **in__l___d** very well, so it's always cold in the winter.

5 I try to **r__y___** glass, plastic and paper, but nothing else.

6 I'm careful to turn the computer and TV off at night, and not leave them **o_ s___d__**.

7 I buy a lot of **s____dh___** clothes – I like them and they're cheap.

8 I think **p____ss__** food is great because you can always make a quick meal at home.

B Write two statements that are true for you using the words/phrases in bold. Compare your sentences with a partner.

REPORTED SPEECH

2 Rewrite the reported conversation using direct speech.

Samantha introduced me (Franco) to Tom who said he was pleased to meet me. I replied that it was a pleasure to meet him, too, and that I hoped Tom was enjoying his stay in Milan. He said he thought Milan was a beautiful city, and he had very much enjoyed his stay there. He said that he had met lots of wonderful people and eaten some delicious food. I asked Tom if he had had the chance to do any sightseeing. Tom told me that unfortunately he hadn't had very much time at all, but that he had enjoyed seeing the cathedral. I asked Tom if he planned to visit Italy again soon. He replied that he would have loved to, but that Italy was a long way from Queensland. I said that was true, and then invited Tom to come and join us for a coffee before he had to leave for the airport. Tom accepted.

Samantha: Franco, this is Tom.
Tom: Pleased to meet you, Franco.
Franco: It's …

3A Work in pairs. Take turns to ask and answer questions 1–5. Make a note of your partner's answers.

1 What are your plans for your next holiday?

2 Where did you grow up? Is it different there now?

3 What do you usually do on a Saturday afternoon?

4 What are you going to do later?

5 What two promises can you make concerning your English studies?

B Work with another student. Tell them what you learned about your partner using reported speech.

REPORTING VERBS

4 Work in pairs and take turns. Student A: choose a word from the box. Don't say the word, but say something in the manner of the word. Student B: listen and guess which word your partner is describing.

| explain | refuse | promise |
| warn | invite | suggest | offer |

A: If you do that again, I'm leaving.
B: warn?
A: That's right.

VERB PATTERNS

5A Circle the correct alternative.

1 He promised *to give/giving* me back the money.

2 I refused *to answer/answering*.

3 She invited us *to stay/for staying*.

4 He's offered *pay/to pay*.

5 In the end, everyone agreed *it to be/that it was* the best thing to do.

6 They explained *wanting/that they wanted* our address.

B Work in pairs and discuss. When was the last time:

• you promised to do something?

• you agreed with someone's idea?

• someone explained something to you?

• you warned someone about something?

• someone offered to do something for you?

GIVING ADVICE/WARNINGS

6A Complete the advice/warnings using the words in brackets to help.

1 _____, don't tell the teacher. (whatever)

2 _____ buy a phrase book. (forget)

3 _____ you get fit before you do it. (make)

4 _____ wear that old shirt, _____ you'll never get the job. (else)

5 If _____, I'd buy her some flowers. (were)

6 _____ you don't oversleep and miss the plane. (careful)

7 You _____ look for a hotel on the internet (better)

8 _____ ask your manager who can approve it. (need)

B Match the advice/warnings above with situations a)–h).

a) I haven't done my homework.

b) I forgot my mother's birthday.

c) I arrive in New York late at night. I don't know where I'm going to stay.

d) My plane leaves at 6a.m., but I don't have an alarm.

e) I'd like to have a holiday but I'm not sure who I have to get permission from.

f) I'm planning to run a marathon, but I haven't done any training.

g) I can't speak the language.

h) I've got a job interview, but I don't have any clean clothes to wear.

C Work in pairs. Take turns to give each other advice using the situations above.

BBC VIDEO PODCAST

Download the video podcast and view people talking about what they think are the biggest problems facing the world at the moment.

Authentic BBC interviews

www.pearsonlongman.com/speakout

IRREGULAR VERBS

VERB	PAST SIMPLE	PAST PARTICIPLE
be	was	been
beat	beat	beaten
become	became	become
begin	began	begun
bend	bent	bent
bet	bet	bet
bite	bit	bitten
bleed	bled	bled
blow	blew	blown
break	broke	broken
bring	brought	brought
broadcast	broadcast	broadcast
build	built	built
burn	burned/burnt	burned/burnt
burst	burst	burst
buy	bought	bought
catch	caught	caught
choose	chose	chosen
come	came	come
cost	cost	cost
cut	cut	cut
deal	dealt	dealt
dig	dug	dug
do	did	done
draw	drew	drawn
dream	dreamed/dreamt	dreamed/dreamt
drink	drank	drunk
drive	drove	driven
eat	ate	eaten
fall	fell	fallen
feel	felt	felt
feed	fed	fed
fight	fought	fought
find	found	found
fly	flew	flown
forbid	forbade	forbidden
forget	forgot	forgotten
forgive	forgave	forgiven
freeze	froze	frozen
get	got	got
give	gave	given
go	went	been/gone
grow	grew	grown
hang	hung	hung
have	had	had
hear	heard	heard
hide	hid	hidden
hit	hit	hit
hold	held	held
hurt	hurt	hurt
keep	kept	kept
know	knew	known
lay	laid	laid
lead	led	led
leap	leapt	leapt
learn	learned/learnt	learned/learnt

VERB	PAST SIMPLE	PAST PARTICIPLE
leave	left	left
lend	lent	lent
let	let	let
lie	lay	lain
light	lit	lit
lose	lost	lost
make	made	made
mean	meant	meant
meet	met	met
mistake	mistook	mistaken
pay	paid	paid
put	put	put
read /riːd/	read /red/	read /red/
ride	rode	ridden
ring	rang	rung
rise	rose	risen
run	ran	run
say	said	said
see	saw	seen
sell	sold	sold
send	sent	sent
set	set	set
shake	shook	shaken
shine	shone	shone
shoot	shot	shot
show	showed	shown
shrink	shrank	shrunk
shut	shut	shut
sing	sang	sung
sink	sank	sunk
sit	sat	sat
sleep	slept	slept
slide	slid	slid
smell	smelled/smelt	smelled/smelt
speak	spoke	spoken
spell	spelt	spelt
spend	spent	spent
spill	spilled/spilt	spilled/spilt
split	split	split
spread	spread	spread
stand	stood	stood
steal	stole	stolen
stick	stuck	stuck
sting	stung	stung
swim	swam	swum
take	took	taken
teach	taught	taught
tear	tore	torn
tell	told	told
think	thought	thought
throw	threw	thrown
understand	understood	understood
wake	woke	woken
wear	wore	worn
win	won	won
write	wrote	written

LANGUAGE BANK

GRAMMAR

1.1

question forms
object questions

Object questions use the word order: question word + auxiliary verb + subject + infinitive.

question word	auxiliary verb	subject	verb
Where	do	you	work?
What	did	she	say?
When	are	they	coming?

yes/no questions

Yes/No questions don't use a question word. The answer to the question is *Yes* or *No*.

auxiliary verb	subject	verb
Does	he	smoke?
Did	we	win?
Have	they	arrived?

subject questions

When the *wh-* question word is the subject of the question:

- we don't use an auxiliary verb (*do, did*, etc.).
- we use the same word order as in an affirmative sentence.

question word	verb	object
Who	wants	ice cream?
What	happened?	---
Who	ate	the cheese?

questions with prepositions

When we use a verb + preposition expression (but not multi-word verbs) such as *look for, depend on, write about*, etc., we usually keep the verb and preposition together.

*What did you **talk about**? Who are you **looking for**?*

In very formal English we sometimes move the preposition to the front of the sentence. Compare:

*What does it **depend on**? On what does it **depend**?*

1.2

review of verb tenses
present simple

+	He **looks** happy.
-	He **doesn't look** happy.
?	**Does** he **look** happy?

Use the present simple to talk about something that is always or generally true, habits, routines, with *be* and other state verbs (see below).

present continuous

+	We**'re staying** here.
-	We **aren't staying** here.
?	**Are** we **staying** here?

Use the present continuous to talk about an activity happening at the time of speaking or a temporary activity happening around now. It may be happening at the moment, but maybe not.

past simple

+	They **worked** hard.
-	They **didn't work** hard.
?	**Did** they **work** hard?

Use the past simple to talk about finished actions, events or situations in the past.

past continuous

+	I **was living** there during the 90s.
-	I **wasn't living** there during the 90s.
?	**Were** you **living** there?

Use the past continuous to talk about an action or situation in progress at a particular time in the past. This action was not finished at that time.

state verbs and dynamic verbs

State verbs are not usually used in the continuous form. The most common state verbs are:

- attitude verbs: *love, hate, like, want, prefer*
- thinking verbs: *believe, know, remember, understand, mean, imagine*
- sense verbs: *see, hear, sound, appear, seem*
- belonging verbs: *own, possess, belong to, have, contain, include*

Some state verbs can be used in the continuous form when they describe actions, e.g. *see, have, think*.

*I**'m seeing** Phil tonight.* (see = meet)

*We**'re having** a party.* (have = organise)

*I**'m thinking** of going to university.* (think = consider)

1.3

talking about yourself

introducing a question
Could I ask a question?
There are a couple of things I'd like to ask about.
Can I ask you about that?
I have a query.

introducing an opinion
For me (the most important thing is) …
I'd have to say …
In my opinion, …
One thing I'd like to say is that …

PRACTICE

1 Write questions for the answers in italics.

1 Where _____ ?
  I live *in Madrid.*

2 Who _____ ?
  Nick won the game.

3 Does _____ ?
  No, he doesn't eat meat.

4 What _____ ?
  They are *sleeping.*

5 What _____ ?
  I'm writing about *my first holiday.*

6 When _____ ?
  We arrived *yesterday.*

7 Who _____ ?
  We ate the chocolate.

8 Did _____ ?
  Yes, we liked the film.

2 Put the words in brackets in the correct places to make questions.

1 the President? (killed, who)
  _____

2 were you thinking? (what, about)
  _____

3 to the old theatre? (happened, what)
  _____

4 Where your great-grandparents come? (from, did)
  _____

5 your ancestors from here? (come, did)
  _____

6 she here for a long time? (worked, has)
  _____

7 is all that noise? (who, making)
  _____

8 house you looking for? (are, which)
  _____

1 Underline the correct alternatives.

'Like most translators, I ¹*'m speaking/speak* several languages. At the moment, I ²*'m attending/attend* a conference. I ³*was doing/did* some work for an internet company when I ⁴*was hearing/heard* about this conference. I ⁵*was arriving/arrived* three days ago and I'm going to stay until Monday, when it ends.'

My best friend is called Gina. We ⁶*aren't speaking/don't speak* to each other every day, but we're very close. I ⁷*was meeting/met* her on my first morning at university. I ⁸*was looking/looked* for the library when she came up to me and asked, 'Excuse me, ⁹*do you know/are you knowing* where the library is?' We ¹⁰*were finding/found* it together!

2 Put the verbs in brackets into the correct tense.

1 Sit down and watch the game! We _____ (win) 2–1. Ronaldo scored two minutes ago.

2 John wasn't here last summer. He _____ (travel) around Africa.

3 Fifty years ago, my favourite writer _____ (die).

4 I didn't do the homework because I _____ (not listen) when the teacher told us what to do.

5 DVDs _____ (not work) very well on my laptop, so I use the TV and DVD player.

6 What's that smell? Can you turn off the oven? I think the food _____ (burn).

7 _____ (see) that film last night? What did you think?

8 Everyone knows that smoking _____ (cause) cancer.

1 Find and correct the mistakes in the conversation below. There are six mistakes.

1 A: There are a couple of things I'd like ask about.

  B: Go ahead.

  A: Firstly, which of your films do you think is the best?

  B: I'd having to say *Millennium Dreamer.* For me, it's my best film and it was my first comedy.

  A: Can I ask you around that? You've never done comedy before. Why not?

  B: I don't know. I suppose people think I'm a serious actor.

  A: Could I ask question about your image? Is it accurate? Are you really the strong silent type in real life?

  B: No. One of thing I'd like to say is that these images are invented by the media. By my opinion, good actors are never just one thing. That's why they're actors.

2.1

present perfect/past simple

time up to now

+	I've been to Marrakesh.
-	He hasn't been here.
?	Have you tried it?

Use the present perfect for actions which have happened in your life before now. These are often general experiences. It isn't important exactly when these things happened.

He's played in an Indie band for a couple of years. I haven't travelled to other countries.

We often use the adverbs ever and never with the present perfect.

We've never been to China. Have you ever been to the Opera?

recent events

Use the present perfect to talk about events which happened a short time ago. We often use the adverbs just, yet and already.

I've just finished his book. It was brilliant.

We've already eaten.

Have you done your homework yet?

We've seen a lot of Jude recently.

present perfect or past simple?

Use the past simple to talk about a specific event which happened at a specific time.

I've been to Sweden. (At some time in my life up to now. We don't know when.)

We went to Stockholm in 2002. (Not We've been to Stockholm in 2002. This is a specific occasion and date, so we use the past simple.)

2.2

narrative tenses

past simple

Use the past simple for states and actions in the past. We often specify the time when they happened.

I left university in 1996. He didn't know the way to Sal's house.

past continuous

Use the past continuous to talk about the background information for a story. Use the past simple to talk about the main events.

As I was walking through the park, the sun was shining and the birds were singing. Suddenly, I heard a loud noise.

Often the past continuous action is interrupted by another action (in the past simple).

I was having a bath when the phone rang.

We can use conjunctions like as and while to talk about two actions which were happening at the same time.

While I was reading the paper, I watched the women buying vegetables in the market.

For more information on state and dynamic verbs section 1.2, page 148.

past perfect

+	I had finished my work.
-	They hadn't had time.
?	Had they been there before?

Use the past perfect to make it clear that one action happened before the other.

```
            PAST                                   NOW
     I lost my wallet.    I didn't have any money.
_____X_____X_____|
     past perfect         past simple        present
```

I didn't have any money because I had lost my wallet.

When before or after is used in the sentence, it's already clear which action comes before the other, so we can use the past simple instead of the past perfect.

She had lived in London for five years before she moved to New York. She lived in London for five years before she moved to New York.

We often use the past perfect with 'thinking' verbs like remember, realise, think, discover, find out, etc.

When I got to the school, I realised I'd left my books at home.

2.3

telling a story

beginning the story	This happened when ...
	In the beginning, ...
describing what happened	Well, ...
	Anyway, ...
	So, ...
	Before long, ...
	And then, all of a sudden ...
	The next thing I knew, ...
ending the story	In the end, ...
	Finally, ...

questions to keep a story going	So, what happened?
	What did you do?
	What happened next?
	Really?
responses to show interest	I don't believe it!
	Oh no / Oh dear.
	How embarrassing!
	That's really funny.
	You must be joking.
	Yes, I know.

PRACTICE

2.1

1 Tick the correct sentences, a) or b).

1 a) I've been to India last year.
   b) I went to India last year.
2 a) I finished my studies in 2005.
   b) I've finished my studies in 2005.
3 a) Did you have lunch yet?
   b) Have you had lunch yet?
4 a) Did you ever see Metallica play live?
   b) Have you ever seen Metallica play live?
5 a) Is this the first time you've tried judo?
   b) Is this the first time you tried judo?
6 a) It's the most beautiful place I've ever been to.
   b) It's the most beautiful place I ever went to.

2 Use the prompts to make short conversations.

1 A: you / be / here / before? (ever)
   B: no / not
2 A: you / see / the film *The Reader?*
   B: no / not / see (yet)
3 A: he / be / to Budapest?
   B: yes / go / last summer
4 A: you / finish / that book? (yet)
   B: yes / start / the next one (already)
5 A: you / see / Maria?
   B: yes, she / leave / a message for you
6 A: he / decide / what job / want to do? (yet)
   B: no / have / not

2.2

1 Underline the correct alternatives to complete the story.

I remember when Marvin Gaye [1]*died/had died*. I [2]*had been/was going* to one of his concerts a few months before. In fact, he [3]*hadn't played/wasn't playing* very well and I was disappointed. I also remember when JFK was shot. I [4]*had lived/was living* with my parents in New York and I [5]*studied/was studying* at the time. I remember the cleaning lady [6]*came/was coming* into the room, and said to me, 'Hey, President Lincoln has been shot.' I [7]*replied/was replying*, 'I know that.' 'No,' she said. 'President Lincoln has been shot!' So I said, 'What do you mean?' And she said, 'Oh no, I mean … President, you know, what's his name, the one now. President Kennedy's been shot.' So then I [8]*was turning/turned* on the radio.

2 Find and correct the mistakes. One sentence is correct.

1 I was leaving the room when I had heard someone shouting.
2 I couldn't open the door because I left my keys at home.
3 We drove through the tunnel when the car broke down.
4 As soon as the film started I realised I seen it before.
5 I never been to Egypt before, so I was really excited to see the pyramids.
6 By the time we arrived at the party, everybody else is leaving.
7 We had waited for nearly an hour before the waiter took our order.
8 I looked through some old photographs when I found this one of you.

2.3

1 Complete the conversation with the words and phrases in the box.

| In the end   don't believe it   The next thing I knew
| So, this happened when   So, what happened   Well
| really funny   Anyway   You must be joking |

A: Well, [1]_____ I was working in a photographic store.
B: [2]_____?
A: [3]_____, one day, a woman came in and asked if we could fix the problem she had with a photograph. [4]_____, I asked her what the problem was.
B: OK.
A: [5]_____, she had taken this old photo out of her bag which showed an old man sitting behind a cow, milking it.

[6]_____, when I asked her what she wanted us to do to the photo, she said, 'Can you move the cow?' 'Move the cow?' I asked. 'Yes,' she replied. 'I want to see what my grandfather looked like. She pointed to the feet sticking out from under the cow.
B: Oh no. [7]_____.
A: No, seriously. She wanted us to move the cow, so that she could see her grandfather's face.
B: I [8]_____! So, what happened next?
A: [9]_____, when I told her we couldn't do it, she got quite angry, and left the shop saying, 'Then I'll have to take it to someone else.'
B: That's [10]_____.

GRAMMAR

3.1

the future (plans)

be going to

+	I'm going to start university next year.
-	He isn't going to get a job this year.
?	Where are you going to stay?

When using *be going to* use the word order: subject + *am/are/is* + *going to* + infinitive. Use *be going to* to talk about future plans or intentions. When the verb is *go* or *come*, we often use the present continuous.

We're going to (go to) Spain. We're going to Spain.

I'm going to come and see you later. I'm coming to see you later.

present continuous

+	I'm starting my course in September.
-	We're not going away for very long.
?	What time are you leaving in the morning?

The present continuous is formed: subject + *am/are/is (not)* + verb + *-ing*. Use the present continuous to talk about future plans, when arrangements have already been made. We usually specify a future time such as *next week*, *on Friday*, etc., unless it is already clear that we are talking about the future.

We're flying to Greece on Friday. (We've already bought the tickets.)

She's staying in a hotel near the airport. (The hotel is already booked.)

In some cases it doesn't matter if it's the present continuous or *be going to*.

I'm playing football on Saturday. I'm going to play football on Saturday.

will

+	We'll meet you at the station.
-	I won't see you tomorrow.
?	Will you want a taxi?

When there is no plan or arrangement (when we make a decision at the time of speaking), we often use *will*.

I'm tired. I think I'll go to bed.

(subject + *will* + infinitive)

For use of *be going to* and *will* for prediction, see section 3.2 below.

might

+	I might go out later.
-	We might not be able to finish all this work tomorrow.

Use *might* (+ infinitive) to talk about plans, when we are unsure what the plan is.

I might stay at home and watch a DVD. (But I'm not sure. I might go out.)

spoken grammar

We do not usually use *might* + infinitive in the question form. It seems old-fashioned and formal. *Do you think* you might see Evelyn? NOT *Might you see Evelyn?*

3.2

the future (predictions)

will

Use *will* to make predictions.

Smartphones will organise our lives. She's so talented that I'm sure she'll become famous.

We often use *I think* and *I hope* with *will*.

I think John will become a doctor. She hopes she will work in the theatre.

be going to

Use *be going to* to make predictions when there is present evidence.

We only have two cars. It's going to be difficult to take eleven people tomorrow.

We use *probably* to make the prediction less certain. *Probably* usually comes after *will*.

The dollar will probably get stronger this year.

Probably comes after *to be* when we use it with *be going to*.

E-readers are probably going to become cheaper.

may and might

Use *may* or *might* to make predictions which are less certain. The negative forms are *may not* and *might not*.

Some of our workers may lose their jobs because of the restructuring.

We might not go away this year because we don't have any money.

could

Use *could* to make predictions which are less certain.

Global warming could destroy large parts of Asia in the next thirty years.

be likely to

Use *be likely to* to make predictions when something is probable. The negative is *be unlikely to* or *not be likely to*.

Regina is likely to be late because she works until seven.

We're unlikely to reach Paris before lunch because of all the traffic.

Are you likely to be hungry later?

Likely/Unlikely are adjectives.

Will we start at 5.00? It's unlikely.

spoken grammar

Might is more common than *may* in spoken English. *May* is a little bit more formal.

3.3

dealing with misunderstandings

saying you didn't hear something	I didn't catch any of that.
saying you don't understand someone's opinion	You've lost me.
	I don't get what you're saying.
asking someone to explain something more clearly	What exactly do you mean?
	Do you mean to say …?
asking someone to repeat something	Can you say that again?
	Could you repeat the last part/name/thing you said?

PRACTICE

3.1

1 Complete the conversation. Use the prompts in brackets where necessary.

A: Where ¹_____ you going?

B: I'm ²_____ to Paul's house. We' ³_____ going to watch the football.

A: OK. Who ⁴_____ ? (play)

B: Real Madrid versus Barcelona.

A: I see. And what time are you ⁵_____ home? (come)

B: I don't know.

A: How ⁶_____ getting home?

B: I'm not sure. I ⁷_____ his dad to drive me home, or I ⁸_____ catch the bus. (ask/might)

2 Find and correct the mistakes. There is one mistake in each sentence.

1 Will you going out this weekend?

2 I'm sorry I can't come. I playing tennis after work.

3 I don't feel very well. I think I stay at home.

4 What you going to do?

5 We go for a picnic, so I hope it doesn't rain.

6 Is that the phone? Don't worry – I'm going to get it.

7 They might going to a concert.

8 I'm sorry we can't come, but we're to visit my mother this weekend.

3.2

1 Rewrite the sentences below using the words in brackets.

1 We probably won't win the cup this year. (might)

We _____ .

2 I may be late. (likely)

I'm _____ .

3 That company will close in July. (going)

That company _____ .

4 He probably won't call after 10.00. (unlikely)

He _____ .

5 I'm not going to give up exercise. (won't)

I _____ .

6 We might have a problem with the flight. (may)

There _____ .

7 She'll get angry when she sees this. (going)

She _____ .

8 Are you going to visit us? (will)

_____

9 I would love it if he comes to the party. (hope)

_____

10 It is thought prices will rise if they complete the development. (could)

Prices _____ .

2 Put the pairs of words in the box into the correct place to complete the sentences.

| will be | aren't going | won't know | might not |
| likely to | may arrive | is going | not likely |

1 Jenny be able to meet us tonight because she has to work late.

2 Several of our workers are lose their jobs this year because of the economic recession.

3 In twenty years' time, cars able to fly.

4 The predicted storm at any moment.

5 The children to stay with me because I'm busy.

6 I my exam results until August.

7 It's that we'll arrive before 6.00 because there are train delays.

8 Watch out! That painting to fall off the wall!

3.3

1 Match 1–7 with a)–g) to make sentences and questions.

1 I didn't catch   a) you're saying.

2 You've lost   b) you mean?

3 I don't get what   c) that again?

4 What exactly do   d) to say …?

5 Could you repeat the   e) any of that.

6 Do you mean   f) last name?

7 Can you say   g) me.

You're where? Don't shush me!

SUSHI BAR

LANGUAGE BANK

GRAMMAR

4.1 must, have to, should (obligation)

must, have to

+	I **must** get up at 5 tomorrow.
	They **have to** start work early.
	We **must** start on time.
	She **has to** get there early.
-	You **mustn't** do that!
	We **don't have to** worry.
	They **mustn't** be late.
	He **doesn't have to** bring anything.
?	Do *I/we/you* **have to** bring …?
	(**Must** you go so early?)*
	Does *he/she/it* **have to** go?

* Question forms with *must* are not very common, and sound quite formal. We usually use *Do I have to …?* instead.

Use *must* and *have to* to talk about obligations. These things are necessary or important. *Must* is often used for a personal obligation (something we have decided for ourselves that we must do).

*I **must** give up eating chocolate.*

Must is also used in written rules.

*All applicants **must** provide proof of identity.*

Have to is used for external obligation.

*We **have to** wear a uniform.* (It's a company rule.)

Often you can use *must* or *have to* with the same meaning, but in spoken English *have to* is more common.

Don't have to and *mustn't* have different meanings. *Mustn't* means 'it is not allowed'. *Don't/Doesn't have to* means it is not necessary, but you can do it if you want.

*You **mustn't** smoke cigarettes anywhere in the building.* (It is not permitted and it's dangerous.)

*You **don't have to** work after 6.* (It's not necessary.)

Must can only be used to talk about present or future obligation. To talk about a past obligation, use *had to*.

*We **had to** get up early to catch the plane.*

spoken grammar

Have/Has got to means the same as *have/has to* in the context of obligation and is used a lot in spoken English.

*I**'ve got to** get some money from the bank. She**'s got to** get another job.*

should/shouldn't

+	I/You/He/She/	**should** see this film.
-	It/We/They	**shouldn't** smoke in the house.
?	Do you think we **should** …?*	

**Should we …* is more formal, and not very common.

Use *should* to talk about weak obligations (not as strong as *must* or *have to*). Often it is used for things which you think are a good idea (advice), e.g. *You **should** come to work in smart clothes.* Use *shouldn't* to talk about things which are not a good idea, e.g. *You **shouldn't** go to bed so late.* *Ought to* has the same meaning as *should*, but is not usually used in the negative or questions, e.g. *You **ought to** call her. = You **should** call her.*

4.2 used to, would

used to

+	I/You/He/She/	**used to** live in France.
-	It/We/They	**didn't use** to see my parents.
?	Did they **use** to visit?	

Use *used to* to talk about past habits/states, which have often changed or are not true now. You can also use the past simple.

*As a child, I **used to** love eating sweets. As a child I **ate** a lot of sweets.*

We can also use *would* to talk about past habits, but not to talk about past states.

*I **would go** to the sweet shop every day.* (habit)

*As a child, I **was** happy. As a child I **used to be** very happy.* (state) NOT *As a child, I would be happy.* (state)

Do not use *used to* to talk about things that happened only once, or for a specific number of times/length of time. Use the past simple for this.

*My family **moved** to America last year.* NOT *My family used to move to America last year.*

*We **went** to Italy twice on holiday.* NOT *We used to go to Italy twice on holiday.*

*I **studied** at university for three years.* NOT *I used to study at university for three years.*

spoken grammar

Never used to is more common in spoken English than *didn't use to*.

*We **never used to** see them, except for during August.*

In spoken English, we often leave out the verb or phrase after *used to*

*Do you smoke? No, I **used to**, but I **don't** any more.*

4.3 reaching agreement

giving opinions	suggestions	commenting on other opinions	
I (really) feel that …	What about …?	That's a good idea.	I (don't) see what you mean.
The way I see things, …	I suggest we focus on …	That's a good point.	I'm not sure that I agree, actually.
The way I see it, …	I think we should think about …	That's fine by me.	I'm not sure that … is a good idea.
	I suggest we think about …	That's OK by me.	
	How about if / Why don't we (call it)…?	Exactly!	

PRACTICE

1 Underline the correct alternative to complete the text.

The worst jobs in the world?

If you like travelling to exotic places, perhaps you [1]*should/ shouldn't* try this job. Helge Zieler is a mosquito researcher. In order to study the biting habits of the mosquito which spreads malaria in Brazil, Helge [2]*has to/doesn't have to* sit inside a mosquito net while hundreds of mosquitoes bite him. Every time he sees a mosquito land on his body, he [3]*must/have to* suck it into a tube in his mouth, and then blow it into a container. On a good evening, Helge can catch 500 mosquitoes in three hours. But to do this, he receives 3,000 bites (an average of seventeen bites per minute for 180 minutes). He [4]*mustn't/must* forget his anti-malaria tablets. Once he caught malaria and it took him two years to recover.

You [5]*shouldn't/don't have to* drive too fast on the roads, especially when you're driving in the countryside. Why? Because more than 400 million animals are killed on the roads every year. Joanne Keene knows, because she [6]*has to/shouldn't* remove them. Car drivers [7]*don't have to/must* pick the animals up, so Joanne drives around in a huge truck full of dead cats and raccoons. 'It's a hard job,' she says, 'because we work very long hours. We [8]*mustn't/must* be on call 24 hours a day.'

2 Match 1–8 with a)–h) to make sentences.

1 It's a good job but we …
2 I love Saturday mornings, because I don't have to
3 I think you should
4 The doctor told me that I
5 You mustn't
6 You don't have to
7 Francois is very lucky. His father is very rich, so he
8 I really must

a) have to work hard.
b) should do more exercise.
c) come to work dressed in jeans. You have to look smart.
d) doesn't have to work at all.
e) give up smoking. It's not good for my health.
f) get up for work. I can stay in bed until 10a.m.
g) send the forms in until September, but it's a good idea to send them early.
h) think about whether you really want to apply for the job.

4.1

---

1 Cross out the alternative which is <u>not</u> possible.

1 I *used to play/played/play* a lot of tennis when I was younger.

2 After school I *would take/used to take/take* the bus home.

3 He *never used to play/would play/ played* the guitar, but he doesn't play any more.

4 I *didn't use to enjoy/didn't enjoy/ wouldn't enjoy* school, but I worked hard anyway.

5 Tim *used to have/would have/had* long hair.

6 I *studied/used to study/didn't use to study* French for five years.

2 Make sentences with *used to* or *would* using the words in brackets. Sometimes both may be possible.

1 In Ancient Greece, people _____ (think) the world was flat, but Aristotle thought it was round.

2 In the olden days, people _____ (not have) cars, so they rode horses.

3 _____ people really _____ (enjoy) watching gladiator fights in Ancient Rome?

4 In the sixteenth century, ladies _____ (put) a white powder containing lead on their faces. It was poisonous.

5 Two hundred years ago, they _____ (not use) anaesthetics to perform operations.

6 Before iron was invented, soldiers _____ (fight) using bronze swords, but they weren't very strong and often changed shape in battle.

7 The Romans _____ (make) themselves sick, so that they could eat more during their huge banquets.

8 Why _____ people _____ (eat) garlic in Ancient Egypt? It was to cure toothache.

4.2

---

1 Using the words in italics, rewrite the second sentence so it has the same meaning as the first.

1 Let's begin.
 I think we ___should begin___.

2 I suggest we look at the emails first.
 Why _____?

3 I don't understand.
 I _____ you mean.

4 I agree with that idea.
 It's _____ me.

5 From my point of view, it works very well.
 The way _____ things, it works very well.

6 I agree with what you have just said.
 That's _____ point.

4.3

comparatives and superlatives

one-syllable adjectives and two-syllable adjectives ending in -y

adjective	comparative	superlative	notes
cheap	cheap**er**	**the** cheap**est**	+-er/the +-est
fast	fast**er**	**the** fast**est**	
easy	eas**ier**	**the** eas**iest**	-y changes to -i
friendly	friendl**ier**	**the** friendl**iest**	+ -er/the +-est
big	bi**gg**er	the bi**gg**est	adjective ending in *CVC double final consonant
large	larg**er**	**the** larg**est**	adjective ending in -e, add -r / the + -st

two-syllable and longer adjectives

adjective	comparative	superlative	notes
important	more/less important than	the most/ least important	+ more/less ... than, or the most/the least ... in the ...

irregular adjectives

adjective	comparative	superlative
good	better	the best
bad	worse	the worst
far	further/farther	the furthest/farthest

5.1

ways of comparing

Here are some common expressions used for making comparisons: *It's exactly/about the same as ...,   It's very similar to ...,   It's not as ... as.*

It's **exactly the same as** the one we had last year.

It's **very similar to** somewhere I stayed last year. He's **not as tall as** I expected.

It's a lot/much/far more + adjective: It's **far more beautiful** than I imagined.

It's a little/a little bit/slightly: It's **slightly smaller** than the last flat I lived in.

using superlatives

Here are some common expressions used with superlatives: *by far the most ..., one of the most ... the second (third/fourth) most ...*

It's **by far the most** delicious meal I've ever eaten.

It's **one of the most** beautiful places in the world.

We often use superlatives with a phrase beginning in the ...

She's by far the best student **in the class.**

It's one of the tallest buildings **in the world.**

*CVC – consonant, vowel, consonant

question tags

To make question tags, add auxiliary verb + pronoun at the end of the question. For a positive sentence, use a negative tag: *You **play** tennis, **don't you**?* For a negative sentence use a positive tag: *They **weren't** here, **were they**?*

Use contractions in the tag, not the full verb: *He's nice, isn't he?* NOT *He's nice, is not he?* N.B. Use a comma before the question tag and a question mark after it.

5.2

	positive verb + negative tag	negative verb + positive tag
present	You're twenty, aren't you?	She doesn't swim, does she?
past	They came back, didn't they?	You didn't see Tim, did you?
present perfect	You've lost it, haven't you?	He hasn't seen us, has he?
future	I'll be back by 10.00, won't I?	We won't lose, will we?

Use question tags to check information that you think is true. Also use question tags to sound less direct (a way to sound polite).

If we are sure of the information, the intonation falls on the question tag.

You're coming tomorrow, aren't you? (expect the answer 'yes'.)

If we are really not sure, the intonation rises on the question tag.

She's from Europe, isn't she? (maybe she isn't)

polite requests

request	responses
Could you carry this bag **for me**? **Could you** bring your laptop with you?	Yes, of course. I'm afraid I can't/I'm sorry, I can't.
Could you tell me the way to the hotel? **Could you tell me** what time it is?	Yes, I can. It's ... Let me have a look.
Do you know what time the shops open? **Do you know** how to get there?	I'm not sure.
Would you mind coming a little bit earlier? **Would you mind** booking us a table?	Of course not. OK./Sure.

5.3

watch out!

Could you tell me ...? and *Do you know ...?* are not direct questions; the word order is the same as for statements.

Could you tell me what time it is? NOT *Could you tell me what time is it?*

Do you know what time the shops open? NOT *Do you know what time do the shops open?*

Would you mind ...+ -ing

Would you mind watering my plants when I go away? NOT *Would you mind to water ...?*

Would you mind ...? is followed by a negative response.

Would you mind helping me? No, of course not. (I'm happy to help you) NOT *Yes, of course* (I would mind helping you = I'm not happy to help you)

PRACTICE

1 Complete the sentences with the comparative or superlative form of the adjectives in brackets.

1 We usually fly to Italy instead of going in the car, because it's _____. (quick)

2 They had to travel _____ than they wanted to find a hotel. (far)

3 When I was a teenager, I was much _____ than I am now. (not confident)

4 He's one of _____ children in the class. (naughty)

5 Exams are much _____ now than they were when I was at school. (easy)

6 Sweden is _____ than Norway. (big)

7 K2 is the second _____ mountain in the world. (high)

8 This book is slightly _____ to understand than his last book. The plot is very complicated. (difficult)

9 He used to be a teacher, but he's decided to become a firefighter. It's a much _____ job. (dangerous)

10 It's by far _____ film I've ever seen. (good)

2 Rewrite the sentences using the words in bold, so that they have the same meaning.

1 My brother is slightly taller than I am. **bit**

_____

2 The journey to the coast took much longer than we had expected. **far**

_____

3 It's easily the most expensive restaurant I've ever been to. **by**

_____

4 Your shoes and my shoes are almost the same. **similar**

_____

5 People here are much healthier now that they have clean water. **lot**

_____

1 Match 1–8 with a)–h) to make tag questions.

1 Clive was an engineer,	a) have they?
2 You're from Ethiopia,	b) won't he?
3 Shania isn't an actress,	c) has she?
4 They haven't been here before,	d) aren't you?
5 He'll be home soon,	e) is she?
6 You work here,	f) will they?
7 She hasn't met you,	g) wasn't he?
8 They won't finish on time,	h) don't you?

2 Find and correct the mistakes. There is one mistake in each question.

1 You weren't happy, weren't you?

2 It'll probably rain, doesn't it?

3 She researched her roots, didn't her?

4 They always ask tricky questions, they don't?

5 I take after my dad, doesn't he?

6 You've met Kevin's fiancée, have not you?

7 I put my foot in it yesterday, haven't I?

8 My mentor will give me a hand, he won't?

9 You had a lot on your mind, doesn't you?

10 Phil and Luke are on holiday, are not they?

1 Find the mistakes and correct them. There is an extra word or two in each line.

1 A: Excuse me, could you is hold the door for me?

   B: Yes, I do of course.

2 A: Do you know when the next train does to leaves?

   B: I'm not OK sure.

3 A: Would you to mind staying behind after the meeting?

   B: It's Sure. That's fine.

4 A: Could is possible you tell me what Tim's phone number is?

   B: Let me have a to look.

5 A: Would you mind to looking after my bag while I go to the bathroom?

   B: No, of course not mind.

6 A: Could you tell for me the way to the station?

   B: Yes, so I can.

5.1

5.2

5.3

zero and first conditionals

Zero and first conditionals are sometimes called ' real conditionals' because they talk about situations which are always true, or events which are possible or probable in the future.

zero conditional

if/when +	present simple +	present simple
If/When	You* **heat** water to 100° Centigrade,	it **boils**.

* Here *you* is a general subject meaning 'anyone' or 'people in general'.

Use the zero conditional to talk about a general situation, or something which is always true (a fact).

*If plants **don't have** water, they **die**. Ice **melts** if you **heat** it.* (*You* here refers to 'anyone', or people generally, not 'you' specifically.)

6.1 *If/When* can come at the beginning or in the middle of the sentence.

If I'm not in the office by 8a.m., my boss gets angry. My boss gets angry if I'm not in the office by 8a.m.

If and *when* have the same meaning in zero conditional sentences. In this case *if* means 'when this happens' or 'every time this happens'.

When I'm feeling stressed, I eat chocolate. If I'm feeling stressed, I eat chocolate.

first conditional

if/when +	present simple +	will/could/might + verb
If	you **give** me your phone number,	I'll **call** you when we're ready.
When	you **go** into the kitchen,	you'**ll see** the keys on the table.

Use the first conditional to talk about possible situations in the future and their consequences. If you are sure about the result, use *will/won't*. If you're not sure, use *could/might*.

We can change the order of the sentence, but *if/when* is always followed by the present simple.

*If my train **arrives** on time, I'll meet you at ten o'clock. Or I'll meet you at ten o'clock if my train **arrives** on time.* NOT *if my train will arrive on time.*

In first conditional sentences, *if* and *when* have different meanings. Use *if* when you are not sure if the situation will happen: **If** *I pass my exams, **I'll be very happy.*** Use *when* for a situation which you know will happen: **When** *I pass my exams, **I'll have a party.***

Unless has the meaning of 'if not' or 'except in this situation'.

*I'll go straight to the restaurant, **unless** you call me first.* (I will go straight to the restaurant, if you don't call me first.)

Note the difference between zero and first conditional in the sentences below.

*If you sit in the sun, you **get** sunburn.* (Zero conditional for a general situation/ fact. 'You' means anyone, or people in general.)

*If you sit in the sun, you'**ll get** sunburn.* (First conditional for a specific situation. I'm talking to you (personally) about what will happen today.)

---

second conditional

if +	past simple +	would clause
If	I **lived** to be 100,	I **would** probably **be** very tired.
	he **was** the President,	he'**d make** a lot of changes.
	we **bought** the house,	we'**d need** to sell our car.

6.2 Use the second conditional to talk about an unreal or imaginary situation and its consequences.

In spoken English, *would* is contracted in the positive and negative form.

*I'**d** be there if I had time. If she had enough food, she'**d** feed us all.*

Would is not usually contracted in the question form.

*If you passed your exam, **would** you go to university? **Would** you help me if I paid you?*

Use *If I were you …* to give advice: **If I were you,** *I'd change teams.*

Instead of *would*, we can use *could* or *should*: *If you got really fit, you **could** probably play again.*

It is common to use other expressions in the *would* clause: *would be able to*, *would need to* and *would have to*.

*If I lost my job, I'**d need to** find another one!*

*We **would have to** cancel the game if it rained.*

*If you bought a larger quantity, we'**d be able to** offer you a better deal.*

---

giving news

good news	I've got some good news (for you).
	I'm really pleased to tell you …
	You'll never guess what.
bad news	Bad news, I'm afraid.
	I'm sorry to have to tell you, but …
	I'm afraid/Unfortunately, …
	I'm afraid I've got some bad news …
	There's something I've got to tell you.
good or bad news	You know …? Well, …
	I've/We've got something to tell you.

6.3

responding to good news	Wow! That's fantastic/great news.
	Congratulations!
	You're joking!
	You lucky thing!
	Well done.
	Have you?/Did you?
responding to bad news	That's a shame.
	That's terrible/awful.
	That's really annoying.
	I'm really sorry to hear that.

PRACTICE

1 Complete the sentences with the correct form of the verbs in brackets.

1 If I _____ (pass) my exams, my teacher _____ (be) very surprised.

2 When we _____ (visit) my mother, she usually _____ (look after) the children.

3 When Gaby _____ (leave) her job in the summer, she _____ (worry) about what to do next.

4 If I _____ (not find) any cheap tickets, we _____ (not go) to Malta.

5 If you _____ (not water) plants, they _____ (die).

6 I _____ (be) surprised if Martha _____ (come) to the party. She said she wasn't feeling well.

7 If you _____ (get) lost, do you usually _____ (ask) someone for directions?

8 They _____ (not come) unless you _____ (invite) them.

9 If it _____ (be) a nice day, I _____ (like) to go for a run in the morning.

10 I _____ (listen) to classical music when I _____ (want) to relax.

2 Underline the correct alternative.

1 You can't come to the conference *unless/if/when* you're invited.

2 I'm not talking to you *unless/if/when* you calm down first.

3 They'll arrive as soon as dinner *is/will be/won't be* ready.

4 They'll cancel the flight *if/unless/when* the weather is bad.

5 If you eat all of that chocolate mousse, you *'ll feel/feel/won't feel* ill.

6 We'll organise a taxi when we *know/will know/might know* what time the concert starts.

7 When I see a spider, I always *scream/might scream/will scream*.

8 I'll get some money as soon as the bank *will open/opens/might open*.

6.1

---

1 Complete the sentences with the correct form of the verbs in brackets. Use contractions where possible.

1 If I _____ (sell) my house now, it _____ (not/be) worth very much.

2 _____ (your parents/come) if I _____ (organise) a party?

3 He _____ (not/be) able to study here if _____ (not/pass) that exam.

4 If you _____ (lose) your passport, _____ (need) visit the consulate.

5 They _____ (be) healthier if _____ (not/eat) so much junk food.

6 If you _____ (write) a novel, what _____ (call) it?

7 If the students _____ (not/have) internet access, _____ (find) it difficult.

8 We _____ (not/work) there if the boss _____ (not/give) us a lot of freedom.

9 Where _____ (she/live) if _____ (have) to move to a different country?

10 If he _____ (can) study on Tuesdays, _____ (not/need) to come on Wednesday.

2 Write answers to the questions using the prompts. Use contractions.

1 A: Can we walk to the game?
   B: No. (be/late)
   If we _walked to the game, we'd be late_____.

2 A: Why doesn't the team enter the competition?
   B: (it/lose)
   If the team _____.

3 A: Can I borrow his car?
   B: No. (get/angry)
   If you _____.

4 A: Why don't we call her now?
   B: No. (we/wake her up)
   If we _____.

5 A: Why can't we start the project again?
   B: (waste/money)
   If we _____.

6 A: Can we extend our holiday?
   B: No. (miss/school)
   If we _____.

6.2

---

1 Complete the conversations.

1 A: You'll never _____ what.
   B: What?
   A: I'm moving to Australia.
   B: You're _____!
   A: No, I'm leaving in March.
   B: You _____ thing.

2 A: I've passed my exams!
   B: _____ you? Congratulations!
   A: Yes, I got the results this morning.

3 A: There's _____ I've got to tell you.
   B: What is it?
   A: I've decided to leave my job at the university.
   B: I'm _____ to hear that. What's the problem?

4 A: I'm _____ we're going to be late.
   B: Why? What's happened?
   A: The flight's been delayed.
   B: Oh, that's a _____. That's really _____.

6.3

LANGUAGE BANK

present perfect simple vs continuous
present perfect continuous

7.1

+	I	've/have	been	reading a book.
	She	's/has		playing the piano.
-	You	haven't		listening to me.
?	Have	you		going there for a long time?

Use the present perfect simple or continuous for actions/ activities which started in the past and continue until now.

I've studied German for six years. *I've been studying* German for six years.

Often, there is little change in meaning between the two tenses (especially for verbs such as *live, work, teach, study*).

I've lived here for years. *I've been living* here for years.

Use the present perfect continuous to emphasise the length or duration of an activity.

I've been doing yoga for years. (but I'm still not very good at it)

He's been playing football since he was three.

As with other continuous forms, do not use the present perfect continuous with state verbs (e.g. *love, hate, enjoy, know*, etc.). With these verbs, use the present perfect simple.

I've known him for ages. NOT *I've been knowing* him for ages.

We often use *for, since* and *How long have you …?* with the present perfect simple and continuous.

How long have you been waiting *for*? She's been working here *since* 2010.

present and past ability
modal verbs to talk about ability

7.2

	present	past
+	I **can** cook.	I **could** run fast.
-	I **can't** drive.	He **couldn't** do maths.
?	**Can** you **speak** Spanish?	**Could** you **cook** when you were younger?

We can also use *be able to* to talk about ability.

	present	past
+	She**'s able to** write well.	Aged three, I **was able to** read.
-	He**'s not able to** drive.	Aged two, he **wasn't able to** walk.
?	**Is** he **able to** speak French?	**Were** you **able to** get a job?

Expressions to talk about ability at a particular moment

We can use *be able to* to talk about one particular situation.

*We **are able to*** offer you a special discount on the fridge today. *She didn't answer her phone so I **wasn't able to** speak to her.*

Use *manage to* to show that an action is/was difficult.

	present	past
+	I usually **manage to** finish my work on time.	We **managed to** book a great hotel.
-	I **don't** always **manage to** speak to my parents every week.	She **didn't manage to** pass the exam.
?	**Do** you **manage to** see the grandchildren regularly?	**Did** you **manage to** finish washing the dishes?

clarifying opinions

7.3

giving opinions
The reason I say this **is that** he didn't ask our permission.
For me, there are two options here.
In my view, we should stop selling the product.
I do think we should talk to them first.
I must say I agree with Robert.

giving examples
For example, she forgot her keys yesterday.
Let me give you an example: there was a festival last week.
For one thing, I don't like caviar.

PRACTICE

1 Complete the sentences with the present perfect simple or continuous form of the verbs in the box. Where both forms are possible, choose the present perfect continuous.

> do   sit   (not) listen   hate   (not) watch
> study   teach   (not) know   read   live   wait

1 I'm tired. I _____ in boring meetings all day.

2 They _____ for their exams since five o'clock this morning.

3 I'm glad you're here. We _____ for you all day.

4 I can't listen to jazz. I _____ always _____ it.

5 He _____ karate for nearly twenty years.

6 You _____ to me. You haven't heard what I said.

7 She's got a new job. She _____ economics at the university since June.

8 How long _____ you _____ in the UK? When did you move here?

9 I _____ TV. I _____ my book.

10 We _____ each other for very long.

2 Underline the correct alternative to complete the sentences.

1 Hi Tariq. I haven't *seen/been seeing* you for ages!

2 I have *been knowing/known* Justin since we were at school.

3 Yes, we've *met/been meeting* each other before.

4 I *'ve been playing/did played* the guitar for as long as I can remember.

5 My brother *has been travelling/have been travelled* around the world for the last two years.

6 He has always *been enjoying/enjoyed* travelling.

7 Excuse me. I *'ve been waiting/have wait* for this phone call all morning.

8 I *have studying/have been studying* Mandarin for more than ten years, and I still find it difficult.

---

1 Find and correct the mistakes. There are five mistakes in the text.

Johnny isn't able make full sentences but he can to say several words such as *Mama* and *Dada*, which he couldn't a month ago. He able to understand various commands like 'No!' and 'Come here' and he recognises his name. He's becoming more mobile; yesterday he managed crawl from the living room to the kitchen. He's also getting better with his hands. He can hold a pen and he sometimes manages to drawing simple pictures.

2 Rewrite the sentences using the words in brackets. Write three words (contractions are one word).

1 She knows how to ride a motorbike.

_____ a motorbike. (can)

2 I'm not able to play any instruments.

_____ any instruments. (can't)

3 Seyi and Denia couldn't come last night.

They _____ come last night. (able)

4 Were you able to take any photos?

_____ to take any photos? (manage)

5 Can you make pizza?

_____ to make pizza? (able)

6 I can usually sleep for eight hours even on a plane.

Usually I _____ for eight hours even on a plane. (manage)

7 Were you a fast runner when you were a child?

_____ fast when you were a child? (could)

8 I haven't finished my homework.

I _____ finish my homework. (managed)

---

1 Underline the correct alternative.

1 Jackie has been so nice. *For example,/For me,* she took us to the cinema.

2 You all think that new restaurant is great, but *for one thing/in my view* the food isn't that good.

3 Ibrahim said the concert was disappointing, and *I must say/the reason I say* I agree.

4 Shakespeare borrowed most of his stories. *Let me give you an example:/I must say* the plot of *King Lear* is taken from a much older story.

5 I like that laptop. *For one thing/I do think* it's a bit heavy, though.

6 People love the Rolling Stones, but *for me,/the reason I say this is* Led Zeppelin is the greatest rock band.

7 Dogs are the best pets. *For another/The reason I say this is because* they are so faithful.

8 You should buy that mobile. For one thing, it looks fantastic. *For another,/For example,* it's cheap.

7.1

7.2

7.3

8.1

articles

Use *a/an* (indefinite article):

- the first time something is mentioned. *I saw **a** mouse in the kitchen.*
- before singular nouns. *She's watching **a** film.*
- with jobs. *I'm **a** doctor. He's **an** artist.*

Use *the* (definite article):

- when there is only one of something. *I see **the** sun.*
- when something has been mentioned before. ***The** mouse (that I was talking about) was huge!*
- with seas, oceans, rivers and country names that are plural or use extra words like Kingdom, e.g. *the River Danube, the Pacific Ocean, the United Kingdom*
- before the names of some areas, e.g. *the south of France, the coast of Italy*
- with superlatives. *Ali was **the** greatest boxer.*
- with some defining expressions, e.g. *the first, the only*
- in some phrases with prepositions, e.g. *in the morning, at the end, by the next day*
- with dates in spoken English, e.g. *the fifth of June*

Use **no article** (zero article):

- to talk generally about things or people. *Doctors make more money than nurses.*
- with most names of towns, cities, and countries.
- before plural nouns. *I bought six bottles of water.*
- in some phrases with prepositions, e.g. *on Monday, at work, for lunch, on foot*
- with sports. *I like tennis. He plays football.*

quantifiers

Use ***some*** and ***any*** when talking about 'a limited amount/number' (not a large or small amount/number). We often use *some* in positive sentences. In this instance *several* can also be used. *I have **some** close friends. I have **several** close friends.*

We also use *some* in questions, especially in requests and offers. *Can you give me **some** sugar? Do you want **some** help?*

We often use *any* in negatives and questions. *I don't have **any** children.* Use ***much*** and ***many*** in questions and negatives. *Much* is used with large amounts of an uncountable noun: *How **much** time do we have? Many* is used with large numbers of a countable noun: *I don't have **many** friends.*

All means 'everything/everyone'. We can use it with or without *of*. ***All** the people here are friendly. **All of** the people here are friendly.*

We use ***a lot***, ***lots of***, and ***plenty of*** with large amounts/numbers. We usually use these in positive sentences. *Plenty of* means 'more than enough' (so there won't be a problem). *I spend **a lot of** time in Paris.*

Too and ***too much/many*** mean 'more than necessary'. We use *much* with uncountable nouns. We use *many* with countable nouns. *This film is **too long**. There's **too much** salt on this meat.*

Enough means 'as much as we need'. We use it in positive and negative sentences and questions. *I don't want this task because I have **enough** to do. There isn't **enough** time. Do you have **enough** sugar?*

None and ***no*** can mean 'zero'. We use *none of* + noun/pronoun. We use *no* + noun (without article or possessive adjective). ***None of** the cinemas showed the film. There are **no** reasons for this.*

A few means 'a small number'. We use it with countable nouns. We usually use it in positive sentences. *She knew **a few** actors.*

A little and ***a bit of*** mean 'a small amount'. We use them with uncountable nouns. We usually use them in positive sentences. *I asked for **a little** water. I need **a bit of** help.*

8.2

relative clauses

defining relative clauses

Use relative clauses to talk about what a person, place or thing is or does.

Use relative pronouns to join the main clause and the relative clause:

- *who* for people *He's the man **who** sold me the coat.*
- *where* for places *This is the town **where** I was born.*
- *which* for things *That computer **which** you showed me is very cheap.*
- *when* for times *This was the moment **when** Mr Moran knew he was in trouble.*
- *whose* for possessions (it means 'of which or of who') *This is Sarah, **whose** husband you met yesterday.*

We can use *that* instead of *which* or *who*. *Are you the lady **who/that** I spoke to on the phone? Is that the book **which/that** you lent me?*

We can leave out *who*, *which* and *that* when these words are not the subject of the relative clause. Compare: *She's the girl (**who**) I saw yesterday.* (The subject of the relative clause is *I* (not *who*). So we can omit *who*.) with *She's the girl **who** speaks French.* (The subject of the relative clause is *who*. So we cannot omit *who*.)

non-defining relative clauses

Use non-defining relative clauses to add extra non-essential information about a place, person or thing. The sentence is grammatically correct without the non-defining relative clause. Use a comma before the non-defining relative clause. Use a comma or a full-stop after it. We cannot omit the relative pronoun (*who*, *which that*, etc.) *They spoke to Tara, **who** was in a good mood.* We cannot use *that* instead of *which* or *who*. *I saw his latest film, **which** was terrible.*

8.3

being a good guest

asking for advice	
Is it OK if I (do this)?	Yes, of course. / No, you'd better not.
What should I do (in this situation)?	If I were you, I'd …
Do I need to (take off my shoes)?	Yes, you should. / No, it's not necessary.
Did I do something wrong?	It's OK. We can sort it out. / Don't worry about it.
Is this a bad time?	No. Come in. / Can you come back later?

apologising
Sorry about that. I didn't know (you were in a meeting).
My apologies. I didn't realise (you were busy).

PRACTICE

1 Find and correct the mistakes. There is one mistake with quantifiers or articles in each sentence.

1 Why don't you come and join us? There are plenty the seats.

2 Bobby's girlfriend is engineer.

3 Thousands of people were at the game, so there was lot of noise.

4 Yesterday we saw a doctor about my illness. Fortunately, a doctor said it was nothing serious.

5 Laila was hungry so she ate a bit bread.

6 The women live longer than men.

7 We went to the party but there weren't much people there.

8 We looked up and saw an aeroplane in sky.

9 I can't buy it because I only have a few money left.

10 My wife and I have lived in United States for several years.

2 Complete the story with the words in the box.

| a   an   the (x3)   much   many   few   little   lot |

¹_____ old man reaches his 120th birthday. ²_____ journalist comes to interview him. 'What is the secret of your long life?' he asks. 'Well,' says ³_____ old man, 'I don't have ⁴_____ problems, I don't drink ⁵_____ alcohol, I eat a ⁶_____ of good food, and I spend a ⁷_____ time every day relaxing. But do you want to know my real secret? I never disagree with anyone.' 'That's ridiculous!' says ⁸_____ journalist. 'There must be another secret.'
A ⁹_____ moments later, ¹⁰_____ old man says, 'OK, you're right.'

8.1

---

1 Complete the sentences with who, which, where, when or whose.

1 I met a man _____ house had burned down.

2 This was the moment _____ we knew we would win.

3 I spent several months in Rome, _____ is my favourite city.

4 The village, _____ Teresa grew up poor but happy, was very small.

5 The girl _____ sold you the carpet is from Morocco.

6 That blog, _____ he writes every day, is one of the most popular in the country.

7 Jill married a guy _____ she met on a dating site.

8 I don't want to be with someone _____ whole life is spent surfing the net.

2 Rewrite the sentences using relative clauses. Use the words in italics and the words in the box.

| that   who (x2)   which (x2)   where   when   whose |

1 What's this programme? Did you want to watch it?
   Is this the programme _____that you wanted to watch_____?

2 Last year I met a translator. She spoke six languages.
   Last year I met a translator _____.

3 It was six o'clock on the fifth of August. At that moment, the world changed forever.
   It was six o'clock on the fifth of August _____.

4 They gave Jodie an apple. She ate it quickly.
   They gave Jodie an apple, _____.

5 You see that apartment? Felipe lived there.
   That's the apartment _____.

6 She spent a month in Manchester. She loved it.
   She spent a month in Manchester, _____.

7 The boss's office is next to mine. He's always shouting!
   The boss, _____.

8 My boyfriend is coming to visit me. He lives in Barcelona.
   My boyfriend, _____.

8.2

---

1 Put the words in the correct order to make conversations.

1 A: do / to / hand / I / everyone's / shake / need / ?
   B: no, / necessary / not / it's

2 A: / is / if / it / I / into / take / meeting / coffee / OK / the / ?
   B: yes, / course / of

3 A: I / to / realise / didn't / I / send / by / the / information / had / email.
   B: It's OK. we / out / it / sort / can

4 A: did / wrong / something / do / I / ?
   B: don't / it / about / worry

5 A: what / I / late / do / if / should / am / I / ?
   B: if / you / I / were, / I'd / an / train / earlier / catch

6 A: / sorry / that / about. I / you / know / here / were / didn't
   B: No problem.

7 A: is / a / bad / time / this / ?
   B: fine. / it's / No,

8.3

third conditional

9.1

if clause	*would* clause
if + *had* + past participle	*would have* + past participle
If I **had seen** my friend,	I **would have spoken** to her.

Use the third conditional to talk about hypothetical or imaginary situations in the past. It describes an unreal or impossible situation, e.g. Real situation = I woke up late. Hypothetical situation (third conditional): *If I had heard my alarm clock, I wouldn't have woken up late.* (I didn't hear my alarm clock. I woke up late.)

We can start sentences and questions with the *if* or *would* clause.

*They **wouldn't have been** late if they had caught the bus.*

*If they **had caught** the bus, they **wouldn't have been** late.*

*What would you **have done** if I hadn't called? If I **hadn't called**, what **would you have** done?*

Note: When the sentence starts with *if*, we use a comma after the *if* clause.

In written and spoken English, we use contractions with third conditional sentences except in very formal documents.

She'd have told us if she'd heard anything. We wouldn't have left early if we'd known you were coming.

The defendant would not have been caught if he had stayed in his home. (formal)

active vs passive
the passive

9.2

	active	passive
present simple	The shop **doesn't accept** credit cards.	Credit cards **aren't accepted** here.
present continuous	**Is** anyone **using** that computer at the moment?	**Is** that computer **being used** at the moment?
past simple	Someone **told** us to be here at 8.00.	We **were told** to be here at 8.00.
present perfect	No one **has asked** us about the date.	We **haven't been asked** about the date.
will	Someone **will give** me a car on my next birthday.	I'll **be given** a car on my next birthday.

Use the active voice to talk about the things people do, e.g. *Sam ate the chicken.*

To make the passive, use subject + *be* + past participle. Use the passive voice:

• to talk about what happens to things or people. *Khaled has been given a prize.*

• when we don't know the doer (the person or thing that does the action). *The film star was murdered.*

• when the identity of the doer of the action is not important. *This cheese is made in Italy.* (It's not important who actually makes it.)

• if the doer of the action is obvious. *The thief was arrested.* (The police are the only people who could arrest the thief.)

If we want to say who does/did the action, we use *by*. *The microwave oven was invented by Percy LeBaron Spencer.*

We sometimes use the passive to emphasise a particular part of the sentence. Compare:

Frank Lloyd Wright designed the Guggenheim Museum of Art in New York. with *The Guggenheim Museum of Art in New York was designed by Frank Lloyd Wright.*

In the second sentence, the emphasis is on Frank Lloyd Wright.

The passive is often used in newspaper reports and other formal writing.

expressing uncertainty

9.3

saying you don't know
I have no idea.*
I haven't a clue.*

*These are both informal.

saying you are not sure, but you have an idea
I'm not a hundred percent certain* but it might be …
I'm fairly sure* it's …

*Sure and certain mean the same thing. We can use either of them in these expressions.

saying you know what it isn't
It's definitely not …
I'm sure it isn't …

saying you used to know
I can't remember.
I've forgotten.

PRACTICE

1 Match 1–8 with a)–h) to make sentences.

1 If we had arrived earlier,
2 I wouldn't have told her
3 If he hadn't fallen asleep,
4 We would have called you
5 If I'd done all my homework,
6 John would have brought a present
7 If the teacher hadn't helped him,
8 I would have bought that computer

a) he would have failed the exam.
b) if he'd known it was your birthday.
c) he wouldn't have crashed the car.
d) we wouldn't have missed the plane.
e) if it had been on sale.
f) if I'd known it was a secret.
g) I would have passed the course.
h) if we'd had your number.

9.1

2 Rewrite the sentences using the third conditional.

1 Maya was late for the meeting. Her car broke down.
If Maya's car hadn't _____.
2 She felt ill so she didn't come to the concert.
She would _____.
3 I didn't get the job. I wasn't qualified.
If I had _____.
4 They didn't buy the house. They didn't have enough money.
They would _____.
5 We lost the game. Our best player was injured.
If our best player hadn't _____.
6 You didn't tell me you were coming so I didn't cook a meal.
I would _____.

---

1 Underline the correct alternative.

1 Oh no! My wallet *has being stolen/has been stolen/has stolen*!
2 Were those documents *be sent/send/sent* by email or by post?
3 Not many houses *are been built/are being built/are being build* at the moment.
4 That piano *isn't been played/hasn't be played/hasn't been played* for years.
5 Cars that are parked illegally will *be removed/ being removed/ to be removed*.
6 Are those toys *make/be made/made* by hand?
7 We *weren't employed/not were employed/weren't employ* by the government until 1998.
8 We can't use the photocopier because it's *being repaired/repairing/be repaired* right now.

9.2

2 Complete the sentences with the active or passive form of the verbs in brackets. Use the verb tense in italics.

1 The magazine _____ (read) mainly by teenagers. It _____ (publish) every month. *present simple*
2 Most of his programmes _____ (not film) in Europe; he usually _____ (work) in Asia. *present simple*
3 The book _____ (write) by an ex-soldier. It _____ (describe) the war in Vietnam. *past simple*
4 My last company _____ (make) clothes. It _____ (buy) by a multinational company called Zed. *past simple*
5 The buildings _____ (clean) and the walls _____ (paint). *present perfect*
6 I _____ (give) a new office but I _____ (not move) my things in there yet. *present perfect*
7 Today this dish _____ (not cook) in the oven. Instead, we _____ (use) the grill. *present continuous*
8 English _____ (not spoken) everywhere in future. Lots of people _____ (not speak) it. *future (will)*

---

1 Underline the correct alternative to complete the sentences.

1 What's my PIN number? *I'm forgetting/I forgotten/I've forgotten*.
2 Can you smoke in the restaurant? *I'm sure isn't/I sure it isn't/I'm sure it isn't* legal.
3 What is this drink? It's *definitely am not/definitely not/definite not* orange juice.
4 How old is he? I'm *surely fair/fair sure/fairly sure* he's twenty.

9.3

5 What's Maria's second name? I *haven't the clue/have a clue/haven't a clue*.
6 What's the world's biggest building? I *have no idea/have not idea/am no idea*.
7 Where do the Smiths live? I *not remember/can't to remember/can't remember*.
8 When does the game start? I'm not *a hundred percent certain/certain hundred percent/the hundred percent certain* but it might be at 2.00.

reported speech

direct speech (actual words)	reported speech
'I always **buy** organic food.'	He said (that) he always **bought** organic food.
'I'm **going** to see my mother tomorrow.'	She told me she **was going** to see her mother **the next day**.
'I've **passed my** exams.'	He said he **had passed his** exams.
'We **saw** her at the station.'	They said they **had seen** her at the station.
'I'll **meet you here.**'	He said he **would** meet me **there**.
'I **can't** hear you.'	She said she **couldn't** hear me.
'We **might** be late.'	They said they **might** be late.
'I **must** leave at midday.'	He said he **had to** leave at midday.

10.1

Use reported speech to report what someone said earlier. After a past tense reporting verb, e.g. *said, told,* etc., the original verb often moves one tense back (this is sometimes called 'backshifting').

There may be other changes to pronouns, possessive adjectives, and to references of time or place.

'I'll go.' → **She** said **she would** go.

'It's my car.' → **He** said it was **his** car.

'We'll see you tomorrow.' → **They** said they would see **us the next day.**

'I'll be here.' → **She** said **she would** be there.

Must changes to *had to*, but *mustn't* doesn't change.

'We mustn't be late.' → **They** said **they mustn't** be late. NOT ~~They said they didn't have to be late.~~

Could, would and *might* also don't change in reported speech.

'We **might** see you later.' → **They** said (that) **they might** see us later.

Say and *tell* are the most common reporting verbs. Note the different verb patterns.

He **told me** *that he'd be late.* *She* **said** *(to me) that she wanted to stay.*

Sometimes there is no need to change the tenses (no backshift). This is the case when the reporting verb is in the present tense.

'I'll meet you at the airport.' → *He* **says** *he'll meet us at the airport.*

If the information we are reporting is still true in the present, we do not need to change the tenses but if the reporting verb is in the past, we can.

'It's a great film.' → *She said* **that it's** *a great film.* (This is still true now.) or *She said* **that it was** *a great film.* (Implies she's seen it and thought it was good at the time.)

reported questions

Reported questions have the same tense and word changes as reported statements. To report a *yes/no* question, use *if/whether* after the reporting verb.

'Do you live in Peru?' → *She asked me* **if** *I lived in Peru.* or *She asked me* **whether** *I lived in Peru.*

To report a *Wh-* question, use the question word.

'Where is the restaurant?' → *She asked me* **where** *the restaurant was.*

In reported questions, the word order is the same as for statements. We do not use an auxiliary *do/does/did.*

'Do you like eating sushi?' → *She asked me* **if I like eating** *sushi.*

verb patterns

Many different structures can follow a verb in English. Some verbs are followed by an *-ing* form, and some are followed by the infinitive.

I can't **stand listening** *to opera.* *He* **learned to speak** *Mandarin when he moved to China.*

verb + infinitive with *to*: agree, ask, tell, expect, learn, manage, help, decide, offer, promise, want, refuse, need

10.2

We **managed to get** *to the theatre on time.* *They* **agreed to give** *us cheap tickets.*

verb + *-ing*: like, love, hate, can't stand, (be) keen on, look forward to, miss, enjoy, fancy, give up, practise

I **miss spending** *time with my friends and family.* *We* **look forward to seeing** *you.*

Reporting verbs use many different verb patterns, so it's important to learn the patterns. Some verbs can use more than one structure, e.g. *suggest*

He **suggested that** *we meet at 6p.m.* *She* **suggested having** *lunch in the cafeteria.*

verb + infinitive with *to*: offer, promise, refuse, agree

They **offered to give** *us a lift to the station.* *They* **promised to phone** *when they arrive.*

verb + object + infinitive with *to*: invite, warn, tell, ask

They **invited us to stay** *for the weekend.* *He* **warned them not to tell** *anyone.*

verb + *-ing*: suggest, recommend

They **suggested trying** *another restaurant.* *He* **recommended eating** *at Café Fish.*

verb + *that*: explain, warn (someone), promise (someone), suggest

She **explained that** *she had to leave the meeting.* *He* **promised that** *he would take me out tonight.*

giving advice/warnings

10.3

advice	warnings
Make sure you … / If I were you, I'd …	Watch out for … / Be careful to/of …
Don't forget to … / You need to …	Don't … (or else …) / You'd better …
The most important thing is to …	Whatever you do, don't …

PRACTICE

1 Complete the reported statements using tense changes (backshift).

1 'We're going to have a baby.'

_He said (that) _____ _____ going to have a baby._

2 'I've lived here for more than twenty years.'

_She _____ that she had lived _____ for more than twenty years._

3 'We grew these carrots in our garden.'

_They told us that they _____ grown the carrots in _____ garden._

4 'I have to go to the dentist tomorrow.'

_He said (that) he _____ to go to the dentist the _____ day._

5 'I've lost my passport.'

_She said that _____ had lost _____ passport._

6 'I'm feeling a bit stressed.'

_She _____ me that she _____ feeling a bit stressed._

7 'We'd never been to the US before.'

_They said that _____ _____ never been to the US before._

8 'I can't stay long because I have to go to a meeting.'

_She said that she _____ stay long because she _____ to go to a meeting._

2 Using the words in italics, rewrite the sentences as reported speech.

1 'I think that La Tasca's is my favourite restaurant.'

_She said that _____._

2 'I'm going to meet Mr Susuki this afternoon.'

_He told me _____._

3 'Maja called me yesterday.'

_He said that _____._

4 'We'll meet you here tomorrow.'

_They told us that _____._

5 'We haven't received your application.'

_We told her that _____._

6 'I might see you at the party, Matt.'

_She told Matt _____._

7 'I've already sent you an email explaining the situation.'

_He said that _____._

8 'I can't type very fast.'

_She told her boss that _____._

1 Complete the reported statements below with the verbs in the box and any other necessary words.

| refuse | agree | promise | suggest | offer | warn | invite | explain |

1 'I'm afraid I'm not going to pay for this meal.'

_He ___refused to pay___ for the meal._

2 'You need to show your passport to immigration,' she said to him.

_She _____ he _____ his passport to immigration._

3 'If you book your tickets in advance, you'll get two for the price of one,' she told us.

_She _____ our tickets in advance._

4 'I'll pick you up on the way to the station.'

_He _____ pick me up on the way to the station._

5 'Why don't you all come for lunch on Sunday?'

_She _____ us _____ for lunch on Sunday._

6 'I'll definitely cook something for dinner.'

_He _____ something for dinner._

7 'Be careful to hold on to your bags at the station.'

_She _____ on to our bags at the station._

8 'Yes. It's a good idea to have the meeting on Tuesday.'

_He _____ the meeting on Tuesday._

2 Find and correct the mistakes. There are mistakes in six of the sentences.

1 The company has agreed that pay for the trip.

2 They recommended going to a different hotel.

3 I suggested to that she look for another job.

4 She suggested to call an ambulance.

5 We offered helping, but there was nothing we could do.

6 The manager refused let us leave the hotel before we met his wife.

7 We promised to sending her a postcard.

8 I explained that there had been a delay.

1 Make sentences giving advice/warnings using the prompts.

1 forget / set / alarm.

2 you / need / buy / ticket / before / get on the train

3 if I / you / call them / before you leave

4 watch out / speed cameras. There / lots on the road.

5 make sure / apply for a visa

6 whatever / do / don't / leave valuable items / the room

7 important / thing / check / flight times

8 forget / take your mobile phone

VOCABULARY BANK

FAMILY

1 Complete the family tree with the words in the box.

~~in-laws~~   sister-in-law   niece   nephew   grandparents on my mother's side   ex-husband   stepfather   stepdaughter

COLLOCATIONS with *take, get, do* and *go*

1 Add the words/expressions in italics to the correct places in each word web.

1 *your best, exercise, nothing for you, the cleaning*

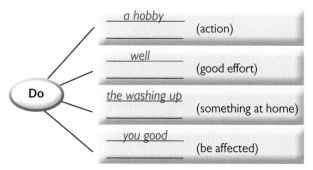

a hobby	(action)
well	(good effort)
the washing up	(something at home)
you good	(be affected)

Do

3 *a look, the blame, sugar, ages*

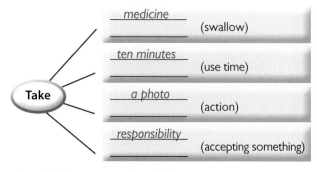

medicine	(swallow)
ten minutes	(use time)
a photo	(action)
responsibility	(accepting something)

Take

2 *fired, a prize, excited, food poisoning*

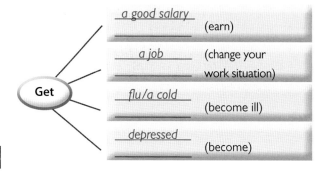

a good salary	(earn)
a job	(change your work situation)
flu/a cold	(become ill)
depressed	(become)

Get

4 *on holiday, crazy, together, badly*

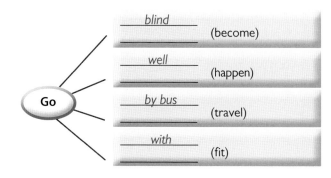

blind	(become)
well	(happen)
by bus	(travel)
with	(fit)

Go

PREPOSITIONS of place

1 Match descriptions 1–5 with pictures A–E.

1 They drove <u>along</u> the motorway, and <u>over</u> the bridge.
2 They went <u>around</u> the city.
3 They drove <u>through</u> the main square, <u>past</u> the post office and turned left <u>by</u> the station.
4 The hotel is <u>near</u> the city centre, <u>between</u> the National Museum and the cathedral.
5 The house is <u>next to</u> the supermarket, <u>opposite</u> the cinema.

A

B

C

D

E

NEWS

1 Read the text and match the words/phrases in bold with definitions 1–13 below.

1 continued to _____ _____
2 a group of criminals who work together _____
3 took someone away because they have done something illegal _____
4 thieves carrying weapons _____ _____
5 an attack by criminals on a bank, shop, etc., to steal money or valuable things _____
6 (doing something) while threatening to shoot someone _____ _____
7 people whose job it is to protect people or a place, or to make sure that a person does not escape _____ _____
8 leave a place or dangerous situation when someone is trying to catch you _____
9 people who saw the crime _____ _____
10 tried _____
11 warn people that something bad is happening _____ _____ _____
12 made someone do this _____
13 a vehicle for the escape _____ _____

Two **security guards** were kidnapped and held hostage for twelve hours by a **gang** of **armed robbers**, who **attempted** to **raid** a security depot. The robbers held the guards **at gunpoint** and **forced** them to hand over keys and security information. They then **proceeded to** fill a lorry with more than £53 million in notes. Another £150 million was left behind because there was no more room in the **getaway vehicle**. Luckily, one of the guards managed to **raise the alarm**, and the police arrived and **arrested** the gang before they could **escape**. **Eye witnesses** said that they saw at least eight men being arrested.

VOCABULARY BANK

COMMUNICATION

1A Underline the phrases in sentences 1–8 which involve communicating.

1 She tried to <u>get hold of you</u> but your mobile was dead.
2 I'm going to have a chat with Tom about his appearance.
3 The film director got in touch with him through his agent.
4 I don't get what you mean.
5 She goes on and on about her problems – it's so boring!
6 I'm so pleased we've stayed in touch all these years.
7 We said sorry for the mess.
8 They sometimes have arguments about money.

B Match the underlined phrases in Exercise 1A with phrases a)–h) below.

a) talk to
b) disagree
c) contact you *get hold of you*
d) apologised
e) understand
f) maintained contact
g) contacted
h) talks too much

IDIOMS

1A Match pictures A–F with the idioms in the box.

| be in two minds   let your hair down   break the ice   travel light |
| learn (something) by heart   go window shopping |

A

B

C

D

E

F

B Complete the sentences with the idioms above.

1 Tomorrow there's a test on this poem. I have to _____ it _____ _____.
2 I'm _____ _____ _____. I don't know if I want the black one or the red one.
3 Everyone was nervous, so Jackie told a few jokes to _____ _____ _____.
4 He always _____ _____. He only takes one suitcase even for long trips.
5 I've got no money at the moment but we can go _____ _____ if you want.
6 You've been working non-stop. Why don't you go out and _____ _____ _____ _____?

C What do you think the idioms mean? Use a dictionary to help you.

PERSONAL QUALITIES

1A Complete the sentences with the adjectives in the box.

> reliable   sensible   easy-going
> aggressive   clever/bright   honest
> lazy   punctual   moody
> independent

1 She is very _____. She works well by herself.

2 You never know what to expect. She's very _____, so one minute she's happy, and the next minute, she's shouting at you.

3 She's very _____. I'm sure she will know what to do if there's a difficult situation.

4 He's extremely _____. He is never late for appointments.

5 My new manager is very _____. She doesn't mind what time we get to work, what we wear. She never looks stressed.

6 He always tells the truth. He's very _____.

7 She likes to do as little work as possible. She's a bit _____.

8 He's very _____. He learns very quickly.

9 You know that you can trust and depend on him. He's hardworking and very _____.

10 He nearly attacked one of his employees when he arrived late for the meeting. He's very _____.

You're late!

B Look at the adjectives in the box again. Do they describe positive or negative characteristics? Do you have any of these characteristics?

WORKING LIFE

1 Match descriptions 1–3 with jobs A–C.

1 I work as a _____ for a large corporation. I usually **work nine-to-five**, but sometimes I have to work late. My job involves **checking and responding to emails, answering phone enquiries** and **organising** my boss's diary.

A Window cleaner

2 I'm an _____. I tend to **work long hours. I'm responsible for** a small team of people. I spend a lot of my time **attending meetings**, and **dealing with problems. I advise clients** on their accounts and **write updates and reports** for the website.

B Personal assistant

3 I'm a _____. Lots of people wouldn't like what I do, because it's **an outdoor job**, and it's a **physical job**, but I love it. **I work for myself**, so I can be very independent, and I **work flexible hours**, which is good for me. It's a very sociable job, too. I talk to people all day long. I couldn't do **an office job**. I would die of boredom!

C Accountant

B Work in pairs. What do the phrases in bold mean?

CONFUSING WORDS

1A Choose the correct option from the words in bold to complete the pairs of sentences.

1 **actually • currently**

a) I expected the first week in my new job to be awful, but _____ it was fine.

b) I am _____ working in London, but before I was working in Paris.

2 **career • course**

a) She's doing a Spanish _____ at the moment, and she's really enjoying it.

b) Ted spent most of his _____ as a teacher.

3 **borrow • lend**

a) Do you think you could _____ me a pen?

b) I had to _____ some money from a friend.

4 **argument • discussion**

a) We had an interesting _____ about the Prime Minister and we all agreed he should resign.

b) I had an _____ with my mother. She's always telling me what to do!

5 **miss • lose**

a) Hurry up, or we'll _____ the bus.

b) Why do I always _____ my car keys?

B Check your answers in a dictionary.

VOCABULARY BANK

TECHNOLOGY

1 Match words/phrases 1–10 with pictures A–J.

1 plug it in
2 press the button
3 have an injection
4 have an operation
5 run out of petrol
6 break down
7 (not) get a connection
8 restart/reboot the computer
9 do an experiment
10 switch it on/off

A

B

C

D

E

F

G

H

I

J

WORD-BUILDING nouns (suffixes)

1A Look at the table which shows six different suffixes used to form nouns from verbs and adjectives.

-ation	education relaxation imagination immigration
-ion	pollution instruction depression competition
-ment	entertainment improvement employment agreement
-ing	running smoking laughing eating
-ness	weakness loneliness happiness kindness
-ity	creativity stupidity sensitivity responsibility

B Cover the table and complete sentences 1–10 with the correct form of the verbs/adjectives in brackets.

1 I think a bit of _____ (compete) in schools is a good thing.
2 There has been a great _____ (improve) in his work recently.
3 Dealing with problem clients is not my _____ (responsible).
4 _____ (lonely) is one of the worst aspects of getting old.
5 He suffers from _____ (depress).
6 Try to use your _____ (imagine).
7 I couldn't believe my own _____ (stupid)!
8 There is live _____ (entertain) from 8p.m.
9 I was amazed by his _____ (kind).
10 I didn't hear the last _____ (instruct).

EMOTIONS

1 Complete definitions 1–10 with the correct form of the adjectives in the box.

> exciting/excited   terrifying/terrified
> astonishing/astonished   tiring/tired
> fascinating/fascinated
> disappointing/disappointed
> disgusting/disgusted
> frustrating/frustrated
> depressing/depressed
> interesting/interested

1 you want to know more about it and you give it your attention: *I was _____ in what he had to say.*

2 being happy, interested and hopeful because something good has happened, or is going to happen: *The kids are getting really _____ about the trip.*

3 very surprising: *It's _____ that you didn't know about this!*

4 making you feel that you want to sleep or rest: *It was a long, _____ journey.*

5 extremely interesting: *Istanbul is a _____ city.*

6 unhappy because something you hoped for did not happen: *I was _____ that I hadn't won.*

7 making you feel sad: *It's a very _____ book. I didn't like it at all.*

8 extremely unpleasant and making you feel sick: *What's that smell? It's _____!*

9 feeling annoyed, upset or impatient because you cannot control/change a situation: *He gets _____ when people don't understand what he's saying.*

10 very frightened: *I'm absolutely _____ of spiders!*

MULTI-WORD VERBS

1A Match the phrasal verbs in sentences 1–10 with meanings a–j.

verb + off

1 I called him on the phone but we got **cut off**.

2 They had to **call off** the football match because of the weather.

3 I have to do this work. I can't **put** it **off** any longer.

verb + out

4 I'd like to **check out** some other options.

5 He's wearing a pink jacket so he'll **stand out** from the crowd.

6 I can't **work out** what to do about the problem.

verb + after

7 My neighbour is **looking after** my cats when we go away.

8 He **takes after** his father. They are both very good-looking.

verb + in

9 Can you print out and then **fill in** the form and send it back to me?

10 Saskia, please **let** me **in**!

a) delay doing something

b) the phone suddenly stopped working.

c) look/behave like an older member of the family

d) get more information about something

e) allow someone to come in

f) decide that a planned event won't happen

g) be easy to see/notice

h) take care of something or someone

i) write the necessary information in an official document

j) decide/plan something to solve a problem

B Label pictures A–E with the sentences above.

A   B   C   D   E   F

VOCABULARY BANK

SUCCESS

1A Match expressions 1–10 with definitions a)–j).

1 be on a shortlist *b)*
2 come first *a)*
3 be nominated
4 be awarded
5 win a medal
6 win an award
7 be on the winning team
8 be a runner up
9 get an 'A'
10 win a prize

a) win
b) be named in a list (chosen from a larger group) to be considered for a prize or job
c) be officially suggested as a possible prize winner (or candidate for an important job)
d) be given an official prize/money
e) receive a prize/money because of an achievement
f) receive a valuable piece of metal because of success in a competition (or bravery, e.g. in war)
g) be part of a group that wins a game/competition
h) come in second place in a competition, race, etc.
i) get something because you are successful in a competition, race, etc.
j) get the highest grade for a piece of academic work

B Look at the situations opposite and complete the captions with the words in the box.

| awarded | winning | medal | award | got | prize |
| nominated | runner up | shortlist | came | | |

'I ¹_____ first.'
'I was the ²_____.'
'I won the bronze ³_____.'

'I won a ⁴_____ for best student! I ⁵_____ A's in all my exams!'

'I was ⁶_____ for Best Actor but I didn't win. The Oscar was ⁷_____ to Rick Rooney.'

'My book was on a ⁸_____ for Book of the Year, but it didn't win. I've never won an ⁹_____.'

'I was on the ¹⁰_____ team!'

VERB PHRASES with prepositions

1A In each sentence the same preposition is missing twice. Complete the sentences with the prepositions in the box.

| to | on | in | for | about | with |

1 I couldn't cope _____ my boss any more so I decided to part _____ the company.
2 The journalist wrote _____ the farm workers, who were protesting _____ their low salary.
3 Always stick _____ what you believe in; this will lead _____ true happiness.
4 She worked _____ a rich family, and her job was to care _____ the sick grandmother.
5 The scientists started working _____ a project, but without any money they couldn't go _____.
6 Aged ten, she took part _____ a play and this resulted _____ her love of the theatre.

B Match the verb phrases in Exercise 1A with definitions a)–k).

a) create a text *write about*
b) look after
c) refuse to change your mind
d) be involved in
e) be employed by
f) cause something to happen (two phrases)
g) spend time and effort doing something
h) leave
i) continue
j) deal with a difficult problem or situation successfully
k) show publicly that you think something is wrong

GETTING ON

1A Match 1–6 with a)–f) to complete the sentences.

My neighbour:

1 is very helpful. For example,
2 sometimes borrows my tools
3 pops over most days, because
4 lends me sugar or milk
5 is really unfriendly. She
6 is always gossiping

a) but he never gives them back!
b) he fixed my car last year.
c) doesn't even say 'good morning'.
d) she likes to chat.
e) about people who live in the street.
f) if I need it.

B Underline the words/phrases in 1–6 which match definitions a)–f).

a) comes to my house (informally)
b) not friendly
c) uses my possessions
d) gives me things (which I will later return)
e) helps a lot
f) talking about other people (usually bad things)

COMPOUND NOUNS

1A Put the words next to the correct key word to make compound nouns. Which compound nouns are written as one word? Use a dictionary to check.

~~racket~~   office   barrier   cream   code   shop
machine   player   lab   tan   court   cup   learner
card   glasses

1 tennis   _racket_
           _____
           _____

2 coffee   _____
           _____
           _____

3 post   _____
           _____
           _____

4 language   _____
           _____
           _____

5 sun   _____
           _____
           _____

B Put the key words in the correct places. Which compound nouns are written as one word? Use a dictionary to check.

book   machine   phone   room   shoes

1 running
   sports   _____
   high-heeled

2 cheque
   picture   _____
   text

3 bed
   dining   _____
   changing

4 sewing
   washing   _____
   drinks

5 mobile
   pay   _____
   cell

HISTORY

1 Use one word from each row in the table to complete sentences 1–12.

noun	verb	adjective	person
invasion	invade		invader
history		historical/historic	historian
colonisation/colony	colonise		coloniser
democracy	democratise	democratic	democrat
liberation	liberate		liberator
discovery	discover		discoverer
leadership	lead		leader
politics		political	politician
development	develop	developing	developer
invention	invent	inventive	inventor
foundation	found	founding	founder
independence		independent	

I   1066 is the date of the Norman _invasion_ of Britain.

2   Edward Gibbon was a great _____. He wrote *The History of the Decline and Fall of the Roman Empire*.

3   India was a _____ of Great Britain until 1947.

4   South Africa's first _____ elections, in which black people could vote, took place in 1994.

5   In the eighteenth and nineteenth centuries, William Wilberforce led a movement to _____ slaves.

6   Alexander Fleming is known for his _____ of penicillin.

7   Fidel Castro was the _____ of the Cuban revolution of 1959.

8   The Kennedys and the Bush family are known for their involvement in American _____.

9   The World Bank lends money to _____ countries, particularly in Asia and Africa.

10 In 1901 Wilhelm Rontgen won the Nobel Prize in Physics for his _____ of the X-ray.

11 Bill Gates is the _____ of Microsoft.

12 Angola gained its _____ from Portugal in 1975.

COLLOCATIONS with *come, give, have* and *make*

1 Put the words/expressions in italics into the correct places in each word web.

I   *across the mountain, with instructions, to dinner, nearer*

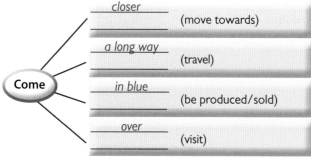

closer _____ (move towards)
a long way _____ (travel)
Come in blue _____ (be produced/sold)
over _____ (visit)

3   *a cold, a chance, ideas, 100 calories*

210 pages _____ (contain)
memories _____ (thoughts)
Have a disease _____ (illness)
a choice _____ (opportunity)

2   *a prize, permission, orders, me a headache*

advice _____ (tell someone something)
a donation _____ (present)
Give responsibility _____ (allow)
me a shock _____ (cause feelings)

4   *a living, an agreement, a film, an effort*

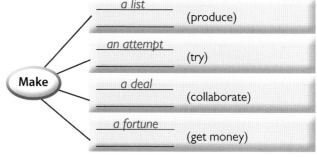

a list _____ (produce)
an attempt _____ (try)
Make a deal _____ (collaborate)
a fortune _____ (get money)

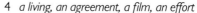

THE ENVIRONMENT

1A Complete the text with words/phrases from the box with the same meaning as the words/phrases in brackets.

> global warming   pollution   aerosol cans   protect   industrial waste
> factory smoke   natural resources   destroys the environment
> harmful   environmentally-friendly   car exhaust fumes
> destruction of the rainforest

Many people are worried about the state of the planet, and the effects of [1]*global warming* (an increase in world temperatures, caused by an increase in carbon dioxide around the Earth). A growing human population is putting pressure on the Earth's [2]_____ _____, (things that exist in nature and can be used by people, for example oil, trees, etc.) like food and water. Also, a lot of human activity is [3]_____ (causes damage), either because it causes [4]_____ (dirty air, water or land), or because it [5]_____ _____ _____ (damages the air, water and land so badly that it might not recover). Some of the most common causes of damage are:

* [6]_____ _____ (chemicals and unwanted materials which factories throw away)
* [7]_____ _____ and [8]_____ _____ _____
* [9]_____ _____ (which contain CFCs – a chemical which damages the ozone layer)
* [10]_____ _____ _____ _____ – which increases the amount of carbon dioxide in the atmosphere.

Environmentalists try to [11]_____ the environment (keep it safe from harm) by encouraging people to change the way they live (recycling more, using [12]_____ _____ or 'green' products which do not damage the environment, wasting less, etc.) and persuading governments to take environmental issues more seriously.

B Complete the table with words from the text in Exercise 1A.

noun	verb
[1]_____	destroy
protection	[2]_____
[3]_____	pollute
[4]_____	damage
waste	[5]_____

WORD-BUILDING (prefixes)

1 Look at the prefixes in the table and complete sentences 1–12 with a suitable form of the words in brackets.

in-	**in**visible
	inappropriate
	inaccurate
	inadequate
	inability
im-	**im**mature
	impossible
	impolite
	immobile
	immoral
ir-	**ir**responsible
	irregular
	irrelevant
	irrational
ex-	**ex**-girlfriend
	ex-Prime Minister
	ex-husband
	ex-boss
	ex-wife

1 The number is not correct. It's _____. (accurate)

2 Let me introduce you to my _____, Amelia. (wife)

3 I can't do it. It's _____! (possible)

4 It's difficult to travel because the buses and trains are very _____. (regular)

5 You can't leave without saying goodbye. It's _____. (polite)

6 She behaves like a child. She's very _____. (mature)

7 You can't come to the office dressed like that. It's _____. (appropriate)

8 He left his laptop on the train. He's very _____. (responsible)

9 I used to work for him. He's my _____. (boss)

10 There is no good reason for it. It's completely _____. (rational)

11 It doesn't do the job. It's _____. (adequate)

12 She refused to move at all. She was _____. (mobile)

1.2

4C Look at your drawing. Does it include these things?

1 wheels   2 handlebar   3 saddle   4 chain

5 crossbar   6 pedals

1.2

8B Read the text and check your answers.

Stella magazine commissioned YouGov, a research agency, to interview over 1,000 women in the UK about what they really think. Here are some of the results.

80% of women say that losing their health is their greatest concern, followed by putting on weight (52%) and losing their jobs (24%). It seems that British women aren't too happy with their bodies: 23% of women are on a diet now and 58% have **gone on a diet** in the past. Only 4% of women **do** more than 7 hours' **exercise** per week, while 21% do no exercise at all.

The biggest challenge for modern women is balancing home and work life (82%), followed by bringing up happy children (56%) and finding time for themselves (52%).

As for their love lives, 9% of women aged 45–54 met their husbands through the internet, and 49% of women believe that the best age to **get married** is between 25 and 29.

And what about the relationships between men and women? 59% think fathers should **take** more **responsibility** for their children. These women are also less than content with their husbands' efforts at home: 51% say they currently **do** over 75% of the **housework**. Despite this, over 70% of women would prefer to have a male boss than a female.

And their heroes? The woman they most admire is ex-Prime Minister Margaret Thatcher (7%), followed by the Queen (5%).

1.3

8A Student B: read your instructions below.

You want to do a course at a famous business school which is well-known for its practical courses. It will give you contacts in the business world. Think about these things:

- the business you want to start
- relevant work experience you have with another company

Student A will interview you for the course. He/She will ask about your:

- reason for doing the course
- work experience
- expectations of the course
- plans for the future

Prepare your answers and think of some questions to ask about the school.

2.1

2A Read and check your answers.

Fact or fiction:

1 Fiction: the film *The Last Samurai* does tell the story of the samurai rebellion, but the character Nathan Algren did not exist.

2 Fiction: in truth, we know very little about William Shakespeare's personal life, or what provided his inspiration.

3 Partly true: whilst *Gladiator* did take a few liberties with history, it's true that the Emperor was killed by a gladiator in the Roman baths.

4 Partly true: the film *Braveheart* does tell the story of how William Wallace fought to free Scotland, but kilts were not worn in Scotland until 300 years later. And there are many other historical inaccuracies.

5 Partly true: the film *Apollo 13* was praised for its accuracy. Much of the dialogue was taken directly from recordings. However, the pilot's exact words were, 'OK, Houston, we've had a problem here'.

9.3

Student A

7A Check Student B's answers to your questions.

1 Canberra; 2 India; 3 Paraguay

9.1

Student B

2B Read the texts below and make notes with the following prompts.

- What?
- Where?
- When?
- Why was it important?

Galileo explores the heavens

When Galileo became the first person to look at the sky through a telescope, it changed our view of the universe. His discoveries about the Sun, Moon and other planets completely disagreed with older theories. He then wrote a book, *Two World Systems*, published in Italy in 1630, which led to his problems with the Roman Catholic Church. At his trial, Galileo was found guilty and it was only in the twentieth century that the Vatican finally agreed with him. If Galileo hadn't defended his theories, he would have been a free man, but we wouldn't have understood the science of our universe.

The steam engine

For most of human history we were not very different from other animals, which also have language, act as a group, and have organisational systems. But the steam engine gave us the ability to do things faster and to do things that other animals couldn't. This development, which took place in Britain in the 18th century, was not one invention, but many. Different people were involved at different stages: Thomas Newcomen, James Watt and George Stephenson. The steam engine allowed us to transform the way we use energy. It changed so many things, including transportation, manufacturing and communication. Life would have been totally different if we hadn't invented it.

4.1

7A Work out your score. Add up the number of points (0, 1 or 2) for each answer. Use your total to find out if you work like a millionaire.

Question 1: a) 0 b) 1 c) 2
Question 2: a) 1 b) 2 c) 0
Question 3: a) 0 b) 1 c) 2
Question 4: a) 1 b) 2 c) 0
Question 5: a) 0 b) 1 c) 2

Key:

Score 8–10 You work like a millionaire!
You are very ambitious and enjoy your work. Keep going. Sooner or later all your hard work will pay off and you can live like a millionaire, too.

Score 6–7 You have millionaire potential!
You understand hard work, and if you make it your top priority, you could be a millionaire, too. Keep focused on your goal.

Score 0–5 You don't work like a millionaire!
The clearest characteristics of self-made millionaires is that they work hard and they enjoy their work. You seem to prefer a work–life balance, where work and money are not your top priorities.

4.1

9B Read the vocabulary notes and check your answers.

remember • remind
If you **remember** something, a fact or event from the past, or something you earlier decided to do, comes back into your mind:
He suddenly remembered he had to go to the bank.
If someone **reminds** you to do something, or something reminds you of something, they make you remember it:
Remind me to call him later today.

forget • leave
If you want to talk about the place where you have left something, use the verb **leave**, not the verb **forget**. Compare:
I've forgotten my book and I've forgotten my keys.
I've left my keys in the car.
Don't say: *I've forgotten my keys in the car.*

listen • hear
If you **hear** something, you know that sound has been made, and can often recognise what it is:
Did you hear that noise?
If you **listen** to something or someone, you pay attention to the words, sounds and music that they are making:
I am sorry, could you repeat the question? I wasn't listening.

fun • funny
Use **fun** to talk about events and activities that are enjoyable, such as games and parties:
Let's go to the beach and have some fun.
Funny is an adjective that describes someone or something that makes you laugh:
Bob's jokes are really funny.

earn • win
Use **earn** to talk about getting money by working:
She earns about $50,000 a year.
Use **win** to say that someone gets a prize in a game or competition.
Brian won first prize in the skating competition.

COMMUNICATION BANK

2.1

10A Student B: make *Have you ever ...?* questions using the prompts.

1 win an award/competition/some money

2 eat something very unusual

3 break a bone in your body

4 lock yourself out of the house

5 ride a horse/donkey/camel/motorbike

6 climb a mountain/run more than 2 km

3.2

8C Check your answers.

1 False. Compare: *I said the wrong thing.* (formal) *I **put my foot in it**.* (informal) *Not everyone will want them.* (formal) *They are not **everyone's cup of tea**.*

2 True. *I hate **small talk**. I just want to talk about the important business.* We can't say: *I hate talk small.*

3 True. *They don't have much time. They're **working against the clock**.* (present continuous) *Tomorrow we have a lot of things to do. We're **going to work against the clock**.* (*be going to* for future plans)

4 True. *What's **on your mind**? = What are you thinking?* or *It's an issue **close to my heart**. = I feel passionate about it.*

3.3

1B Read the end of the story.

The waiter said, 'Mr Carson has already paid your bill.' The producer thought this was incredibly generous. So the next morning he called Carson and said, 'That was so nice of you. How generous you are!' Carson started to laugh and said, 'I didn't know that all those people outside were with you. I thought it was just the people at the table!'

The bill? About ten thousand dollars.

9.1

Student B

7A Look at the notes and describe a big moment in history. Think about the questions on page 105 to help you.

The rise of the computer

1981 – IBM launched the first personal computer. Microsoft wrote the software.

By 1984 IBM was selling three million PCs a year. Apple launched a rival, the Macintosh, which used a mouse and icons.

1985 – Microsoft launched Windows and used some of the same tools.

5.2

1B Check your answers.

1 Nobody has ever done it, but in theory, yes it is possible.

2 Any heavy meal can make you dream more (because you spend more time in REM sleep). But cheese doesn't cause more dreams (good or bad) than any other food.

3 Because the heavier you are, the more difficult it is to push you out of the ring (which is how you win a sumo wrestling match).

4 No. Wasps do drink nectar from flowers but they don't use it to make honey.

5 Yes. If you travel, you'll notice that you can see different constellations of stars. This is because the surface of the Earth is curved.

6 When we cut an onion, it releases a substance called lachrymatory-factor synthase. When a very small amount goes in your eye it irritates the eye. We then produce tears (we cry) to wash the substance away.

9.3

5B Check your answers.

1 Michelangelo; 2 Al Gore; 3 F W de Klerk; 4 Gael Garcia Bernal; 5 Sony and Philips in a joint project; 6 J R R Tolkien; 7 Spain (in 2010); 8 *Jurassic Park*

10.3

8A Student B: read the instructions below.

You work in the Tourist Information centre. A customer would like to visit the Australian Outback. Give him/her some advice, using the prompts below:

1 whatever do / don't approach dingoes – they can bite. Remember / throw away any leftover food.

2 watch out / snakes – some are poisonous. If see one / move slowly away.

3 flies – If I were you / buy fly net to fix onto your hat

4 not forget / wear / hat / suncream / take plenty of water / drink

5 don't wear high heels / new, expensive clothes – land is rough and rocky

B Change roles and role-play the following situation. Student B: you are a tourist. You want to go snorkelling on the reef. Ask the dive instructor for advice, e.g. Are there any special clothes you should wear? What equipment do you need?

I'd like some information about going diving. First of all, what clothing do I need to wear?

9.3

Student B

7A Check Student A's answers to your questions.

1 Uruguay; 2 The body of a 5,000-year-old man; 3 1999

5.1

6B Which do you think is the best form of transport, A–E for each challenge? Why? Compare your ideas with other students.

Hi, I'm James May. I'm a car journalist and BBC presenter. Welcome to my Big Ideas. In this challenge, we're going to explore some of the ways of getting from A to B using a range of transport options.

Mostly we're looking at transport available today but there's a couple that are just around the corner, so we'll pretend we're a few years into the future.

Challenges

1 Challenge: Get to Scotland – easily
I'm in London and need to get to Scotland. I need to get there as quickly as I can. The only problem is I'm too tired to actually drive anything. I want to put my feet up and do the crossword on the way.

Transport: _____

2 Challenge: Get to concert in Hyde Park – without sitting in traffic
OK, for this challenge I've got to get to a classical music concert in Hyde Park (Central London). If I fly, I'll need transport from the airport. Got any good ideas?

Transport: _____

3 Challenge: Go to see elephants in Africa – quickly
Do you ever want to experience the wonders of the world? Me, too. Right now I want to see elephants, maybe even feed a few and I'm not talking about a trip to a zoo here in Great Britain. I want to see them in their natural environment. Get me to Africa. And get me there, and back again, fast.

Transport: _____

4 Challenge: See Moulin Rouge in Paris – efficiently
I fancy an expensive night out, let's go to Paris to see the Moulin Rouge. But, I want to be green, so I want to get there using the most energy-efficient way possible.

Transport: _____

5 Challenge: Get out of here – quickly
Oh dear – I've upset someone. I need to get out of here quickly.

Transport: _____

7.2

4B Student B: read the text below to see if your ideas were mentioned.

The human computer

Daniel Tammet says he was born on a blue day, 31st January 1979. He knows it was blue because Wednesdays are always blue, like the number nine or the sound of people arguing.

As a child, Daniel was diagnosed as autistic. He couldn't make friends. He was too different from the other children. Aged eight, he was able to calculate 82 x 82 x 82 x 82 in his head, but he couldn't tie his own shoe laces, or ride a bicycle.

The thing that makes Daniel special is that he has an incredible ability with numbers. He imagines them as shapes and colours ('289 is an ugly number', he says) and is able to do extremely difficult mathematical calculations. On the TV programme that made him famous in the UK, he managed to recite 22,514 numbers from pi perfectly. If you tell Daniel your birth date, he can tell you what day of the week you were born on, and what day of the week it will be on your 65th birthday.

Daniel counts everything. He eats exactly forty-five grams of porridge for breakfast each morning and he brushes his teeth for exactly two minutes. He doesn't like walking on the beach near his home because there are too many pebbles to count.

Daniel's other great love, besides numbers (which he calls 'his friends'), is learning languages. He speaks ten, and he managed to learn Icelandic in a week for a TV programme in Iceland. He now runs a language teaching business on the internet and in 2007 published a book, *Born on a Blue Day*.

* **porridge** – a type of cereal

* **pebbles** – small stones

* **pi** – a mathematical expression represented by the Greek letter π

C Read the text again and answer the questions.

1 How was his behaviour different to the other children's?
2 What special talents does he have?
3 How did the public learn about his special talents?
4 What country/countries has he been to and what did he do there?
5 What has he published?
6 What is his 'job' now?

D Tell your partner about your text. Use questions 1–6 to help.

10.1

Group B

6A Look at the photo and read the fact file below. Then discuss the questions.

The carbon problem

Did you know ...?

- Transport is responsible for 25 percent of the UK's carbon footprint, and that doesn't include flying. In the UK, there are more cars than the number of households. In California, there are more cars than the number of people living there.

- Currently cars are used for 18 percent of trips under a mile and for 62 percent of trips of between one and two miles. 38 percent of car trips are taken by one person alone, and 34 percent are shared by two people.

- Lighting and household appliances like washing machines are responsible for around 35 percent of the carbon pollution from your home, and most of your electricity bills. If every household in the UK put a solar panel on their roof, we would produce more electricity than we need as a nation.

1 Do you think every family needs to have access to a car? Why/Why not?

2 What do you think should be done to reduce the number of miles people drive in cars/fly in aeroplanes?

3 Do you think people should generate their own electricity using wind/solar power, etc., or should governments choose options like nuclear power?

4 What laws/schemes would you introduce to deal with these problems?

9.3

Student B

7 You are going to ask Student A the questions below. First, add two more questions of your own. The answers can be found on page 160.

> History
>
> 1 Which football team won the first World Cup in 1930? Was it Brazil, Argentina or Uruguay?
> 2 What was discovered in the Alps mountain range in 1991? Was it the body of a 5,000-year-old man, the body of a hairy elephant, or a World War II aeroplane?
> 3 When did the European Union introduce the euro? Was it 1979, 1989 or 1999?
> 4
> 5

3.3

B Change roles and role-play the situation.

Student A   **Student B**

You are a guest at a hotel. Your room is too small. Ten minutes ago you called reception to ask if there are any suites available. Then room service arrived with a trolley of sweets (cakes, ice cream, etc.). Call reception to make your complaint.

You are a receptionist at a hotel. A guest calls to make a complaint. Start the conversation by saying 'Reception. How can I help you?'

'Hello. Yes, I'm afraid I have a problem ...' Explain the problem again and ask if there is a suite available.

Apologise for the misunderstanding. Explain that there are no suites available at the moment, but there will be tomorrow.

Check details and thank the receptionist for their help.

Confirm details, apologise again and end the call.

9.1

Student A

7A Look at the notes and describe a big moment in history. Think about the questions on page 105 to help you.

Twenty-first-century natural disasters

Boxing Day Tsunami, 2004, killed 230,000 in eleven countries. Badly affected India, Thailand, Indonesia and Sri Lanka. Underwater earthquake measured approximately 9.2 on the Richter scale (second largest recorded in history).

Hurricane Katrina, 2005, killed 1,836, affected mainly poor blacks in New Orleans, USA.

Earthquake in L'Aquila, Central Italy, 2009, killed over 300 people.

4.2

11 Choose one of the job advertisements below and write your covering letter.

Fashion designer wanted:

We are looking for a graphic designer with a background in the fashion trade. You should have relevant experience and be up-to-date with fashion trends. Strong hand illustration as well as computer design is essential. Please submit a copy of your CV with relevant samples of work.

Teaching assistant, Bahamas

Primary school is looking for a teaching assistant to start ASAP. The school is a short walk from the beach. No formal qualifications are necessary; however, a genuine love for the job is required. Please forward CVs or contact me for further information.

Travel writer required.

Travel writer wanted to join our small team. The successful applicant will travel around the world, staying in luxury hotels, and dining in fine restaurants. He/She will need to send a weekly update, including a short review. No previous experience required, but good communication skills and a love of travel essential.

10.4

6A Choose one of the places below. Then plan a three-minute report. Use the prompts and key phrases on page 125 to help.

The Taj Mahal

The Taj Mahal receives 3–4 million tourists each year, but the crowds and the air pollution are eating away at the white stone facade. Now there are plans to close the Taj Mahal to the public, leaving its famous domes visible only from a distance.

The Forbidden City

It may have been forbidden once but nowadays nearly seven million visitors come to see the ancient emperor's palaces in Beijing, China every year. Now traffic pollution is a real problem which is damaging the palaces. A huge restoration is planned, but should the government stop people visiting?

Mount Kilimanjaro, Tanzania

The famous snows of Kilimanjaro are melting and may soon be gone. A combination of evaporation, too little snowfall, and internal heat from the dormant volcano have reduced the mountain's ice and snow cover by 90 percent from historic levels and it continues to retreat about 1m (3.25 ft.) per year.

The Pyramids of Giza

Unrestricted development around the area, and the way in which the city of Cairo grows closer and closer to the pyramids, threatens both the pyramids and the Great Sphinx. There are now plans to run a multi-lane motorway around the city of Cairo, which could create further problems.

The Grand Canyon, Arizona

Why might it disappear? There are more requests each year to mine near the Grand Canyon. The number of mining claims increased from ten in 2003 to more than 1,100 in 2008, bringing with them the risk of stream and groundwater contamination from cyanide and other chemicals. Should permission for the mining claims be stopped because of the threat?

AUDIO SCRIPTS

UNIT 1 Recording 1

W = Woman   M = Man

W: So, do you know a lot about your family history?

M: I do actually. Yes, erm, cos, one thing we have got is a family tree, so, erm, I've put it all on the computer. So, er, I know quite a lot about them.

W: Did you ever meet your great-grandparents, for example?

M: No, I never met them. Erm, in fact, I've only ever met one grandparent.

W: Oh?

M: Yeah, they all died rather young so I only had … I met my granny. Erm, that was from my mother's side. Mellows, they were from Yorkshire.

W: Oh, I was going to say, where did your ancestors come from?

M: Well, yeah, no, erm, my mother's side they all came from Yorkshire, but my father's family, er, originally came from Holland. They came over with, er, with William of Orange in 1689.

W: Ah! That's fascinating!

M: And my ancestor was William of Orange's, erm, closest advisor. And, er, so that was for the glorious revolution.

W: Wow! And what happened to the other ancestors? Do you know anything about your other side?

M: What?

W: What might have happened to …

M: What, my mother's side?

W: … more recently perhaps?

M: Well, all of, most of my ancestors were either soldiers, erm, or in the church, or sailors, and, erm, very dull apparently. My father's side, incredibly dull lot until, er, my father's ah father married ah a woman whose ah surname was Knowle and they're all eccentrics – barking mad – lovely and great fun, so I like to think that I'm descended from that lot, rather more than the boring lot.

W: So on that note, which members of your family do you feel close to, would you say?

M: Well, I've only got, I don't have. Both my parents are dead now so, my immediate family is the answer to that question, my wife and my two sons who are twenty-five and twenty-one years old.

W: And who tells the best family stories?

M: Me!

W: I thought so!

UNIT 1 Recording 3

P = Presenter
Part 1

P: Is your brain male or female? A strange question? Maybe, maybe not. In a moment, you will be asked to draw a picture of a bike. Make sure you have a pen or pencil. Pause now, and play when you're ready.

Part 2

P: OK, you have exactly one minute to draw a picture of a bicycle. Go!

Make it as beautiful or normal as you like. Include as much detail as you can. You've got forty-five seconds left.

You've got another fifteen seconds.

You've got five seconds left … four, three, two, one, zero, stop. Right, stop drawing please. Now, you have to write down on your piece of paper, whether you, the artist, are male or female. That's all we need to know for the experiment. Now turn to page a hundred and fifty-eight to see what a real bike looks like. Please pause the recording now.

UNIT 1 Recording 4

P = Presenter
Part 3

P: Now, count up the parts on your drawing. Did you include wheels? A handlebar? A saddle? A chain? A crossbar? Pedals? Did your bike have at least five parts? And could it work? Now for the difference between the men's drawings of a bicycle and the women's: female drawings often include a person riding the bike; men's drawings don't usually include a person. This is a clear indication that women think people are important. Men, on the other hand, are more interested in getting the machine right.

UNIT 1 Recording 5

P = Presenter   W1 = 1st woman
M1 = 1st man   W2 = 2nd woman
Part 4

P: Here are some comments from men and women who did the test.

W1: Hmmm. Well, I only got four parts right. How many did you get right?

M1: I only got four. How many did you get?

W2: I've got, I've got five, but none of us got the chain, did we, so …

M1: Mine hasn't even got pedals …

W2: No, mine hasn't got pedals …

M1: Pedals nor chains so mine will never work!

W2: But if you've got pedals and no chain it's not going to work anyway …

M1: It'll have to be going downhill …

W2: And also that, um, that means the explanation for men making the bike work doesn't work because you, you …

M1: That's right … of the two women and one man none of us drew …

W2: Have made the bike work.

M1: … yeah, and none of us drew a person … so the explanation about women wanting to put a person on there is hasn't proven correct for you two …

W1: No, not with us … no.

M1: And mine is meant to be all about functionality and it hasn't … ah, I've got a little bird on my handlebars though …

W2: It's a very clear drawing though, yours …

W1: I think mine is more male than yours, maybe? Yes …

M1: I think you're right …

W2: Yours is much more accurate … yours is the most accurate one.

M1: The way you've used the biro to just kind of make the lines more solid … that's quite a masculine …

W1: And you've got lights on yours and you've got, you've got five, five parts.

W2: Yeah.

UNIT 1 Recording 6

1 I think I'm a good employee as I always do my best at work.

2 At my school we have a system of mentors who help the younger pupils, and I'm one of the mentors.

3 My nice news is that I recently became godmother to my best friend's little girl.

4 I'm the boss of a small company that sells phone cards.

5 I'll introduce you to my fiancé later. We got engaged two weeks ago.

6 I took up judo six months ago and I'm a member of a local club.

UNIT 1 Recording 7

Conversation 1
T = Teacher   S = Student

T: And what about your expectations of the course?

S: Well, as I said, I've studied English for many years and spent time in Britain, but that was a few years ago. So for me the most important thing is to just refresh … and try to remember my English and practise speaking and listening.

T: OK. You've got a very good level of English so we'd put you in the advanced class. Is there anything else?

S: Could I ask a question?

T: Of course.

S: I can take the morning class from 9.00 to 12.00. Is that right?

T: Yes, that's right.

S: And in the afternoon there are options? Optional classes?

T: Yes, these are special classes with a special focus like English idioms, conversation, pronunciation. We have the full list here.

S: I see. Thank you.

T: No problem. OK, well, thank you very much.

Conversation 2

I = Interviewer   A = Applicant

I: There are a couple of things I'd like to ask about, Jade. Your CV says you have some experience of looking after children?

A: Yes, I was a tutor on a summer camp last year.

I: Can I ask you about that? What type of things did you do?

A: Um, well, I organised games.

I: Games for?

A: The children.

I: OK. And what age were the children?

A: Um … seven to ten.

I: OK. And you enjoyed it?

A: Yes.

I: What aspect, what part did you enjoy, would you say?

A: I suppose I'd have to say I liked the games best.

I: And any problems?

A: Um, no.

I: What about the different ages? We often find that different ages together can be difficult.

A: It depends. In my opinion, you can usually get the older children to help the younger ones.

Conversation 3

I = Interviewer   S = Student

I: I think that's about it. Do you have any questions? Any queries?

S: Um, yes, actually I do have a query.

I: Yes, go ahead.

S: It's about online classes at the university.

I: Right.

S: If I'm accepted, I saw that there are … urm, that it's possible to take some courses online.

I: That's right.

S: So I wouldn't need to attend classes?

I: Not for the online courses. But, erm … well, one thing I'd like to say is that the online courses are, in many ways, more difficult than face-to-face courses. Certainly in terms of reading and writing, they're really quite demanding.

UNIT 1   Recording 8

A = Annabel Winter

A: I heard about Second Life, um, BBC breakfast TV, and um I decided to sort of get on it because I wanted to see what it'd be like to interact in a, a virtual world so, um, and also to see how it was presented onscreen on our computers. So, um, I went on and you can create your own avatar which means to create a, a sort of a different version of yourself, so um, I … it … I, I … created a new image of myself, um I didn't change my appearance that much. You can choose different parts of, ah the body so you can change your face, I made myself, I made myself with dark hair

rather than with blonde. I'm not sure why. Um, one thing I decided to alter was my job. I, um, decided to be a businesswoman rather than, um, an actress … um, but one thing that hasn't changed is my personality. You get to talk to people online um as your avatar, so obviously my responses are um still as me. Um, but you can also set up, ah … your own buildings, you can, you can, um, pay for and build your own buildings, so you can be your own businesswoman in your own shop and people can come in and actually buy things from your shop. So it's really interesting to sort of interact as this alternative being, different version, different version of me.

UNIT 2   Recording 1

R = Rosie (A film historian)   P1 = 1st presenter   P2 = 2nd presenter

P1: Hi and welcome to *The Film Show*, where today we're looking at the Hollywood biopic and why it's become so popular. Now, Hollywood has always used true stories in its films. In fact, they began making successful films in the 1920s, and since then there have been thousands of films based on true stories.

P2: That's right, but in recent years, there've been more and more biopics. Directors have turned to the lives of famous people as a source of material. So, why is it that some of the best films in recent years have been based on true events, or inspired by real people?

P1: Today, we're talking to Rosie Truman, an actor and a film historian. Rosie, why do you think Hollywood is doing so many biopics?

R: Well, one reason is that it seems that audiences really enjoy films about people that they already know something about, but they want to know more. So, from these films we've learned something. We've learned about the difficult lives of some of the biggest music legends, like Ray Charles and Johnny Cash. We've learned about their history and how they grew up. And we've learned about the lives of politicians, like George Bush, or sporting heroes, like Muhammad Ali. It's a way in which Hollywood can actually teach us about history in an entertaining way. And it's interesting.

P2: Yes, I think that's right.

UNIT 2   Recording 2

R = Rosie (A film historian)   P1 = 1st presenter   P2 = 2nd presenter

P2: But what about the actors, Rosie? I mean, many of the actors have won Oscars for their roles in these films. What's it like for them?

R: Well, I think actors just love these roles. I mean, that's another reason why the films work so well. For an actor, this is a great challenge – you know, taking on a role like

this. And it's very exciting to be asked to play a character who everyone already knows. Look at Helen Mirren. She won an Oscar for her role playing the Queen, and it's probably one of her greatest successes.

P1: Oh, absolutely! And I mean there have been some fantastic performances.

P2: Yes, that's right …

P1: So, how do they do it? How does an actor prepare for a role like this? Do they get the chance to meet the person that they're going to play? I mean … What happens?

R: Well, yes, obviously, if that person is still alive, then that's a great way for the actor to study the character: how this person moves, how they respond to people. In fact, I know that Helen Mirren met the Queen for tea, you know, very English. And she has talked about how this really helped her to understand her character. And Will Smith, who played Muhammad Ali … well, when they met, they got on really well, and … and they became friends.

P2: But what about playing a difficult character, like George Bush, for example?

R: Yes, it's funny actually, when you're playing a character everyone knows, you have to work really hard at it. And especially on the voice, to get it exactly right. Josh Brolin played George Bush. And when he was preparing for the character, he talked to himself all day in a Texan accent. He even phoned up hotels in Texas, just so he could learn the accent.

P1: Really? That's funny. What about actors who can't meet the character in person? What do they do?

R: Well, there are lots of other ways to prepare. Audrey Tatou, for example. She played Coco Chanel. So she couldn't meet her in person, but she watched hours and hours of film footage. She watched her in interviews, and she looked at the photographs. In a way, you have a little bit more freedom to do what you want with the character, when people are not so familiar, you know, with how the person behaves, and with their voice. Tatou wanted to look like Coco Chanel when she was on screen, so that we would recognise the image.

P2: That's right. And it was a beautiful film.

R: It was, and you know one of the things …

UNIT 2   Recording 5

1 I lived there for ten years.

2 We've never met before.

3 He won an Oscar.

4 They've spent all the money.

5 You decided to stay.

6 I've learnt a lot.

AUDIO SCRIPTS

UNIT 2 Recording 6

P = Presenter N1 = 1st news clip
N2 = 2nd news clip N3 = 3rd news clip
N4 = 4th news clip
P: Hello. I know what I was doing. Do you?
N1: Buckingham Palace has announced the death of Diana, Princess of Wales. The Princess, who was thirty-six, died late last night in a car crash in central Paris.
N2: It's one small step for man, one giant leap for mankind.
N3: Breaking news in here at five live. There are reports that a plane has crashed into the World Trade Center in New York. That's a plane is reportedly crashed into the World Trade Center in New York, setting it on fire …
N4: President Kennedy and Governor John Connally of Texas were shot today from an ambush as President Kennedy's motorcade left the centre of Dallas …

UNIT 2 Recording 7

W = Woman M = Man
M: OK, so, tell me all about it …
W: Well, in the beginning, I was at home, and … um … this was just one morning before a very important interview …
M: Uh-huh.
W: And … um … I didn't feel well, so my mother had given me some pills, and um … then I didn't think anything more about it. So, anyway, erm … I then got on to the tube, um … to go for my interview.
M: Right, and what happened then?
W: Well, um … clearly I must have fallen asleep, because I wasn't feeling great by this time. And um, I'm starting to feel sleepy, so I'm thinking I must have fallen asleep. Anyway, erm … I was getting some funny looks, even before I fell asleep, but anyway. I fell asleep, and then I realised, before long, um … I must have been having a dream, I suppose, about my mother. And all of a sudden, I've woken up, but I haven't just woken up, I've woken up shouting the word, 'Mum!'.
M: No! You're joking!
W: At the top of my voice, in a packed, quiet tube.
M: Oh no!
W: Yes, and everybody's staring at me, and that did not help, er, matters. Anyway, I've got off the tube, and I've then arrived at my interview, put all that behind me, I'm not, I'm still not feeling a hundred per cent perfect, but nevertheless arrived at my interview on time, and go in, and think, actually 'This is going rather well. They're not saying an awful lot, and come to think of it, they're looking at me in a rather strange way.'
M: Right …Then what?
W: Well, the next thing I knew, I have left

the interview, and said 'thank you very much for seeing me, blah-di-blah … and gone to the ladies' room. And there in the mirror, I could see what everyone was looking at, and why they couldn't say anything,
M: What was it?
W: My face had swollen up!
M: Ah! No way!
W: It was bright red, and …
M: No!
W: and covered in blotches, spots …
M: Oh! You're kidding!
W: Yes, and the pills that my mother had given me were so out-of-date that they had caused an allergic reaction …
M: Oh! How embarrassing!
W: I know.

UNIT 2 Recording 8

W = Woman M = Man
W2 = 2nd Woman
M: OK. What do we reckon? True or false?
W2: Erm … I don't know. I think it might be false because … I don't know …
M: Yeah, she was a little bit slow in telling the story …
W2: I don't know if your mum would give you out-of-date pills …
M: Yeah, would a mother giver her daughter out-of-date pills?
W2: I think false.
M: It sounded like she was trying to think of what to say next, so … you think false, I think false.
W: Yes, it was false!

UNIT 2 Recording 10

C = Chris Harris
C: OK. Well, in this story, the painting which Finch has stolen is a Van Gogh. Er, he has stolen it for a Russian art dealer, who offered to pay him huge amounts of money for the painting. The problem is that Finch isn't a very good thief. In fact, he's been in prison before. So, when he's in the airport in Rio, he realises that security men are watching him. They're talking on their radios. Also, he sees a newspaper which has headlines about the stolen painting. He decides to put the painting inside a locker in the airport. Er … He keeps the key, and flies back to the UK hoping that in a few weeks' time, he can go back to Brazil and collect the painting. However, when he leaves the airport in the UK, he realises that he is being followed by customs officers. Oh, also, he meets the art dealer who wants the painting, and the dealer threatens to break his legs if he doesn't get the painting. So, Finch is worried, but he has an idea. He tells a friend of his about the painting, and gives him the key to the locker. He

arranges for the friend to fly to Brazil and collect the painting, and to meet him in Argentina, where they can share the money. What he doesn't know is that the friend has seen that there is a reward being offered for the painting. So he decides to call the police and tell them about the plan. Because of this, when Finch arrives at the airport, he is arrested.

UNIT 3 Recording 3

Conversation 1
W1 = 1st woman M1 = 1st man
W2 = 2nd woman M2 = 2nd man
W1: Erm, so there are many, many ways we communicate with people at the moment and, um, in the near future – I wanted to talk about something that, um, is going to be with us which is, um, a system for translating foreign languages. Um, so potentially you could be on the phone talking to someone from another country who's speaking in a different language and it's being, um, translated into your ear so you can communicate that way. What do we th-
M1: Like an intermediary or something?
W1: Um, yes …
M1: Or by technology?
W1: By technology so you can do this on Skype you know where you've got the erm, the camera filming you and you are talking to someone um in another country … How, how do we feel about that?
M1: Well, it might work in the future but it certainly doesn't work at the moment. I mean if you go to a website that's in a foreign language and you can get these, you know, these online translation services …
M2: It, erm …
W2: It's not quite right.
M1: It's very funny.
M2: He gets it wrong.
M1: He gets it completely wrong, especially English to Japanese and back from it.
W1: See, you see will this type of communication affect the way we work, and … and?
W2: Well, businesses, I mean it works very well for businesses because you will be able to communicate with someone from a different company in a different country and maybe … erm, that will stop barriers in that way.

Conversation 2
W = Woman M = Man
W: I heard a TV programme the other day and they said that they don't think that handwriting will exist in the next ten years. What d'you think about that?
M: Oh really? What, what did they suggest would take its place?
W: Er, well, for things like, erm, signatures, you know, for bank cards, or whatever, or

signing things, erm, they suggested that we would use thumbprints or er, digital …

M: Kind of retina scans, things like that?

W: Yeah, that's it, yeah.

M: Well, I personally think that handwriting will be with us y'know for a long time. Erm, I think in years to come, people will still carry a pen around in their top pocket rather than anything else, and erm, that will be the quickest, easiest, and most straightforward way to communicate.

W: Well, maybe in the short term but if you think about – I don't know – sort of kids ten, twelve years old, they're using more and more y'know computers at school and things, and they might actually just stop writing, stop the practice of writing.

Conversation 3
W1 = 1st woman M1 = 1st man
W2 = 2nd woman M2 = 2nd man

W1: Well, before I give my opinion I'd like to know what you all think about the future of television.

M1: Well, it won't be on a television set, that's for sure.

W2: No, it'll be on a computer.

M2: Absolutely.

M1: Through broadband on a, on a computer, and it'll be on demand. Y'know, the difference between push and pull technology.

W1: Yes, I absolutely agree that it will be on demand, but I don't think that it will still be … I don't think … I think there'll be a place for computers, for YouTube, all those things, but ultimately it will not replace a very large screen in your living room.

M1: But the large screen in your living room will still be there. It's just the method of delivery and whether or not it's broadcast to you when you don't want it or whether you …

W2: Oh, I absolutely agree.

M1: … pick it up when you do want it.

M2: How soon do you think it'll change then? I mean are we talking long term? Short term?

M1: It won't be in a month … It won't be in a month or two, and it won't be in the short term, but certainly in the long term this will be the future.

W1: I think, I think it will be in the short term, actually. I would say in the next …

W2: Everything is so quickly changing, isn't it?

W1: Yes, absolutely.

M1: You've already got y'know on-demand, with the iPlayer and …

W1: Yes …

M1: and YouTube where y'know if you want to see it you can go and see it when you want to see it.

W1: And that is phenomenally successful.

UNIT 3 Recording 4

Conversation 1
W = Woman M = Man

W: Hi. Me again. I've sent an attachment with all the figures for the last six months. That should be all you need.

M: Sorry – I didn't catch any of that.

W: I've sent the figures in an attachment. Is that Tom?

M: You've lost me. Who is this?

W: This is Ana Lucia. Is that Tom?

M: No, this is Willy's Burger Bar. What number are you trying to get?

W: 845 6795.

M: I think you've got the wrong number.

W: Oh I'm sorry.

Conversation 2
M = Man W = Woman

M: I've got a reservation in the name of David Cullinan.

W: Just one moment. Umm, could you repeat the last name?

M: Cullinan. C-u-l-l-i-n-a-n.

W: Cullinan. I can't find the name. Did you make the reservation over the phone?

M: Yes, just yesterday.

W: Sorry, let me just see if there are any messages here. I won't be a moment. I'm sorry. We've got no reservations in the name of Cullinan, and we're fully booked tonight.

M: So you're saying I can't stay here. This is the Sheldon Hotel, yes?

W: No, this is The Felton. With an 'f'.

M: Really? So I'm in the wrong hotel.

W: The Sheldon is on Queen's Road, just around the corner.

M: Oh no. Sorry, can you say that again – where is it?

W: On Queen's Road, just around the corner.

Conversation 3
G = Girl F = Father

G: You've missed the best bits. You're late.

F: What exactly do you mean? The show starts at 7.00, doesn't it?

G: No, it finishes at 7.00!

F: Didn't you say it starts at 7.00?

G: No, it starts at 5.00 and finishes at 7.00!

F: So what you mean is I've missed the whole show.

G: Yes.

Conversation 4
M = Man W = Woman

M: We've got nothing for you, I'm afraid.

W: I don't get what you're saying. You're a car rental company, right?

M: Yes, but today's a holiday and all the cars have been booked already.

W: Do you mean to tell me that there's nothing at all? No cars available?

M: There's nothing till tomorrow, I'm afraid.

W: But I definitely booked a car for today, the third of July.

M: It's the fourth of July today. In other words, your booking was for yesterday.

W: It can't be. Is it?

M: It's the fourth today, madam.

W: Oh no, I've got the date wrong.

UNIT 3 Recording 6

1 So you're saying I can't stay here.
2 Didn't you say it starts at 7.00?
3 So what you mean is I've missed the whole show.
4 Do you mean to tell me that there's nothing at all?
5 In other words, your booking was for yesterday.

UNIT 3 Recording 7

L = Lisa Brown

L: I use the internet all the time to communicate, but I think for giving good news it's much, much nicer to be there and to do it face-to-face, though obviously it depends on what type of good news it is. Maybe the news is for someone you don't know personally or someone in a different country or city so you can't deliver it face-to-face. If that's the case, an email or a phone call are fine.

I'd say the same thing about giving bad news. If you know the person, it's much better to give it face to face. On the other hand, some bad news can be really difficult to give face to face. It can be embarrassing if someone's going to start crying in front of you or if they're going to get upset. So in those circumstances I'd rather send an email because it's less personal. I don't think I'd ever give bad news by text.

For arranging social activities I usually text my friends or do it over the phone. It's more convenient. People have such bad memories we kind of need to see arrangements written down. Also, we're always changing our plans at the last minute so we really need our phones switched on all the time.

For sending a 'thank you' message I think it's really nice to send a letter or, in my case, usually a card. I still send handwritten cards sometimes, and I think people really appreciate them because it shows you made an effort, whereas just sending a text or something isn't much of an effort. And it's not like they're going to keep the message for more than two minutes. But they might keep a card.

AUDIO SCRIPTS

UNIT 4 Recording 1

A = Angela P = Pauline M = Monty

A: As a child, I always wanted to be a model. I used to look at all of the **beautiful** women in the magazines, and on television. And I used to think it looked so exciting. To spend all day wearing beautiful clothes, and going to exciting locations for photo shoots. And I've always loved fashion, so the idea that I could go to fashion shows in Paris, New York, etc. was just **amazing** for me. What I didn't realise is that actually being a model is really, really hard work. The hours are very long, especially when you have to travel. Sometimes, we travel for fifteen hours or more, and when we arrive we need to start work straightaway. And the problem is that you need to look good all the time. But often, you're feeling **terrible**.

P: I have a passion for food, so being a restaurant critic seemed like the perfect job for me. I could spend my days sitting in some of the best restaurants, eating **delicious** food, and get paid for it. The only problem, which I didn't realise at the time, is that actually you can get bored of eating restaurant food. I used to eat three-course meals every day, or sometimes twice a day. And I would often cook at home. So I put on loads of weight. I was **furious**! I used to spend hours in the gym, doing exercise to try and work off the food I was eating. But it was **impossible**. So, in the end, I gave it up.

M: I used to work in a bank, so when I lost my job I decided it was time to do something that I would really enjoy. To follow a dream, if you like. I had this wonderfully romantic idea of owning my own vineyard, making wine, and spending my life in the beautiful Tuscan countryside. But the reality is very different. I had no idea how tiring the job would be. For a start, there're no holidays. For five months of the year, you don't even have weekends. You work seven days a week and you're **exhausted** all the time. And the other problem is the weather. Bad weather can ruin everything. So, in the winter, you have to get up at two o'clock in the morning when it's **freezing** outside, to turn on the frost control. And in September, a bad storm can ruin the grapes in just a few minutes. At least when I worked in an office, I didn't use to worry about the weather. Having said that, I love my life. And the science of making wine is absolutely **fascinating**. I wouldn't change my job for anything.

UNIT 4 Recording 4

W1 = 1st woman M1 = 1st man
M2 = 2nd man W2 = 2nd woman

W1: **First of all** we need to decide what food we want to sell.

M1: OK, well, the way I see things, the most important thing is to make sure, in the catering industry, what we want to do, is we want to make sure that we make a seventy percent profit on everything we sell, right? So, we need to think about food that doesn't cost very much to produce, …

M2: OK, so no smoked salmon, or …

W2: Exactly. But I think we should decide on a name for the company first, like 'Lotus foods' or 'Saffron', something which sounds exotic.

W1: Hmm. I'm not sure that I agree. **Let's focus** on the issue of a theme for our food, you know like Indian, or Mediterranean first, because that will influence the name.

M2: That's a good point. Also, I suggest we think about how we're going to sell. Because if we're going to events, then the type of food we cook might change, but we could have a name like Food4events.

W1: Good idea.

M1: Sorry, I missed that.

M2: We could call the company Food4events, and cater for events, weddings and parties. That kind of thing.

W1: I think that's a great idea. Does everyone agree with that?

All: Yes. That's fine. Yup. That's fine by me.

W1: OK. So, **moving on to the next point**, where do we work from?

M1: We need to be somewhere central, like in central London, and then we can travel to events from there.

W2: Sorry, but I'm not sure that central London is a good idea. It's very expensive. I suggest we look outside the city, where it's cheaper to rent office-space.

M2: Yes, I see what you mean. You're right – we don't need to be based in the centre of the city.

W2: Exactly.

W1: OK, so let's recap: the company is called Food4events and we sell at parties, events, weddings, etc. We're based outside London. Erm … What else do we need to think about?

M2: How is our company going to be different from others?

W1: Ah … **I think we need to come back to** the kind of food we want to sell. I really feel that we need to specialise, so perhaps we could be Italian.

W2: How about Mediterranean?

M1: Yes, Mediterranean's really popular.

W1: OK – good point. I like the idea of Mediterranean, actually.

M2: OK. Why don't we call it Italy On The Move?

M1: Or Buon Appetito?

W1: I like that. It sounds good. Oh, let's go with Italian, so it's an Italian catering company, and it's called Buon Appetito. That will make us different from the others, and we can have Luca as our head chef! So, let's sum up what we've decided. The company …

UNIT 4 Recording 7

C = Candace Parker

C: I'm a kindergarten teacher with a class of two-year-olds. So, um, my daily routine: well, I wake up about six thirty, take a shower, and have breakfast with my husband. I have to be at the Child Development Centre by seven thirty so I leave home by twenty past at the latest. Luckily, I don't have far to drive. The first thing I do is check my mail at work to see if there are any messages. Then I go to the classroom and switch on the lights, and I check everything is ready for the children. They usually start coming in about eight. The first hour is play-time, so we're on the floor with the toys. At nine o'clock we get the children seated at the table for their breakfast, which is usually muffins and apple sauce, or bread and cheese, and fruit juice. Then we clean up. If the weather's good we take the children out to the playground. This is probably the best part of the day because everyone's happy to be outside. We try to do this at least once a day. We have lunch at midday and then most of the children have a little nap for about an hour. After that, we do some art work or play music to the children or read to them. Then it's snack time around three thirty: just biscuits and more fruit juice. Then the parents usually arrive at four to take the children home. When all the children have gone, I write down what we did during the day and clean up a little, and then I make plans for the next day. And that's it! I'm usually home by five. Then I relax by reading or watching TV. It's a lovely job.

UNIT 5 Recording 3

W1 = 1st woman M1 = 1st man
W2 = 2nd woman

W1: Why are the windows round on ships?

M1: Round windows are stronger, aren't they?

W2: Are they? I've no idea.

W1: That's right. According to the book, they're less likely to break.

W2: Ah.

M1: There you go.

W1: What about this second one? How many hairs are there on the human head?

W2: Erm … A million?

M1: No, it's not that many, is it?

W2: It depends whose head, doesn't it?! On my dad's there are about three.

W1: The answer is about 10,000.

M1: Oh, really?

W2: I think that's a bit of a stupid question

because it depends, doesn't it?

M1: Well, it was a four-year-old who asked the question.

W2: Oh yeah, that's true.

W1: Next question: What happens when your plane flies over a volcano?

W2: Ummm.

M1: Nothing happens, does it? Well, it depends on whether the volcano is erupting? Or whether it's active.

W2: Yeah.

W1: Well, according to the book, Jamieson asked a pilot. And the pilot said as he was flying over the volcano, his engines shut down, stopped working completely.

W2: Scary. Did he get hot?

W1: Hmm, it doesn't say. But he obviously survived. So there you go. Anyway, what about this one? Why did The Beatles break up?

W2: Dunno. They got old, didn't they?

M1: No, John Lennon went off with Yoko Ono, didn't he?

W1: Well, Jamieson wrote to Yoko Ono and she replied, 'Because they all grew up, wanted to do things their own way, and they did.'

W2: Oh that's interesting.

M1: I'm amazed she replied.

W1: Me, too. OK, last one. After watching a violent video game, the little boy asked why is there war?

W2: Great question.

M1: That's a really good question.

W2: Hmm, because men like fighting?

M1: Political reasons. One country wants the land or the oil or the gold.

W1: Well, Jamieson asked lots of experts. Most of them didn't or couldn't answer. Then he asked an American army colonel, who said there are four big reasons: different ideologies, a sense of honour, economic reasons, and fear.

M1: Uh-huh.

W2: Good question for a four-year-old.

M1: And a good answer.

UNIT 5   Recording 6

Conversation 1
M = Man W = Woman

M: Arggh. Oh no.

W: What's the matter?

M: Oh. This cash machine's not working. **Do you know if** there's another machine somewhere? I really need to get some money.

W: Hmm … I'm not sure. There might be one in the shopping centre.

M: Thanks.

Conversation 2

W = Woman M = Man

W: Argh!

M: What's the matter?

W: My laptop's just crashed, again. That's the third time it's happened. **Would you mind looking at it for me?**

M: Sure.

W: Thanks. It's so annoying. I keep losing my documents. **Do you know what the problem is?**

M: Let me have a look. There's a lot of stuff on here. Why don't you save the documents onto a memory stick?

W: That's a good idea.

M: And then do you want me to try …

Conversation 3
W = Woman M = Man

W: Customer Services. Good Morning.

M: Um, yes. I've got a problem with my vacuum cleaner.

W: **Could you tell me what the problem is,** sir?

M: Yes, I can. It keeps making a funny noise. And it's just not working properly.

W: You say it keeps making a funny noise …

M: Yes, that's right.

W: OK. Let's see if I can find someone who can help you. **Could you hold the line, please?**

M: Yes, of course.

Conversation 4
M = Man W = Woman

M: Oh. I don't believe it! Excuse me, this machine's not working. It's just taken my money. **Could you give me a refund?**

W: I'm afraid I can't do that.

M: Why not?

W: Well, I'm not allowed to give refunds.

M: But I've just lost my money. And I still need a ticket.

W: I can sell you a ticket, but I can't give you a refund.

M: Well, **could you tell me who I should speak to?**

W: Yes, of course. You need to speak to the manager.

M: OK. **Would you mind calling him for me?**

W: Of course not. I'll just call him.

UNIT 5   Recording 8

Conversation 1
A: I can't concentrate. Would you mind turning the music down?

B: Sure. Sorry about that.

Conversation 2
A: I need to speak to the manager. Do you know if there's anyone in the office?

B: Let me have a look.

Conversation 3

A: I'm afraid Mr Soul isn't here at the moment.

B: Do you know when he's coming back?

A: I'm not sure. Do you want me to check?

B: Thank you.

Conversation 4
A: Could you tell me how this machine works? I don't know how to turn it on.

B: Yes, of course.

Conversation 5
A: I need to take this machine to the repair service. Would you mind helping me?

B: Of course not. Leave it here.

Conversation 6
A: My computer has frozen. Could you tell me who I should speak to?

B: OK. Let me have a look.

UNIT 5   Recording 9

J = James Carn

J: I'm going to tell you about Robo-Chef. Basically, Robo-Chef can prepare and cook all your favourite recipes. It works like this. First of all, it washes and prepares all the vegetables, then it prepares your dish, and cooks it for you on your cooker. Robo-Chef comes complete with hundreds of menus already programmed. But you can also programme Robo-Chef with your own recipes, or, if you want to try something new, you can download new recipes whenever you like. All you have to do is choose the dish you want, decide how many people you want Robo-Chef to cook for, and what time you want the meal to be ready. So, let's say you would like a vegetable lasagne for six people, ready by eight o'clock. Then, just make sure you have all the ingredients in the kitchen, press the button, and that's it. You can go out to work, and when you come home in the evening, your delicious supper will be ready. What could be easier? Robo-Chef is the chef of the future.

UNIT 6   Recording 1

R = Radio presenter C = Clip
P = Professor M = Man

R: Welcome to Start the Day!

C: Hello – can I help you?

Your call is important to us.

Hello – can I help you?

Your call is important to us. Sorry, all our operators are busy at the moment. Please hold.

M: They put you in a queue for ages, listening to this terrible music. When you finally speak to someone, you're so angry, you just want to shout …

R: Anger. We all know the feeling. A report out last year shows that people are getting angrier. One in ten people say that they have trouble controlling their temper. Traffic jams, airports, call centres,

AUDIO SCRIPTS

computer crashes – they can all leave us feeling angry, and anger is difficult to control. Or is it? Professor Miller from The Metropolitan University is here to tell us about two very different therapies to help deal with stress. First of all, destruction therapy. What's that about?

P: Well, basically, the idea is that a lot of people, when they get angry, they don't know what to do with their anger – they don't deal with it very well. They just keep it inside. But, if you don't deal with your anger, sooner or later it will explode. So with destruction therapy, you use your anger to destroy something, but in a controlled way, and the idea is that if you do that, it helps you to feel better.

R: OK, I get angry a lot. Can destruction therapy help me?

P: Perhaps. We can try it. What we do is we take you to a place full of old cars. When we get there, I'll give you a hammer, and you can use it to smash a car to pieces.

R: Really? Is it that simple? If I smash the car to pieces, will I feel better?

P: Yes, a little. But that's only the beginning. Then, I'll ask you to think about a situation in the past when you felt really angry. And when you think about that anger situation, you'll hit the car much harder. And the therapy will be much more satisfying. When we finish the session, you'll feel much better.

R: That's amazing, and businesses are using this kind of therapy in Spain, is that right?

P: Yes, there are some old hotels in Spain. You can pay to go and destroy the hotel. So, some companies who feel that their workers are stressed, or they need to build a team, send their workers to destroy the hotel. And it's a good way for them to get rid of that stress. It works.

R: That's incredible. But there's another idea I wanted to ask you about. People say that laughter is the best medicine. And nowadays, laughter therapy is used in hospitals to help people with pain.

P: That's right.

R: So, how does that work?

P: Well, if people laugh about something, they feel better. On average, children laugh up to 400 times a day, but when we grow up, we only laugh about seventeen times a day. And it's not enough, because when you laugh, your body produces chemicals – and these chemicals make you feel happier. And they also make you feel less pain. So, in Mexico, for example, they use laughter therapy in hospitals. A group of people go around the hospital, visiting the patients, and basically, they make them laugh, by telling them jokes, or doing something funny.

R: And does it really work? Do people feel better afterwards?

P: Absolutely! They feel better, and they don't need medicine.

R: That's brilliant. So, in Mexico, laughter really is the best medicine?

P: Yes, it looks like it. That's right …

UNIT 6 Recording 4

Conversation 1
W = Woman M = Man
W: We've got something to tell you.
M: What's that?
W: We're getting married.
M: Wow! That's fantastic. Congratulations!
W: There's one thing I've got to tell you though.
M: Really? What's that?
W: I'm afraid you're not invited.
M: Oh. That's a shame.
W: It's going to be a very small wedding.
M: I see.

Conversation 2
W = Woman M = Man
W: Hello. You came in for a job interview last week.
M: Yes, that's right.
W: Firstly, I'd like to say that we were very impressed with your interview.
M: Oh. Thank you.
W: However, I'm sorry to have to tell you, but we've offered the job to someone else.
M: Oh. That's a shame. Thanks, anyway.
W: I'm afraid the other candidate had more experience.
M: I understand.
W: But, we'd like to keep your details, in case another job comes up in the future.
M: OK.

Conversation 3
W1 = 1st woman W2 = 2nd woman
W1: You'll never guess what.
W2: What?
W1: I've just won some money on the Spanish lottery.
W2: Oh, you're joking?!
W1: No, really.
W2: That's amazing! How much did you win?
W1: One thousand euros.
W2: Oh, you lucky thing! How fantastic! How are you going to spend it?
W1: Actually, I've got so many bills to pay, I'll spend it on that.
W2: Well, it's good news anyway.

Conversation 4
M1 = 1st man M2 = 2nd man
M1: I'm afraid I've got some bad news.
M2: What is it?
M1: I've crashed the car.
M2: Oh no. That's terrible. Are you OK?
M1: Yes, I'm fine.
M2: That's lucky.

M1: But, I'm afraid the car isn't.
M2: Oh, that doesn't matter. You can get the car fixed.
M1: Unfortunately, it was your car.
M2: My car? You mean you crashed my car? How did that happen?
M1: Well, you see I …

Conversation 5
W = Woman M = Man
W: I've got some good news for you.
M: What is it?
W: You know I was waiting to hear from the university?
M: Yes.
W: Well, I'm really pleased to tell you they've offered me a place.
M: That's wonderful news. Well done! I'm so pleased for you.
W: There's only one problem.
M: What's that?
W: It means I'm leaving home.
M: Yes, of course. But it's fantastic news.

Conversation 6
W = Woman M = Man
W: Guess what!
M: What?
W: I got the promotion.
M: That's fantastic!
W: Yes, but there's something I've got to tell you.
M: What's the matter?
W: I'm sorry, but we'll have to cancel the holiday.
M: What do you mean?
W: Unfortunately, I can't go on holiday. I've got too much work to do.
M: Oh no. That's really annoying. I was looking forward to it.
W: I know. I'm really sorry.

Conversation 7
W1 = 1st woman W2 = 2nd woman
W1: Bad news, I'm afraid.
W2: What is it?
W1: Steve's lost his job.
W2: Oh no. That's awful. I'm really sorry to hear that.
W1: Do you want to hear the good news though?
W2: Yes.
W1: The company is paying him £30,000.
W2: Really?
W1: He's going to travel around the world.
W2: That's amazing.

UNIT 6 Recording 8

S = Stig Vatland
S: One of the most, er, memorable moments, or not moments rather events, in my life … er … was a couple of years ago. Erm … It all started one day when I

was at work and my brother phoned me out of the blue and said, um, 'What are you doing the weekend of Sept 23rd?' or whatever it was. And I said, 'I don't know.' He said, 'Well, book a flight to Norway.' My brother lives in Norway, and I live in England so I said, 'Why?', he said, 'Oh I'll let you know when you get there – it's a surprise.' So weeks went on, and I tried to work out what this could be, but I had absolutely no idea. So the weekend in question came about … went to the airport, got on my flight, and ah I was met there by somebody I'd never met before. He just came up and said, 'Are you Stig?'. I said, 'Yes.' And he said, 'OK. Come with me.' So I went with him to the car. We drove for a little while, and I tried to kind of get it out of him where we were going, but he wouldn't tell me anything. He pulled up outside a hotel, and there was my brother, and my half brother, and my two half sisters there waiting for me. I was thinking 'What on earth is going on?' And my brother just said, 'I realise we don't spend enough time together, so I've gathered you all here and I've planned a weekend for you.' We're like 'Oh, cool! So, what are we doing?' 'I'm not telling you.' 'OK fine.' Next thing we got on a boat and, er, he took us out to a lighthouse. And the first night we spent, er, eating Norwegian prawns drinking beer, and we slept in a lighthouse. Next morning we got up, drove off in his car, we said, 'Where are we going?' He said, 'I'm not telling you.' He took us to a local shopping centre and said, er, 'I realise I've done OK in life. I've done better than you guys. Here have a load of money. I want you all to go shopping and buy stuff that you wouldn't normally buy with this money.' He said, 'The one condition is you're not allowed to buy a gift for me or my family.' So off we went in different directions, spent all his money, and, er, bought some very nice things, met back again. In the evening, he took us out to a blues concert, then he took us for a five-course meal. And, er, we stayed that night in a very nice hotel. The next morning we had breakfast, I got back on a plane and went back to England. Yeah, that weekend is one of my happiest memories.

UNIT 7   Recording 1

P = Presenter I = Ian

P: Hello and welcome back to the *Focus* podcast. I'm Jenny Osmond, the editor of *Focus*, the monthly science and technology magazine from the BBC.

He's the hugely influential author of *Blink* and the *Tipping Point*. His work is quoted by academics, presidents and your mates down the pub. And now Malcolm Gladwell has turned that deft mind of his to a new subject: the science of success. In his new book, *The Outliers*, Gladwell argues that if we want to be successful, we should think less about what successful people are like, and more about where they have come from and the opportunities they have had along the way. Now, Ian's read the book and he joins me. Now … his new book is looking at success …

I: Yes, and what he says is, erm, that if we think about somebody like Bill Gates, hugely successful person, and we want to learn from, from his achievements, then what do we look at? We look at what that man is like, you know, what drives him, what does he do on a day-to-day basis, how can we be more like him? Erm … But what Gladwell argues in the new book is, is that we should pay less attention to that side of stuff, and look at where Bill Gates came from. So, how did he get to where he got to, the opportunities he had along the way. Erm … And what he says is that Bill Gates has one thing in common with another group of very successful people, The Beatles.

P: So, what's that?

I: Well, they both practised what they do, and they practised a lot.

P: Right, so how much is a lot?

I: A lot is 10,000 hours. That's like the magic number if you're going to become world-class at anything in the world, you need to put 10,000 hours' practice in.

P: Oh, OK.

I: So, The Beatles, they, they were doing gigs, you know, like all-night gigs in Hamburg, in these little clubs, and just the number of hours that they put in on the stage, erm, allowed them to master their craft. And the same with Bill Gates. He, er, as he was growing up, got into computer programming, and through a very fortunate series of events, he was able to programme, and programme, and programme, erm, and again …

P: Because he had access to computers at a time when these things were developing.

I: Absolutely! … Exactly! The timing is so, so important. He happened to go to a university, erm, where he had access to er, a computer programming unit. I mean, this was back in the 60s and 70s when computers were the size of rooms and stuff. Erm, and so what Gladwell does throughout the book is pick up on these little things that we really need to go back and look at again if we are to really understand why successful people are as successful as they are.

P: I think the 10,000 hours magic number is really interesting because, as you know, I used to play tennis professionally, and I hit a load of tennis balls when I was younger. And I'm sure, I must have done 10,000 hours' worth, you know, I must have done four hours a day, and stuff. And I remember speaking to Martina Hingis' mum about why she thought her kid was so good, and such a prodigy, and she basically said, 'My daughter has been hitting tennis balls since the age of three and she has hit X number of tennis balls for X number of hours and it's, you know, I'm sure she's … So once you're over that magic number of 10,000 … yeah.

I: The same goes for people like Beethoven, erm … It's incredible how …

P: But at the end of the day you have to have talent.

I: You've got to have raw talent, you've got to have belief in what you can do, and you have to have the will to put those hours in … but you also need the opportunity.

UNIT 7   Recording 4

T = Tim   J = John   P = Peggy

T: So what about your memory, Peggy? How good is it?

P: It's OK, which is lucky 'cos I need to remember lots of things.

J: Like what?

P: Well, I'm a sales rep for a publishing company so I'm usually out visiting schools, trying to sell books.

J: So you need to remember … what exactly?

P: Oh, lots of things. The worst thing when I started was just trying to remember how to get to these schools in my car. I used to get lost all the time. I'm not very good at directions. Then once you're there you have to remember the names and faces of the people you're talking to. I once spent a whole hour calling this woman Sally when her name was Samantha.

T: And she didn't tell you?

P: For some reason she didn't tell me. And then there's all the product information.

J: Product information? What, the books?

P: Yes. We sell about five hundred different books and I have to know the difference between all of them. I mean, it gets easier, thank goodness, but I still make mistakes occasionally. What about you, John? You're an actor, right?

J: Yeah. The main thing I have to remember is my lines. Fortunately, I've got a good memory for words, and I don't find it that hard to memorise them. So, I mean, yeah. The other thing you have to remember when you're in the theatre is the blocking.

T: What's that?

J: Blocking? It's where you stand or move to, y'know? Like, when you say your words you might have to walk quickly across the stage. Or move in front of someone. It's all planned and er, you have to remember it.

T: Oh, I see.

J: But it's funny: for, for other things I have a terrible memory. I'm totally useless. I always forget birthdays and dates. I'm always late for things. It's just … yeah … luckily, I'm OK with my lines.

P: What about you, Tim?

T: I'm probably the same as all other students. At least all other history students. I have to memorise dates and also names. But it's not that difficult because you read about them so much you can't really forget them. But for other things I have a really bad memory. I can never remember jokes or films. Sometimes I'm watching a film and after an hour I realise I've seen it already. I'm completely hopeless like that.

J: Oh, me too …

UNIT 7   Recording 5

M = Man W = Woman

M: It's interesting: one of the most intelligent people I know is a ten-year-old boy from Egypt. He doesn't go to school and he works on a street in Cairo, in one of the touristy areas. And he sells things like small statues of the pyramids, things like that, to tourists. Now, the reason I say he's intelligent is that he can sell you something in about fifteen languages. I once spent an afternoon watching him, and it was incredible. Most of the time he uses English, but he guesses where you're from by looking at you, and then he starts speaking. He can speak just a little bit of French, Spanish, Japanese, Italian, German, etcetera. It's amazing. He knows just enough in all these languages to say hello and sell you something.

W: How did he learn the languages?

M: I asked him that and he said he learned them by talking to tourists.

W: That is quite amazing.

M: So anyway, that's my example. Like I said, he doesn't go to school but, for me, he's super-intelligent. What about you?

W: I can think of loads of people who don't have any qualifications but are able to do really difficult things. I've got a friend, for example, who built his own house. He just taught himself how to do it, bought a piece of land, bought the materials and the equipment and just did it. No qualifications, no certificates, no university degree. In my view, that's a real practical kind of intelligence.

M: I couldn't do that.

W: Let me give you another example. I've got another friend who takes parts of old cars and makes new cars from them. He does it at the weekend as a way to relax. And the new car actually works!

M: I couldn't do that either.

W: I wouldn't know where to start. And this is someone who left school at fifteen to do an apprenticeship. But, you know, having said that, I do think qualifications are useful in some ways. I mean, for one thing, they show that you are able to complete a course, that you're motivated and committed enough.

M: Yeah, I think that's true.

W: But I must say real life experience, travelling, going out and meeting people, talking … I think these give you an amazing education, too.

M: Exactly. That's what I was saying. Just like the boy from Egypt.

UNIT 7   Recording 7

1 In my view, that's a real practical kind of intelligence.

2 I do think qualifications are useful in some ways.

3 But I must say real life experience, travelling and meeting people give you an amazing education, too.

4 For one thing, they show you are able to complete a course.

UNIT 7   Recording 8

T = Tracy Hackston

T: A couple of years ago, er, I learned how to scuba dive which was, um, really exciting, really good experience and when you're learning half of the, the training is in the classroom and half is er, a practical in a swimming pool. So the classroom stuff was fine erm, I found it really quite easy. I was learning with my mum and she was really worried about doing the kind of more academic stuff and passing the exam but I found that part OK. It was the practical stuff that I had trouble with and she was really lucky, she was erm, really good. But you go and you learn all the technical stuff, you know how to go under the water, how to clear your mask if you get water in it, that kind of thing. And then you have to do two dives outside in a, in a kind of reservoir or a quarry or, you know, something like that. But obviously because I'm in the UK it was really, really cold and we woke up on the morning of our dive and there was ice on the water so when we got there we were very nervous and didn't want to get into the water. But once I was in it was so freezing that I tried to go under the water but the more I tried the harder it got and then I got very frustrated and started to cry and then all my ears got blocked up and I couldn't get under. But eventually I managed it and erm, went down, passed my test, did all of the skills that you need to do. Despite the fact that I was so terrible at it I managed to pass and now, erm, now I'm passed I can go anywhere I want so I'll make sure it will be somewhere very hot. So, erm, to sum up, all, altogether it was a really difficult, really difficult challenge, I'm so glad I managed it. Erm … For me, it was quite an achievement and, and I'm proud of myself for having done it.

UNIT 8   Recording 2

L = Lynn

L: In real life my husband and I are both artists, visual artists. We paint landscapes and portraits. Well, we've been using the website for about two years now. And about a year ago we started an artists' colony on the internet, and it's been great. There are people like us, who work in the arts but also other people. And we show our paintings, and it's brought some business for us. It's a very creative kind of community, and we love it. We really do.

R = Rick

R: There is definitely a community of bloggers. It's a very twenty-first century community, which means no one knows one another personally. Bloggers might tell you their thoughts but, er, you don't know them as people. The guy who wrote this, who says he's a fifty-year-old American university professor, might be a sixteen-year-old girl from Bombay – we just don't know. But the best blogs have a following, who are very loyal readers. These are people who log on every day. And they get really engaged in the content. Well, that, to me, is a community.

N = Nathan

N: The place where we live is very small. There's only one shop, which sells all sorts of things like food, newspapers, and everything really. There's a small school, a pub, and then not much else. Actually, our social life is based on the pub, where we have our town meetings. Anyway, when we need to buy other things we shop online. It's cheap and it saves us an hour's drive in the car. And yeah, I've bought all sorts of things there: furniture, clothes … stuff you just can't get where we live.

A = Abbie

A: The website which I use the most is a social networking site. It's like Facebook or MySpace. I put up pictures of me and my family and I write messages – but to be honest, I use it mostly to keep in touch with friends. And the thing that I like is you go onto your friend's homepage to see what they've been doing … and er, you, you can see pictures of all their friends. And then you see pictures of your friend's friends, and it grows and grows so you meet new people. Erm, I think it's great. I check it at least once every day.

UNIT 8   Recording 5

Conversation 1

A: I'm really hungry. Can I have some of this?

B: Help yourself.

Conversation 2

A: Come on in.

B: Thanks.

C: Have a seat.

Conversation 3
A: Hi.
B: What a day! I'm so tired!
A: I'll make you some coffee. Put your feet up.

Conversation 4
A: Can I just quickly use your phone?
B: Be my guest.

Conversation 5
A: Welcome!
B: Thank you. What a nice room.
A: Make yourself at home.

UNIT 8 Recording 6

Conversation 1
W = Woman M = Man
W: Hi Dave. Sorry. Do you mind?
M: Sorry?
W: We don't smoke in the house.
M: Oh, sorry about that. I didn't know.
W: That's all right. It's no problem.

Conversation 2
M1 = 1st man M2 = 2nd man
M1: So they've invited me to dinner at their home.
M2: Wonderful. And they're also from Morocco?
M1: The same as you. From Morocco.
M2: That'll be great.
M1: So, do I need to bring a dish? Like, bring some food?
M2: No, it's not necessary. You can bring a small gift if you want but you don't need to bring food.

Conversation 3
M = Man W = Woman
M: Hello?
W: Hello?
M: Hi, I'm Richard Davies. From Exeter? I'm here to visit your offices.
W: Ah hello.
M: I'm a bit early. Is this a bad time?
W: Umm.
M: I can come back later.
W: I wasn't expecting you so early. Can you come back in ten minutes? I just need to finish some work here, then I'll be able to show you around.
M: Of course. Sorry about that.
W: Not at all. It's fine.

Conversation 4
W1 = 1st woman W2 = 2nd woman
W1: So, I walked into your parents' house but I forgot to take my shoes off. Did I do something wrong?
W2: Oh, I see.
W1: My shoes weren't dirty or anything but I still felt really bad.
W2: It's OK – I'll tell my parents you forgot. Don't worry about it.

W1: I don't know. Should I call them up to apologise?
W2: No, it's nothing. You really don't have to apologise.

Conversation 5
W = Waiter C = Customer
W: Excuse me sir, would you mind putting this on?
C: What?
W: Put on your jacket. In this restaurant you have to wear a jacket.
C: My apologies. I didn't realise.

Conversation 6
W = Woman M = Man
W: So this American family are going to stay with us for Thanksgiving.
M: For what?
W: For Thanksgiving. You know, people from the United States celebrate it.
M: So what's the problem?
W: Americans always eat turkey on Thanksgiving, don't they? But we're vegetarians – we never eat meat. So, well, what should we do?
M: Um … if I were you, I'd tell them the problem, and maybe they can cook a turkey while you and your family just eat something else.

UNIT 8 Recording 7

Extract 1
W = Woman M = Man
W: We don't smoke in the house.
M: Oh, sorry about that. I didn't know.
W: That's all right. It's no problem.

Extract 2
W = Woman M = Man
W: I wasn't expecting you so early. Can you come back in ten minutes? I just need to finish some work here, then I'll be able to show you around.
M: Of course. Sorry about that.
W: Not at all. It's fine.

Extract 3
W1 = 1st woman W2 = 2nd woman
W2: It's OK – I'll tell my parents you forgot. Don't worry about it.
W1: I don't know. Should I call them up to apologise?
W2: No, it's nothing. You really don't have to apologise.

UNIT 8 Recording 8

B = Ben Jacques S = Sharon Hills
B: So Sharon, erm, imagine you had to start a brand new community. Er …
S: Yes?
B: I know it's a difficult question, but ideally where would it be?
S: Erm, I'd probably choose somewhere quite warm, so yeah, so you didn't have

any issues of flooding, or you know, too much snow to deal with something like that. And then I'd choose another place most people would probably choose, not an island … erm ….
B: Where … where exactly?
S: But, I think, hmmmm … somewhere in France, I don't know why.
B: Oh somewhere in France? OK and, and who would be there: the French only or a mixture of people?
S: No, I … well, it would need to be a mix of people and they'd need to be able to help one another.
B: In what way?
S: Well, erm … I'd like to take one person who's an expert in one field, another person who's an expert in another field, so you have – you know – arty people, erm, manually skilled people, erm … good orators, good writers.
B: Ah, so a whole range of skills …
S: Exactly!
B: … all going into the melting pot.
S: Yes, but, I wouldn't have too many people to start with, although if it's too small a group then I suppose you risk, erm, falling out. But I think if you keep that group fairly small to begin with then you can draw up your own special laws, you know, to govern yourselves.
B: Would it need laws do you think … this, this utopian society?
S: Mmmm … well, ideally there'd be no laws but because people are human I think you would probably have to come up with some ground rules yes.
B: What would be the most important one?
S: Oh! Erm, I think, erm … not to physically hurt somebody else I suppose.
B: Right, so pretty much like we have at the minute …
S: Yes, I suppose …

UNIT 9 Recording 2

1 Jeans are worn by people all over the world.
2 Mobile phones are being designed especially for teenagers.
3 Teenagers have always been influenced by the media.
4 A great film about a teenage vampire was made in Sweden.
5 In the past, children were seen as mini-adults.
6 In the future, people will be prevented from smoking until they are twenty-one.
7 In Mexico, a party called quinceañera is held when a girl reaches the age of fifteen.
8 Many of the computer games of the future will be designed by teenagers.

AUDIO SCRIPTS

UNIT 9   Recording 3

1 Yeah, I grew up in the 90s. Erm, for me film and music are two important ah important aspects of my life, and it was a fantastic decade for both of those. In terms of films, there were some ah excellent ones that came out, erm, my favourites being *Forrest Gump*, *Pulp Fiction*, and *The Shawshank Redemption*. In terms of the music ... probably the most famous bands of the time was Oasis and Blur. Ah, one of the most memorable moments of the 90s was Euro 96 ... obviously the football tournament. I was lucky enough to go to the opening ceremony myself. Obviously, as we was entering the end of the millennium the celebrations towards the end of the nineties were huge as were the actual celebrations on the night. Tony Blair was elected, erm, so he was the first sort of Labour government for, for a long time. Um and also Mother Teresa died, sort of Mother Teresa was, erm, the famous charitable missionary.

2 Ah, the 70s, well they were wonderful I think if, if I'm asked were they was it a good decade or a bad decade, personally I have to think it was a good decade to grow up in. I think it's very lucky I think of it as a very lucky experience when generally the world that I lived in, which was London and England, which was the post-war period and therefore an era of a certain amount of erm, restriction was all ending and things were freeing up and that happened just at the time that I was leaving home and finding my own independence. It all seemed as though it happened at the same time. Erm, technology was er, changing and improving, um, everything seemed to be developing and getting better in many ways. The fashion was getting rid of short hair and regimented kind of looks, erm, individuality was very much the order of the day. Great people were emerging in the arts. John Lennon, for example, was an icon for me I think as a creative artist with a message as well in his work. Great artists in film, Scorsese, *Taxi Driver*, Spielberg, *Duel* these were emerging artists of tremendous skill and artistry but they were just starting out then when I was.

3 I was a teenager in the 80s and I remember thinking that um I didn't like a lot of the fashion and the music from back then but now it's obvious in retrospect that I did quite like it. I love looking back on like a nostalgia trip at the way we used to dress and how much hair gel I used and how much hair spray the girls used, and er, now in the 2000s there's sort of a trip back into that time you know, girls are wearing big earrings again and geometric patterns of their clothes. Erm, the music in the 80s became quite computerised sounding, quite electronic and er, disco faded away, although we did still have soul although people like Luther Vandross and Billy Ocean, erm, making soul music. Er, New Romantic was another style that came out in the early 80s where the men started wearing lots of make-up and had big shoulders and small waists and erm, there was Madonna was a big trendsetter for girls and er, at one point she cut her hair really short in the mid 80s and almost like a boy's, and then all the girls started cutting their hair short, too. Erm, I wasn't very fashionable myself, I used to spend most of my money on records not clothes. Erm, there were some good films around in the 80s too things like *Back to the Future* with Michael J Fox, *Desperately Seeking Susan* with Madonna, *ET*, *Police Academy* ... Um, I'm gonna be forty this year and I reckon my birthday party is going to be a big nostalgia trip back to the 80s.

UNIT 9   Recording 4

W = Woman M = Man

W: What about this first one? Who was once kidnapped in France?

M: I have no idea. Maybe Isabelle Allende?

W: It was Chaucer. I think he worked for the British government.

M: Did he? I didn't know that.

W: OK, what about the next one? Who was messy?

M: Umm ... probably Machiavelli.

W: It was Karl Marx.

M: Oh really?

W: And the third one: who was stopped by the US government from entering the States?

M: I'm not a hundred percent certain but it might be Chaplin. I read somewhere that he had some political views that they didn't like in the States. I'm fairly sure it's Chaplin. Is that right?

W: You're right. It was Chaplin.

M: Yeah, I read something about that.

W: OK, number four. Who played the violin?

M: I haven't a clue. I'll guess it was Galileo.

W: It was Einstein. He was a very good violinist, apparently.

M: Was he? That's interesting.

W: Number five.

M: It's definitely not Mandela. Ermm ... Joan of Arc?

W: Didn't you see that film about Che Guevara and his friend travelling across South America on their motorbikes?

M: I don't think I did, actually.

W: Yeah, Guevara was a medical student ...

M: Oh yes, I knew that. I just couldn't remember.

W: Who went on a road trip with his friend?

M: Ah, that's right.

W: And the last one?

M: Umm, well I'm sure it isn't Picasso. Oh, it's da Vinci. He invented lots of stuff but never actually produced any of it, like ... um ... oh I can't remember, but I know he was an inventor as well as an artist.

W: Correct. It was da Vinci. He invented the parachute.

M: Oh yeah, I was just about to say that!

UNIT 9   Recording 6

L = Lili Lowe

L: OK, well, someone whose work really influenced me is Gabriel Garcia Marquez. I like his short stories, but I fell in love with his novels, particularly *One Hundred Years of Solitude*. That book really made its mark on me. Anyway, erm, well, Marquez is a Colombian writer. I think he was born in 1928. He's a Nobel Prize winner – he won the Nobel Prize in Literature – and his books have been translated into dozens of languages. Erm ... He's one of the best-known writers in the style of what's called magic realism. This means he writes kind of realistically but there's magic, I mean magical things happen in his books, like ghosts appear and kind of crazy things happen. I'm a big fan of that type of writing. Anyway, his novels are kind of funny but it's black humour or satire. He invents all these amazing, unforgettable characters, like um, corrupt officials and devoted lovers, vicious policemen and stupid revolutionaries, and through it all you're laughing at the characters but you also see their world is falling apart. I haven't read his work in Spanish, only English, erm, but the style is brilliant. His dialogue is fast and funny and he writes amazing descriptions of places and people. And, um, well, it was finding Marquez's work as a teenager that really made me become a reader.

UNIT 10   Recording 2

1 My favourite food city is ah Hiroshima, in Japan ... Umhmm ... Ah they've got all sorts of food. They've of course got the really famous sushi that everyone thinks about when they think of Japanese food, but they've got so much else to offer. Ah, Hiroshima's really famous for its okonomiyaki which is like a cross between a pancake and a pizza ... and it's kind of egg and like a flour mixture with cabbage and noodles and meat and sometimes cheese. It's really good. One of my favourite restaurants is a place called, ah, Daikichi, which specialises in grilled chicken you can get grilled chicken with cheese, grilled chicken with plum sauce, ah and a really good soup with rice and ginger in it. I'd love to take you to Daikichi, you'd love it. They do good beer, too. Erm, but also

you can get tempura in Hiroshima, which is like prawns and vegetables deep fried in a really light, fluffy batter … it's really good. And then, ah, you have also the informal restaurants that are called Izakaya where you go with a group of friends and you order lots of dishes and everyone shares and eats from the middle of the table so it's a great way to try lots of different kinds of food. Actually I know a really good Izakaya that I should take you to.

2 Well, my favourite food city would be Madrid. I lived in Madrid, in Spain for around ten years on and off and the quality of the food is, is wonderful – it's sensational. Spanish people always say that, ah, Spanish food is the best in the world and I always argued while I lived there, that, er, I felt there was a lot more variety of food in the UK, but when I moved back to the UK I really started to miss the richness, the quality of food in Spain. I think my favourite restaurant in Spain was a tiny little, um, Galician which is a part in the north west of Spain, seafood restaurant in a small little bar, it was a very, it wasn't posh or expensive, it was cheap and basic but just served the most wonderful seafood followed by lots of white wine and er, a great Tarta de Santiago, a great pastry dessert, afterwards. Another great thing, obviously about Spanish food which you'll've heard of is 'tapas' where everyone gets together on a Sunday lunchtime before lunch to have a few bites to eat and, and a few beers together and it's a lovely social atmosphere and it's nice to go out and try a variety of different food. I tried once, ah, pig's ear, which I have to say was possibly the worst thing I've ever tasted [laughs], but generally the quality was sensational.

UNIT 10   Recording 4

Conversation 1
W = Woman   M = Man

W: Is there anything I should know for when I arrive at the airport?

M: Yes, watch out for the taxi drivers who tend to hang around outside the airport. Most of them aren't licensed, so you shouldn't really use them.

W: OK.

M: If you do use one, make sure you find out how much the journey is supposed to cost. Don't get in until you've agreed the price with the driver, or else you could find that you have to pay three or four times the amount you should pay for the journey.

W: Oh right. That's good to know.

Conversation 2
M = Man   W = Woman

M: Hi – I'm going to Heathrow tomorrow, and my plane leaves at 3p.m. Latest check in time is 1.40. What time do you think I should leave central London?

W: For Heathrow? Well, you'd better leave plenty of time, because often there are delays on the tube. Are you going on the tube or the train?

M: The tube, I think.

W: The tube? If I were you, I'd allow about an hour and a half. So, if you want to be at the airport at 1.30., then you'd better leave at about twelve o'clock.

M: OK. That's great. Thanks.

Conversation 3
M1 = 1st man   M2 = 2nd man

M1: Be careful when you take trips into the jungle in the north. Generally, there are a lot of mosquitoes there, so remember to take mosquito nets, and insect cream. It's a good idea to wear long trousers, and shirts with sleeves in the evening. And don't forget to take your malaria tablets.

M2: Oh yes, I must remember those.

M1: And whatever you do, don't drink the water, or you'll get a bad stomach.

M2: Oh, I didn't know that.

M1: Yes, always be sure to boil the water first, or drink bottled water. You have to be careful when you eat raw food, too, like fruit, if it's been washed in water.

M2: OK.

Conversation 4
W1 = 1st woman   W2 = 2nd woman

W1: We're going there on holiday, and I've heard that there's a lot of street crime. Is that true?

W2: Not really no. I mean, it's like any big city. You need to watch out for groups of young children on the streets. They try to distract you, and then sometimes take your bag.

W1: Oh. Right.

W2: It's not very common, but don't walk around the city obviously carrying money in a big money belt or anything.

W1: Of course.

W2: The most important thing is to remember to hold on to your handbag, and things like that, but no, there isn't really much crime. On the whole, it's a pretty safe city.

W1: That's useful, thanks.

UNIT 10   Recording 5

1 Watch out for the taxi drivers who tend to hang around outside the airport.

2 Make sure you find out how much the journey is supposed to cost.

3 Don't get in until you've agreed the price with the driver, or else …

4 You'd better leave plenty of time.

5 If I were you, I'd allow about an hour and a half.

6 Be careful when you take trips into the jungle.

7 Don't forget to take your malaria tablets.

8 Whatever you do, don't drink the water.

9 You need to watch out for groups of young children on the streets.

10 The most important thing is to remember to hold on to your handbag.

UNIT 10   Recording 7

R = Rob Hustin

R: One place that I think everyone should have the chance to see is Venice. But the problem is that this beautiful and charming city is slowly sinking. Ever since the fourteenth century engineers have tried to work out a way to stop the floods in Venice, but so far nobody has managed. Sometimes there are as many as forty floods per year between March and September, and Venice is actually sinking at a rate of two and a half inches every decade. It's very possible that your grandchildren, and their grandchildren will never have the chance to see this fragile city. Everyone should have the chance to enjoy the city, to walk across its famous bridges, through its ancient squares. There are no cars in Venice, and many people think it helps this to be one of the most romantic cities in the world. So, can it be saved?

Well, they are trying. Barriers are being put in to try and stop the water getting too high. This is viewed as a temporary measure, although they should last a hundred years, so the problem is finding a permanent solution. If you want my advice, go there while you still can, and then together we can put pressure on the government to spend the money it needs to find a permanent way to keep this beautiful and historic city for future generations. We have an opportunity now to save this city, and we must, before it's too late.

Pearson Education Limited
Edinburgh Gate
Harlow
Essex CM20 2JE
England
and Associated Companies throughout the world.

www.pearsonlongman.com

© Pearson Education Limited 2011

The right of Antonia Clare and JJ Wilson to be identified as authors of this Work has been asserted by them in accordance with the Copyright, Designs and Patents Act 1988.

First published 2011

ISBN: 978-1-4082-1931-7

Set in Gill Sans Book 9.75/11.5

Printed in Slovakia by Neografia

Acknowledgements
The publishers and authors would like to thank the following people and their institutions for their feedback and comments during the development of the material:

Reporters: Brazil: Stephen Greene, Damian Williams; **Germany:** Rosemary Richey; **Italy:** Elizabeth Gregson, Elizabeth Kalton; **Spain:** Eleanor Keegan; **Turkey:** Grant Kempton; **United Kingdom:** Ben Beaumont, Kirsten Colquhoun, Andrew Doig, Fay Drewry, Eileen Flannigan, Sarah Gumbrell, Tad Larner, Fran Linley, Jacqueline McEwan, Zella Phillips, Chris Rogers, Dan Woodard

We are grateful to the following for permission to reproduce copyright material:

Text:
Extract 2.2 adapted from "I want to believe", *BBC Focus*, 01/12/2008, Issue 197, p59 (Blackmore, M.), copyright © BBC Magazines, 2008; Extract 2.2 adapted from "Fraud fugitive in Facebook trap" 14 October 2009 http://news.bbc.co.uk/1/hi/world/americas/8306032.stm, copyright © 2009, The BBC; Extract 3.1 adapted from "Teenagers: Life on Planet Teen" *The Telegraph*, 20/10/2007 (Kavanagh, M.), copyright © Telegraph Media Group Limited; Extract 3.2 from *Longman Active Study Dictionary*, 5th edition, Pearson Longman (2010) p.445, copyright © Pearson Education Ltd; Extract 4.1 adapted from *Think Yourself Rich: Discover Your Millionaire Potential*, published by Vermilion (Sharon Maxwell Magnus 2003), copyright © Sharon Maxwell Magnus, 2003. Reprinted by permission of The Random House Group Ltd, and PFD www.pfd.co.uk on behalf of Sharon Maxwell Magnus; Extract 4.3 after "Wanted: Paradise island 'caretaker'" 12/01/2009, http://news.bbc.co.uk/1/hi/world/asia-pacific/7823812.stm, copyright © 2009, The BBC; Extract 5.1 adapted from Big *Ideas Transport Challenge*, http://www.open2.net/jamesmay/big_ideas_interactive_html.html, copyright © The Open University; Extract 5.3 adapted from "PC rage hits UK" 29 January 2000, http://news.bbc.co.uk/1/hi/sci/tech/623341.stm, copyright © 2009, The BBC; Extract 6.1 adapted from "Special report on Human Behaviour ", *BBC Focus* 1/06/2004, Issue 139, p53, copyright © BBC Magazines, 2008; Extract 6.1 from *Longman Active Study Dictionary* 5th edition, Pearson Longman (2010) pp.960,375,826, copyright © Pearson Education Ltd; Extract 7.2 from *Longman Active Study Dictionary* 5th edition, Pearson Longman (2010) p.53, copyright © Pearson Education Ltd; Extra

9.1 adapted from "12 Giant leaps for mankind", *BBC History Magazine, Vol 10, no 7*, 1/07/2009, pp.42-47 (Attar, R.), copyright © BBC Magazines; Extract 10.1 adapted from "I am the Ethical Man" by Rowlatt, J., http://news.bbc.co.uk/1/hi/programmes/newsnight/4736228.stm and http://www.bbc.co.uk/blogs/newsnight/2007/04/we_are_all_ethical_men_and_women_now.html, copyright © 2009, The BBC; Extract 10.2 adapted from "Osaka – the World's greatest food city", *The Guardian*, 13/07/2009 (Booth, M.), copyright © Guardian News & Media Ltd 2009; Extract 10.3 adapted from "10 things you should never do in an airport", http://travel.aol.co.uk/, copyright © AOL.

In some instances we have been unable to trace the owners of copyright material, and we would appreciate any information that would enable us to do so.

Illustration acknowledgements: Jurgen Ziewe p17; **Matt Herring** pgs38–39, 44–45, 48, 116–117; **Dan Hilliard** pgs11, 84, 95; **Lyndon Hayes** pgs26–27, 61, 74–75; **Eric Smith** pgs14, 38, 62, 72, 129, 133, 135, 137, 140, 149, 150, 151, 152, 153, 154, 157.

Photo acknowledgements: The publisher would like to thank the following for their kind permission to reproduce their photographs:

(Key: b-bottom; c-centre; l-left; r-right; t-top)

Alamy Images: 15, allOver photography 55 (computer), Ancient Art & Architecture Collection Ltd 110 (Chaucer), James R Clarke 19 (girls), culture-images GmbH 65bl, Design Pics Inc. 31 (mother), 62 (A), Garry Gay 43bl (money), Ian Goodrick 62 (E), Nick Gregory 122tc (pass), Dennis Hallinan 103 (drawing), Andrew Holt 122tr, D. Hurst 62 (C), 76bl (rings), Idealink Photography 57 (E), Inspirestock Inc 47 (A), itanistock 87 (B), John James 86tl, Juice Images 68 (C), Iain Masterton 162, MBI 51tl, Photos 12 110 (Chaplin), PIFood 119 (C), Chris Rout 97, SCPhotos 91 (home), Jack Sullivan 124tl, Daniel Templeton 51tr, Transtock Inc. 57 (A), Trinity Mirror / Mirrorpix 103 (fashion), Penny Tweedie 76cl, Benjamin Volant 115 (garden), Patrick Ward 50tc; **Bananastock:** 148 (brother), 148 (brother's daughter), 148 (brother's son), 148 (brother's wife), 148 (me), 148 (son); **BBC Photo Library:** 36tl, 56r, 111, 116tr; **Bridgeman Art Library Ltd:** Michelangelo at work, English School, (20th century) / Private Collection / © Look and Learn 112bc; **Corbis:** Chris Andrews Publications 67 (stress), Bettmann 19 (moon), 23t, 23b, 110 (Einstein), Sara De Boer 81 (Cowell), Fred De Noyelle / Godong 119 (A), Tim Graham 21 (C), Catherine Ivill / AMA 81 (Beckham), Frans Lanting 100–101 (island), Lorenvu / epa 47 (C), moodboard 29br, NASA 59 (D), Michael Nicholson 110 (Marx), Franck Robichon / EPA 21 (E), Andersen Ross / cultura 52–53 (office), Steve Schapiro 103 (march), Soeren Stache / EPA 43 (models), Buero Monaco / zefa 14; **Fotolia.com:** Gerald Bernard 61bl, Lane Erickson 157 (factories), huyang 28-29 (wall), Monkey Business 148 (grandma, left), 148 (grandpa, left); **Getty Images:** 91 (Tribe), AFP 118, AFP / Don Emmert / Staff 21 (G), Val Doone / Hulton Archive 104 (factories), Asia Images 63, Bruce Ayres 73t, James Baigrie 77br, Barcroft Media 83t, 83b, Hamish Blair / Staff 80 (Williams), Lionel Bonaventure / Stringer 120, The Bridgeman Art Library / Giovanni Stradano 112b, Stephen Derr 7bc (interview), GAB Archive / Redferns 80-81c (The Beatles cover), Martyn Hayhow / Stringer 8 (B), Hulton Archive 110 (Che), Hulton Archive /

Philbey / R   , Tom Stoddart Archive / Contribu   nphonie 82, Roger Viollet 21 e 21 (A), 52 (Stacey), 79 (success), ench); **Hodder & Stoughton Publishers,** orn On A Blue Day' by Daniel Tammet, reproduced with permission of Hodder & Stoughton Publishers, 2006 79 (memory man), 161; **iStockphoto:** Steve Debenport 60, Martina Ebel 148 (mother), Steve Geer 94bc, Bill Grove 115 (airport), ilbusca 64-65 (background), Victor Ioramo 77bl, Kemter 148c (ex-husband), David Newton 43br/team, S. Greg Panosian 92-93t, Tatiana Popova 49, Andrew Rich 48 (astronaut and rocket), Mark Richardson 151 (A), Silvrshootr 151 (B), James Steidl 35 (record player), Brad Wieland 148 (father), Mark Wragg 76 (table top); **Jupiterimages:** 148bl (daughter); **mytinygarden.com:** J. Dykes 59 (B); **Helen Nagel:** 'Streetlife' illustration, copyright Helen Nagel / 2021 91 (neighbours); **NASA:** data courtesy Marc Imhoff (NASA / GSFC) and Christopher Elvidge (NOAA / NGDC). Image by Craig Mayhew (NASA / GSFC) and Robert Simmon (NASA / GSFC). 40br, 41bl, JPL / ASU 95; **Pearson Education Ltd:** 148 (aunty), 148 (uncle); **Photolibrary.com:** A H C. / age fotostock 112-113 (background), Banana Stock 12, Walter Bibikow 67 (people), 71c (people), bilderlounge 86tr, A Chederros 62 (B), Corbis 59 (A), Nick Dolding 68 (B), Nick Guttridge 50c (background), Kelly Han 115 (market), Hola Images 98l, Image 100 68 (A), 55 (expert), Ingram Publishing 10, 98r, Steven Kazlowski 115 (polar), 124-125br (polar), LISSAC LISSAC 91 (cyberspace), John Lund 59 (E), David Madison 68 (E), Roger Marshutz / age fotostock 93br, moodboard RF 87tl, Marvin Newman 103 (statue), Mark Polott 105, Sugar Gold Images 68 (D), Tips Italia 19 (house), 28 (house); **Press Association Images:** ABACA PRESS / ABACA USA / Empics Entertainment 57 (B), Piovanotto Marco / ABACA 81 (Lopez), Martial Trezzini / AP 122tl, Pierre Gleizes / AP 108 (A), Damian Dovarganes 57 (D), Gareth Fuller / PA Archive 79br (challenge), 88bl, 88-89 (background), Fiona Hanson / PA Archive 65cr, Antony Jones 9 (E), Tony Marshall / EMPICS Sport 8 (A), Ian West / PA Archive 50c; **Reuters:** Ian Waldie 23c; **Rex Features:** 52 (Gavin), David Fisher 9 (D), David Hartley 8 (C), Rupert Hartley 9 (F), ITV 81 (Redgrave), Barbara Lindberg 55 (Top Gear), 64cl, Olycom SPA 80 (Branson), 122tc (scan), Marc Sharratt 81 (Hendrix), Sipa Press 24, 80 (Clinton), 81 (Gates), Solent News 57 (C); **Science Photo Library Ltd:** Mark Garlick 31bl (city), 36-37t, Pasieka 104tr (DNA), Maria Platt-Evan 110tl (Da Vinci); **Shutterstock.com:** Tiplyashin Anatoly 33tl; **Thinkstock:** BananaStock 148 (sister), Brand X Pictures 35 (phone), Toby Burrows 96, Comstock 148 (daughter), Creatas Images 151 (C), Hemera 41br, 52tr, 62 (C battery), 94br, 148 (cousin), 148 (husband), 157 (traffic), 157t, iStockphoto 8-9t, 22l, 25, 35 (ink), 35 (tv), 35 (video), 59 (C), 59 (F), 69 (F), 87 (A), 94t, 94bl, 119 (B), 121, 148 (father-in-law), 148 (grandma), 148 (grandpa), 157 (aerosol), 157b, Jupiterimages 79br (qualified), Photodisc 148 (in-laws), PhotoObjects.net 35 (tape machine), 148 (mother's husband), Stockbyte 67 (news), 87 (C), 94c; **TopFoto:** 19 (Braveheart), Stapleton Historical Collection / HIP 104 (plane), ullsteinbild 107; **Professor Richard Wiseman:** 72t

All other images © Pearson Education

Every effort has been made to trace the copyright holders and we apologise in advance for any unintentional omissions. We would be pleased to insert the appropriate acknowledgement in any subsequent edition of this publication.